Adjudication for architects and engineers

John Timpson and Brian Totterdill

Legal Notes by Roger Dyer

Published by Thomas Telford Ltd, 1 Heron Quay, London E14 4JD.
URL:http://www.t-telford.co.uk

Distributors for Thomas Telford books are
USA: ASCE Press, 1801 Alexander Bell Drive, Reston, VA 20191-4400
Japan: Maruzen Co. Ltd, Book Department, 3–10 Nihonbashi 2-chome, Chuo-ku, Tokyo 103
Australia: DA Books and Journals, 648 Whitehorse Road, Mitcham 3132, Victoria

First published 1999

Appendices 1–5 are reproduced by kind permission of Her Majesty's Stationery Office.
Appendix 10 is reproduced by kind permission of The Joint Contracts Tribunal (JCT).
Appendix 11 is reproduced by kind permission of The Construction Industry Council (CIC).

A catalogue record for this book is available from the British Library.

ISBN: 0 7277 2672 2

Typeset by Gray Publishing, Tunbridge Wells.
Printed and bound in Great Britain by The Cromwell Press, Trowbridge, Wilts.

Foreword

I count it a privilege to have been invited to write a foreword to a new book, particularly one whose authors are such outstanding practitioners in their own fields.

Adjudication has been a feature of construction contracts, particularly subcontracts, for at least 20 years; generally, it has been confined to dealing with disputes concerning set-off, but, in more recent years, has been used less and less as ways were found to avoid implementing adjudicators' decisions. All that has changed; following the report of Sir Michael Latham, *Constructing the team*, Government was persuaded that primary legislation was required to give all parties to construction contracts a statutory right to have disputes decided by adjudication, which was to be a rapid and relatively inexpensive process in all cases. That legislation (the Housing Grants, Construction and Regeneration Act 1996) is now in force and disputes are being referred to adjudication.

This book, therefore, could not be more timely. There are many ideas about what adjudication under the Act is and should be, and, undoubtedly, the process will develop and its practitioners will perfect their own expertise; nevertheless, the need for informed guidance is paramount.

The authors—an architect, an engineer and a barrister—all have extensive experience as arbitrators, and although adjudication is not arbitration, the techniques and principles of deciding only on the evidence adduced and respecting the principles of natural justice as far as possible are common to any process of third party intervention.

Written in an easy-to-read style, this book is comprehensive yet easily manageable; learned in the true sense. The combined wealth of experience of the authors is apparent on every page, spiced with sound legal advice but tempered by lessons learned in long years of practice.

The title of the book implies that this text is relevant only to architects and engineers. Nothing could be further from the truth; this book should be an essential companion to all adjudicators, construction professionals, employers and their advisers, contractors and subcontractors, and lawyers involved in adjudication. The book will also be invaluable in the training and continuing professional development of adjudicators.

I have no hesitation in commending this book to a wide readership; I know it will find a welcome spot on my own shelves and, more importantly, on my desk as an essential reference.

Harold Crowter
Chairman, Chartered Institute of Arbitrators

Authors' note

The adjudication process which is discussed in this book is a new process. Standard forms of contract have been amended and rules have been published. As experience is gained, the published amendments and rules are being revised and additional documents are being published.

The authors had to draw the line between delaying the publication of this book in order to wait for further published documents or publishing the book to cover the information which was already available.

For this reason, the reader must check the current versions of any contracts or rules, or the Act itself, to see whether or not further revisions have been made since the date the book was passed for publication.

Contents

Glossary

ADR Alternative dispute resolution. Dispute resolution processes which encourage or facilitate disputants to reach their own solution. Includes conciliation, mediation, and the 'mini-trial'.

Adjudication This is a process in which an impartial person makes a binding decision on a dispute within a fixed time period.

Adversarial System The system by which the advocates representing each side adduce arguments to persuade the tribunal that they have the better legal case. In contrast, the inquisitorial system, qv, which allows the tribunal to find out as many relevant facts as possible, is applied in most legal systems on the mainland of Europe.

Affirmation This is used as a substitute for a religious oath when the witness's beliefs will not permit him to take an oath.

Arbitration A method of resolving disputes between two or more Parties by reference to one or more persons appointed for that purpose. If there is written agreement to refer, the arbitration in England and Wales is normally subject to the Arbitration Act 1996.

Award This is the terminology in arbitration for the decision, which is reached by the Arbitrator.

Burden of Proof The Party who is making an assertion has to produce evidence which proves his assertion for the assertion to be accepted as being true and then the burden shifts to the other Party to produce contrary evidence to rebut the presumption.

Calderbank Letter   An offer made in the course of arbitration or litigation whereby the letter, if properly phrased, has the same effect on costs as a payment into Court. So called after the matrimonial case of *Calderbank v Calderbank* 1976. See also *Sealed Offers* and *Offers to settle*.

Collateral warranties   A form of agreement, assurance, etc., which is independent of, but subordinate to, a contract affecting the same subject matter.

Common Law   The law of the land formulated, developed and administered by the old common law Courts, that is to say the decisions of the Courts. Common law has to be distinguished from equity, statute law, any special law, and the Civil Law (of Rome, i.e. Continental law).

Conciliation   *See ADR.* In conciliation, the Parties in dispute agree that a neutral Third Party should help them reconcile their differences and reach a solution.

Declaratory (Judgement, Award or Decision)   A decision which declares the rights, obligations or liabilities of one or both of the parties.

Discovery (of documents)   The process by which the parties to a dispute disclose to their opponents the documents to which they have (or have had) access. The principle is the litigants should put their cards on the table.

Documents only   A case (often but not exclusively where only small sums are disputed) which does not justify the cost of a hearing or where the case is otherwise self-explanatory on the papers. Such a procedure is not normally suitable where evidence needs to be tested by cross-examination.

Further and better particulars   Information which is requested by one party or the other in order to enable him to answer a case which is not clear from a pleading.

Injunction An order or decree by which a Party to an action is required to do, or to refrain from doing a particular thing.

Inquisitorial This is a procedure used more frequently on the Continent than in England and Wales by which the Tribunal takes a much more active part in the proceedings than it does in the Adversarial system. An Adjudicator fulfils an Inquisitorial role when he makes positive enquiries into the facts and the law of a case rather than waiting for the Parties to present their information.

Jurisdiction The competence of a tribunal to entertain an action or other proceeding. Jurisdiction to determine matters may be restricted by agreement or statute. Equally, a tribunal may exceed its jurisdiction by deciding matters beyond its scope.

Mediation *See ADR.* In mediation, the Parties in dispute agree that a Third Party should actively assist them to reach a solution. A more positive approach than conciliation *(which see)*.

Mini-trial See ADR. The Parties in dispute agree that each shall present its case to a panel or tribunal with authority to negotiate a settlement. The panel will consist of managerial representatives from each side with a neutral adviser in the chair. The mini-trial approach is often adopted for reasons of commercial expediency.

Offers to settle Offers to settle a dispute may be made at any stage in the process of resolution. They may be open, sealed, or without prejudice. They may be intended to limit liability of costs.

Order for Directions An order made by a judge or arbitrator or Adjudicator setting the timetable and procedures for an action or claim. In Court proceedings, this may follow the issue of a Summons for Directions.

Pleadings The written or printed statements whereby the parties to a dispute are required to set out the factual basis of their respective cases. Normally, these are the claim, the defence, and the reply, although there are other categories.

Precedent   The reasoning and judgement of a higher Court in a preceding case which is binding in similar cases occurring later in lower Courts.

Privileged Documents   Documents withheld on the ground of some special reason recognised by law, which need not be revealed to the opposite side and should not be made available to the tribunal before the substantive decision is handed down.

Quantum   The amount of damages or the amount fixed as compensation for particular losses.

Security for costs   A deposit or guarantee given by a Claimant or Counter Claimant to meet the costs of the Defendant/Respondent if the claim fails.

Statement of Case   The written statement made by a claimant but which has to be distinguished from a pleading in which evidence and points of law are not normally allowed.

Statute   An act of Parliament.

Statute barred   A situation where a claim is beyond the period laid down in the Limitation Act 1980 as amended by the Latent Damage Act 1986. Also referred to as being 'out of time'.

Third Party   A Party who is not one of the two Parties involved in the proceedings.

Without prejudice   A term applied to a privileged offer made by a Party which prevents that offer being referred to thereafter in subsequent proceedings. May also be applied to correspondence, procedures or meetings.

1

Introduction

What is Adjudication?

Adjudication was a term used in the Latham Report *Constructing the Team* which was published in 1994. The dictionary meaning of Adjudication focuses on the act of adjudicating or pronouncing judgement. Sir Michael Latham's intention, so far as dispute resolution was concerned, was to bring more emphasis on alternative dispute resolution, conciliation, mediation and a strongly recommended process called 'Adjudication'. The stated intention was to reduce the confrontational ethos within the industry, reduce disputes and assist subcontractors particularly, who were at the end of a long chain when it came to receiving payment.

Adjudication was only one of the measures which Sir Michael Latham had in mind.

Unfortunately, the Latham Report did not explain what was meant by the term 'Adjudication'. At that time, Adjudication existed only within the terms of certain construction contracts, notably the New Engineering Contract, although it also played a part in 'JCT 1981 With Contractor's Design' and in certain sub-contract documents published in connection with JCT Contracts.

While there have been statutes for a period of about three centuries defining the activities of an Arbitrator, prior to the publication of the Act,[1] there was no comparable guidance on the

---

1 When we refer to the 'Act' it is to the Housing Grants Construction and Regeneration Act 1996.

law and practice of Adjudication in construction contracts. The Act and the Scheme[2] do not go very far in giving a full understanding of how the process will work. The shortcomings of both the Latham Report and the Act are covered in *Construction Contract Reform: a plea for sanity*, edited by John Uff (The Construction Law Press, London, 1997).

Previously, the powers and duties of an Adjudicator within a contract arose from the terms of those particular contracts. We then had the statutory arrangements of the Act and in particular from the Scheme which was circulated as a series of drafts intended to be incorporated in the Act. Neither the Act nor the Scheme spell out completely how the Adjudication process should work. The full process can only be derived from an understanding of contract procedures and dispute resolution processes already established in law and practice and by implication translating the requirements of the Act and the Scheme into working arrangements.

In the opinion of the authors, the stated intention and spirit of the Latham Report (so far as Adjudication was concerned) can be summed up as follows: two Parties to a contract have their contractual obligations recorded in writing; if they cannot agree on how the contract is to be interpreted in the circumstances which occur, they call in a respected and impartial person who is knowledgeable about the activities involved and ask him/her to give a quick working decision on the issue which has arisen. This enables the contract to continue and if one Party wishes to go on to have a full Arbitration or Litigation then they can do that at a later date.

A similar concept is embodied in the procedure which is taken from a roads contract dated 14 November 1824.[3] It required that:

> Any doubt, decision or question shall be referred to the decision of two referees, one named and appointed by each Party. If these two people do not agree and issue their decision

---

2 When we refer to the 'Scheme' it is to the Scheme for Construction Contracts Regulations 1998 which are referred to in the Act.

3 Extracted from *A Treatise on Roads* by Sir Henry Parnell, 1838.

within one month, they nominate a third person and refer the matter to him. The third person's decision shall be given within one month of the reference to him and shall be final and conclusive between the Parties.

Contracts which contained provision for Adjudication before the Latham Report generally only allowed certain types of dispute to be referred to Adjudication. 'JCT 1981 With Contractor's Design' included a list of 'Adjudication Matters', which could be referred to an Adjudicator for a decision to be made.

The first edition of the New Engineering Contract included a provision that if the Contractor was not satisfied with a particular action, or failure to act, by the Project Manager then the Contractor could refer the matter to Adjudication. However, the current revisions to contracts allow for *any* dispute under the contract, and sometimes also in connection with the contract, to be referred to Adjudication. This, of course, is a direct result of the Act. The experience of the authors is that some disputes are clearly not suitable for a decision within a very limited time period.

- A dispute which involves the study of complex points of law cannot be fully analysed, with presentations by both sides, responses to opposing arguments, answers to queries and then allow time for the Adjudicator to reach his decision, all within 28 days.

- There is also a group of issues where the consequences of an Adjudicator reaching some decisions will leave the Parties in a legal no-man's-land unless the Adjudicator confines his decision to an award of time or money (which can subsequently be reversed if the matter goes to Arbitration or Litigation). An example could be a dispute regarding the structural sufficiency of a prime, load-bearing element of the building.

- Disputes which may have arisen from a series of events, such as a matter involving determination, failure to agree the final account, allegations of professional negligence, or involving third Party action or expertise such as insurance matters, are unlikely to be resolved satisfactorily within 28 days.

- Disputes involving matters such as health and safety, VAT or taxation may need to be referred to the appropriate authority rather than to an Adjudicator.
- A Party who has been ordered to pay a large sum of money may be reluctant to pay if he feels that the decision has been reached with undue haste, based on an inadequate analysis of the problem.
- Disputes which concern matters such as design or quality of work will need to be carefully delineated in order to avoid further problems arising at a later date. The Adjudicator's decision may be reversed by later Arbitration or Litigation. If the decision is financial then it can be reversed, provided the recipient of the finance is still in business. However, a decision to do something, or to do it in a particular way, may not be capable of being reversed. The right of the Employer to stipulate what he requires in a project must be respected, both by the Adjudicator and by the person who writes the notice which constitutes the instructions to the Adjudicator.
- Any dispute which has not been fully studied, by both sides, before submission to the Adjudicator, is likely to result in an unsatisfactory decision. When a Claimant submits evidence which has not previously been considered by the Respondent then the limitation on the time period may prevent the Adjudicator from receiving properly balanced submissions of allegation and response.

On the other hand, there is a wide range of disputes which may be suitable for a fast decision by an Adjudicator:

- single issue disputes for which one submission by each Party can identify the problem and provide the Adjudicator with the opposing points of view and all the necessary supporting evidence
- single issue valuations or extensions of time claims
- problems of quality or workmanship for which the question of compliance with the specification can be determined by a

person with the appropriate experience, following a site inspection

- disputes for which a decision on one aspect, such as liability, would enable the Parties to continue their negotiations on other matters, such as quantum
- disputes which have already been analysed by both sides and documents exchanged giving the opposing points of view, so that the Adjudicator can be asked to decide between the previously established arguments
- disputes for which the Parties will agree to extend the time period for as long as is required by the Adjudicator.

At the present time, in relation to construction contracts, the term, 'Adjudication' can have any one of three meanings:

- contract Adjudication within the terms of Adjudication as embodied in the Contract which *do not* comply with the statutory arrangements
- contract Adjudication within the terms of a contract which *do comply* with the statutory requirements and
- statutory Adjudication in accordance with the Scheme for Construction Contracts referred to in the Housing Grants, Construction and Regeneration Act 1996.

An Adjudicator then, *must* have regard to the *particular contract arrangements* or to the requirements incorporated in the Statutory *scheme* in each particular case or the decision may not fully cover, or may exceed, the matters referred to Adjudication. If the decision does not deal properly with the matter referred, it may be set aside by a final decision by Litigation or Arbitration. Since the intention appears to have been that Adjudication should be available and accessible to any Parties in a Construction Contract, without necessarily the employment of lawyers, there is also a danger that the Parties to a dispute may not fully appreciate the limits of an Adjudicator's jurisdiction in any particular case, or may not articulate a particular issue properly. There is also the potential problem that where the contract contains Adjudication arrangements which do not comply with the statute, then the Parties may have the option of Adjudication on any particular point under the terms of the contract, or under the Scheme. It would also seem to follow that there could be two tracks of Adjudication, one under the terms of the contract and one under the Scheme, each with its own Adjudicator dealing with the same issue but possibly coming to different decisions. At the time of writing it is not clear how this point would be resolved.

In general terms, the government's intentions for Adjudication appear to have been to combine the merits of Arbitration with the truncated time-scales which would apply to 'palm-tree justice'. The Adjudicator's task therefore must be to attempt to deliver the advantages of both situations and to avoid the disadvantages of those same situations. Parties are ill-advised to opt for Adjudication without taking into account fully the risks inherent in a system which is not fully codified and which is more likely to be approximate in its outcome than to produce the fully considered and thoroughly researched position which Litigation or Arbitration Parties should expect. A fundamental injustice in the situation is that an 'innocent' Party may be dragged into the procedure with insufficient time to prepare their case by an ill-informed, or merely speculative, profit-seeking opponent. As the process would allow the Adjudication procedure to proceed without proper professional advice, it is likely that many of the users will embark on Adjudication with a very imperfect understanding of the contractual duties, rights and obligations. In order to work effectively, the process of Adjudication has to be simpler than that which will typically be encountered in Arbitration, since there is much less time in which to execute the process. The Adjudicator can only be expected to deal with one issue at a time and not, as is often the case in Arbitration, with a whole series of claims and/or counter-claims. It is also apparent that anomalous positions may arise where an Adjudicator makes a decision which is eventually reversed by Arbitration or Litigation but the follow-through events after the Adjudicator's decision cannot be reversed as they can, for example, where the decision simply entails an allocation of time or money. An example could be a decision as to whether the quality of piling is in accordance with the contract or not. If the Adjudicator decides it is, and an Arbitrator decides it is not when the building is complete, what does the unfortunate employer do, and what is the position of the Contractor and indeed of the Consultant?

Several chapters in this book consider the background and development of Adjudication, explain exactly how Adjudication may be expected to work, comment on the Act and the Scheme and review the way in which the process of Adjudication would appear to work or on the face of it, create problems in ICE and JCT Contracts, with a brief view of the situation in regard to some other popular contracts.

The general situation is not assisted by the fact that some legal advisers appear to be going in for something akin to 'genetic engineering' in their modifications to standard procedures. We also look at the question of Consultant's Contracts, review some of the principal rules and procedures which have been published so far. We have endeavoured to keep the book in the most compact format which will make it both easily accessible but also cover the subject sufficiently comprehensively to form a useful reference.

The views expressed are the views of the authors based on their experience in the industry and are not held out to represent a definitive explanation of the legal position. The reader who requires legal advice should obtain it from a legal practitioner.

The diverse nature of disputes arising under what most people would regard as Construction Contracts proper and Consultant's Contracts vary considerably, and arrangements which may work well in one set of circumstances are likely to be ill-suited to another set of circumstances. If you take, for example, the case of a dispute over the proper price to be paid for 10 cubic metres of concrete, placed in quick-sand, following an Engineer's decision under an ICE Contract, the arguments and factual background will be very different in complexity to those which are involved in a dispute over the additional fees claimed under a contract between a building owner and an Architect, Engineer and Acoustics Expert which might occur when they are asked to redesign a concert hall for a different site other than that originally intended, but in both cases one of the Parties concerned could invoke the statutory right to refer the matter to an Adjudicator, who would have to decide the issue in 28 days (or 42 days with the agreement of the referring Party).

The format of this book

The lack of guidance and a desire to bring about a co-ordinated approach to Adjudication lead the authors to conclude that a joint publication, covering both JCT and ICE Contracts and the interest's of both Architects and Engineers would be beneficial to many people in the industry. It is not written primarily with a legal audience in mind. Such publications tend to lapse into terminology which may be clear to lawyers, but tends to leave technical practitioners in difficulty. At the same time, there are obviously legal aspects and Roger Dyer's comments on these areas seemed essential. Roger Dyer has practised as an Architect as well as a Barrister and is often involved with a technical as well as a legal audience, so we were confident that his text would be as accessible as we had sought to make the rest. The book is based on the law of England and Wales. Reference is also made to the Scheme for Scotland in Chapter 6.

The following chapters give the background to Adjudication, our comments on the application of Adjudication to some of the main contracts and to professional contracts and we have added such material as might be useful for reference at the present time.

The authors take the view that dispute avoidance is preferable to Adjudication, whatever its merits, and we include references to this aspect in various places.

How to use this book

We anticipate that readers may intend to use this book in at least four different ways:

- by Architects and Engineers in practice, to understand the process, procedures and Adjudication arrangements generally
- by Employers, Contractors and their advisers, to consider how Adjudication could, or might be used in the circumstances of a particular contract situation
- by Adjudicators and Students as an aid to training
- by Adjudicators or Practitioners faced with a particular problem.

In every case we consider it important to read the whole of Chapters 1–6 inclusive plus those parts of Chapter 11 which apply and also Chapter 12 and then pay particular attention to the section or sections relating to particular contracts, as the consequences of the Act are often affected by particular contract arrangements.

2

Background and development of dispute resolution in construction

The general background to dispute resolution in the construction industry was referred to in Sir Michael Latham's report *Constructing The Team*, published in 1994. It was said that the various factions within the industry had, by that time, developed an increasingly confrontational ethos and it was necessary to turn the tide and improve relationships.

Excessive time and cost expended on dispute resolution

It was not only the construction industry which suffered from what was seen as increasingly litigious attitudes where the time and cost of dispute resolution appeared to be rising in an unacceptable manner. Lord MacKay, the Lord Chancellor at that time, had called for an increased use of alternative dispute resolution processes: 'We must adapt our remedies to changing circumstances. We must not allow the burden of going to seek justice to become so great that instead of guaranteeing freedom it crushes it.' A working Party of the Bar and the Law Society chaired by Hilary Heilbron QC called for a radical shake up to reduce delays and provide more user-friendly justice.[1] The following were cited as contributory factors for the delay or prevention of dispute resolution:

---

1 *Civil Justice on Trial – the case for change.*

- Current Court procedures.
- Absence of sufficient emphasis on ADR in legal education and training.
- Lack of awareness and understanding of ADR techniques and benefits on the part of lawyers.
- Those conducting Litigation are often relatively junior and lack the experience or will to open any form of 'Without Prejudice' negotiation.
- The Parties themselves are often inexperienced and do not realise that it may be unnecessary to pursue a matter through to trial.
- At present there is no stage in the Litigation process at which settlement is suggested by the Court.

This unsatisfactory situation is slowly changing.[2] The 1996 Arbitration Act changed many aspects of the process. Many forms of building and engineering contracts now include reference to incorporated rules, and representatives from many sides of the construction industry have tried to agree a common set of rules for Arbitration in construction industry disputes. The CIMAR Arbitration Rules were published in 1998 and could provide more user-friendly justice. The Construction Industry Council's Adjudication Rules were derived from CIMAR's recommendations for Adjudication.

In the international field, the World Bank which lends some $20 billion each year, introduced in 1995 mandatory arrangements in its procurement documents such that in any contract costing over $40 million disputes are to be referred to a three-person disputes review board. The board is paid a retainer and keeps in touch with the progress of the works. A similar programme was used recently on the Severn Bridge Crossing and in other major construction projects.

---

2 *Access to Justice*. Final Report by The Right Honourable the Lord Woolf, Master of the Rolls. HMSO, London, 1996.

Dispute resolution systems generally: non-binding or imposed

For our purposes we can divide resolution systems into two groups: first we have what we can call non-binding systems in which the

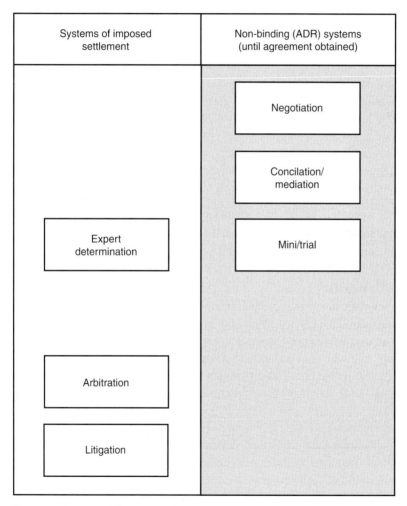

Figure 1. Systems of dispute resolution

Parties agree that their dispute will be explored with the assistance of a Conciliator or a Negotiator or a Mediator or they agree to participate in a mini-trial. They aim to reach an agreement that will resolve the dispute, but the process is not binding until the Parties arrive at an agreement, which they sign and accept as a complete resolution of the defined problem (see Figure 1). Some complain that these systems have no 'teeth', and do not always work because the desired mutual agreement is not achieved. Others report successful cases.

The second group of systems we can call imposed settlement systems in which the resolution is imposed by law. It is the common feature of these systems that there is normally an appeal system and the proceedings are conducted generally in accordance with what lawyers call 'natural justice'. With Adjudication, Latham was seeking an arrangement which would provide a quick process to ensure the cash flow for a Contractor in an industry where cash flow is the life blood, but that such a decision could be superseded by Arbitration, Litigation or any other process which the Parties agreed for use in the longer term. It provided a working decision for the time-being.

Arbitration

At one time the accepted way of dealing with trade or technical disputes cheaply, quickly and effectively was to put the matter before an Arbitrator, someone respected and trusted as an expert in the relevant area of business. Disputes in the construction industry have now become more complex with larger amounts of money at stake and Arbitration is sometimes criticised for being increasingly slow and expensive. The 1996 Arbitration Act may assist in overcoming these problems. The balanced outcome of both Arbitration and Litigation depends not only on the Arbitrator or Judge, but also on the effectiveness of the lawyers and witnesses who are involved. All professions contain members with a wide range of capabilities. The contracts themselves have become more and more complex. The process became more time consuming, while interest rates and the risk of late payment became more draconian in their practical effect.

Expert resolution and the move away from the impartial contract administrator

In this system an Expert, with a duty of care to both Parties, decides how the case should be settled. At one time Architects and Engineers were widely respected and the loss of goodwill occasioned by a major construction dispute served to discourage serious disputes but the imbalance in the industry with an increasingly volatile workload and excessive resources to meet limited demand meant that Contractors sought to make good their losses by contractual manipulation. This position was exacerbated by a tendency no longer to employ Architects or Engineers as impartial Contract Administrators, but to accept a straight 'Employer's representative' to deal with the Employer's position. All these factors have tended to favour some Adjudication process, a 'quick fix'.

Adjudication

The ICE's New Engineering Contract introduced into ICE contracts the use of an 'Adjudicator'. The JCT Contract which is closest to it in concept is 'JCT 81 With Contractor's Design' (WCD). These two Contracts are similar in that neither has what was previously and generally understood as an impartial Architect/Contract Administrator and in the New Engineering Contract the Parties are represented by the Employer in the form of a Project Manager and the Contractor on the other side. In the New Engineering Contract, if the Contractor disagreed with the action of the Project Manager then, as part of the machinery of the Contract, an Adjudicator who has previously been named in the Contract, is called in to reach a decision. The process involves making a decision on one issue at a time and is speedy. JCT 81 WCD had a limited role for an Adjudicator. The Parties could eventually, if necessary, appeal the Adjudicator's decision by way of Arbitration (see Figure 2). At the end of 1995 the DETR drafted the first proposals for a Scheme for

Adjudication under the Act. When these were available for comment they did what few things have achieved previously: they united the construction industry in condemnation of the proposals. Eventually 'The Scheme' was withdrawn but the shell of the Act

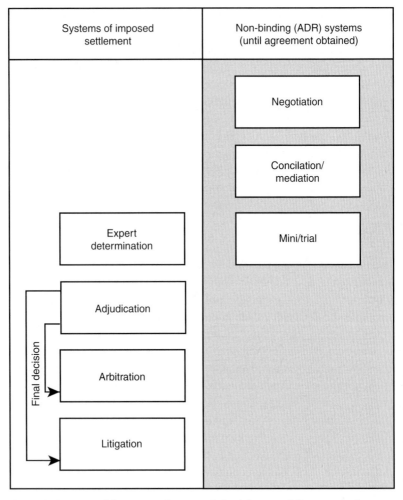

Figure 2. Systems of dispute resolution with final decision following adjudication

was placed on the Statute Book and a further consultation period ensued. A further draft of the Scheme was introduced in August 1997 and still a further draft of the Scheme was published in December 1997 in the form of a draft statutory instrument. The whole process as embodied in the Act and Scheme has been the subject of considerable criticism on the basis of:

- incomplete information for the industry to assess the draft Act and Scheme
- insufficient timing in which to make an assessment
- unsatisfactory drafting of the Act and Scheme.

Adjudication rules

During 1997 both the ICE and the JCT worked on drafts for Adjudication rules which would comply with the Act and mesh with the particular contracts and these were held in draft until the last 'Scheme' was produced. The various professional bodies also started to look at their terms of appointment for consultants. Some might have been willing to allow reference to the Scheme had it generated more confidence, but this was not the case. The picture to emerge was that the Institution of Civil Engineers (ICE) would produce Adjudication rules 'ICE Adjudication procedure 1997' related to their contracts and that Consultant's contracts would either contain their own Adjudication rules or references to Construction Industry Council Rules or would rely on the 'Scheme'. The JCT drafted Adjudication rules and RIBA, Architect's Appointment refers to CIC Adjudication Rules. There was little interest or enthusiasm from the rank and file who generally regarded the whole subject with considerable scepticism, or as a bureaucratic aberration.

The whole process is likely to come into operation in the industry and, among lawyers in particular, with a background of ignorance and distrust. The authors hope that this book will help to overcome the ignorance but would not presume to hope to overcome the distrust.

3

Resolving disputes by Adjudication

This chapter, together with Chapter 4, reviews the Adjudication process from the time when one Party decides to refer a dispute to Adjudication, through to the decision by the Adjudicator. A typical sequence of events is shown in Fig. 3. The detailed Adjudication procedures which are required by particular conditions of contract, or by the Scheme for Construction Contracts, will be considered in later chapters.

The Adjudication process is considered in six parts, following the essential stages of Adjudication:

1. Before the Adjudication.
2. The Notice of Adjudication.
3. The selection and appointment of the Adjudicator.
4. Referral of the dispute to the Adjudicator.
5. Conduct of the Adjudication.
6. The Adjudicator's decision.

Stages 1–5 are considered in this chapter and stage 6 is covered in Chapter 4.

Stage 1 – before the Adjudication

Before any issue can be referred to Adjudication, there must be a dispute. Some contracts define what is meant by the word 'dispute' and prescribe a procedure which must be followed before an objection, a claim, or any other problem can become a dispute. Other contracts do not define a dispute procedure and the first indication that a dispute has arisen could be when one Party to the

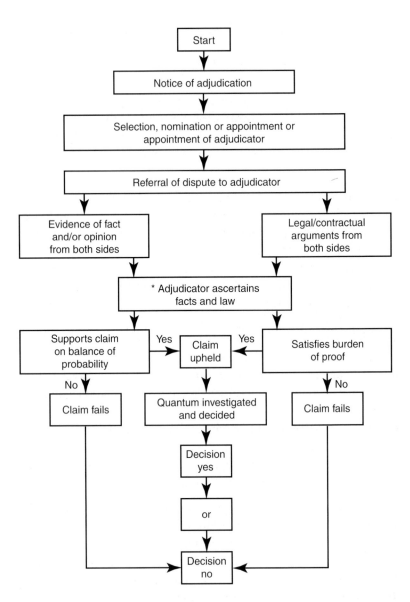

*Note: adjudicator still has to 'ascertain' even if he receives evidence and arguments.

Figure 3. The Adjudication process

Contract issues a notice of intention to refer the dispute to Adjudication.

The fact that an issue can be declared to be a dispute and referred to Adjudication does not necessarily mean that Adjudication is the best way forward. The person who is considering the referral must be satisfied that immediate Adjudication is the best course of action and is in his or her own best interests. This requires consideration of the sequence of questions shown in Fig. 4, which is as follows.

- What is the issue which we are trying to resolve?
- Have I made my views clear to the other side? Do they realise that the initial problem has become a dispute and I intend to involve an independent dispute resolver?
- Would further investigation or tests help to clarify the cause of the problem and resolve the dispute? If so, should the investigation or tests be carried out before I refer the matter to Adjudication?
- Will an impartial decision, within a limited time period, be helpful to the project as a whole?
- Is Adjudication appropriate for this particular problem, or is there a better way forward? Should I try further negotiation, mediation or conciliation?
- Would it be better to refer the problem direct to Arbitration? Is immediate Arbitration permitted by the Contract?
- Is there any procedure which must be followed before the problem can be referred to Adjudication?

The importance of these questions and their implications for disputes under particular Conditions of Contract will be considered in more detail in later chapters of this book.

The execution of a construction contract will always cause problems and problem situations which require actions by both of the Parties to the Contract. Any of these situations or actions may lead to an instruction, request or claim from one Party to the other. The discussions and negotiations may continue for several years or the Parties may quickly reach agreement, decide to drop the matter, or decide to refer the dispute to a third person.

The decision to refer a problem to Adjudication should not be taken without proper consideration of the consequences. Adjudication is, in principle, a procedure which will give an impartial decision within a limited time period. The decision must be

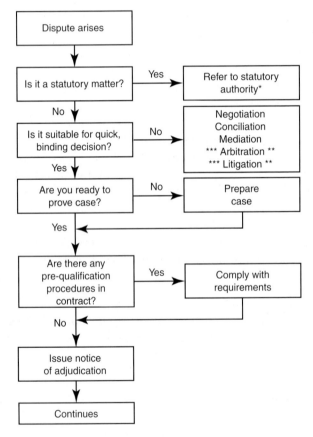

Notes: *   maybe, for example, VAT or health and safety
       ** contract may rule out litigation or early arbitration
       *** responding party may demand adjudication.

Figure 4. What is the most appropriate form of dispute resolution?

implemented but the implementation may later be reversed by Arbitration or Litigation. Some of the problems and disputes which arise in construction may not be suitable for Adjudication, for example:

- Disputes which comprise several issues may need to be considered as separate disputes with separate Adjudications, or as requiring a series of decisions over an extended period.
- Disputes involving complex legal issues are not normally suitable for Adjudication.
- Disputes which require a decision, the consequences of which cannot be reversed, such as a matter of termination, alleged corruption or allegations against a professional person, may not be suitable for Adjudication.
- Matters such as design or quality, which affect the form of the completed project and for which the Contract states that one of the Parties is responsible for the issue of decisions or instructions, are not suitable for Adjudication. Disputes concerning the liability for additional costs as a consequence of such a decision or instruction are more likely to be suitable.
- Matters on which the decision is within the province of some other person or authority, such as VAT, taxation issues, health and safety, or any allegation with criminal implications, must be referred to the proper authority.

When the Party concerned has decided that Adjudication is the best way forward, it must ensure that the problem has been properly identified and that the proper procedures have been followed.

In the construction industry there are two categories of Adjudication:

- 'contractual Adjudication', which is available because it has been included in the contract, and
- 'statutory Adjudication', which is available because the Act has established a statutory right to Adjudication.

When a dispute is referred to Adjudication the Referring Party must be clear whether the reference is being made to a contractual procedure or to Adjudication under the statutory scheme, which has been imposed by the Act.

Contractual adjudication

Most construction contracts include provision for any claims, or other problems, to be notified when the problem first arises, negotiated and finally settled in accordance with certain stated procedures. These procedures may include a process of Adjudication.

The standard forms of contract which are reviewed in this book have been revised to include the requirements of the Act. However, the contract for the particular project may have been modified to suit the requirements of the Employer. If the person considering Adjudication decides that the relevant contract does comply with the requirements of the Act then he will proceed with Adjudication in accordance with the provisions of the contract. As will be seen later, this will include detailed procedures which are in addition to, but compliant with, the requirements of the Act.

Many of the standard forms of contract which were written before the passage of the Act also included provision for Adjudication. These provisions do not comply with all the requirements of the Act. While amendments to the standard forms of contract have now been published there are some contracts which are subject to the Act, but do not incorporate the amendments, possibly because the Contract Documents were prepared before the amendments were published. If, for whatever reason, the Parties have chosen to sign a contract which incorporates a non-compliant Adjudication procedure, then they are presumably entitled to use that procedure. The status of the procedure can be compared to any other matter which depends on the provisions of the Contract. The fact that the government scheme becomes implied terms in a non-compliant contract, probably in conflict with other terms, introduces another source of potential problems.

When the Contract includes a non-compliant Adjudication procedure the person considering referral to Adjudication has a choice. The dispute may be referred to Adjudication in accordance with the contract procedures, or he may exercise his right to Statutory Adjudication under the Act. Clearly, if one Party decides to invoke non-compliant Adjudication under the contract then the other Party may decide to exercise his statutory right to Adjudication under the Scheme. This could result in the confusing situation that the same dispute is being considered, at the same time, by different Adjudicators using different procedures!

When considering whether to refer a dispute to Adjudication under the contract it is necessary to check whether any requirements or procedures in the contract have been followed. The contract may impose restrictions on the type of dispute which can be referred to Adjudication. The procedures may be incorporated into the contract either directly, or by reference to one of the published Adjudication Rules or Procedures. The requirements of the most commonly used standard forms of contract are reviewed in later chapters of this book.

Statutory adjudication
Statutory Adjudication was created by the Housing Grants, Construction and Regeneration Act 1996 (the Act). The statutory rights and procedures are discussed in detail in Chapter 5 and, for present purposes, it is sufficient to note that any Party to a construction contract has the right to refer a dispute arising under the contract for Adjudication. The fact that the non-compliant contract may include a procedure called Adjudication would not prevent either party from making use of the government scheme.

When someone decides that they would like to refer a particular dispute to statutory Adjudication they must first check that the dispute complies with the necessary provisions laid down in the Act. The Contract must be in writing and be a construction contract which is not covered by one of the exclusions which are defined in the Act, and that the dispute arises under the contract. The wording in the Act does not cover disputes which are only 'in connection with' rather than 'under' the contract. Disputes on matters of tort, misrepresentation or some other situations might only be 'in connection with' but not 'under' the contract.

Statutory Adjudication will be conducted in accordance with the Scheme for Construction Contracts (the Scheme) which is reviewed in Chapter 6.

Stage 2 – the notice of Adjudication

For an Adjudication to commence, the person who decides to refer the dispute to Adjudication must inform the other person of his intention. This requires a 'Notice of Adjudication', from the 'Referring Party' to the 'Other Party', who is also known as the 'Responding Party' or 'Receiving Party'.

The Notice of Adjudication should always be in writing, to avoid misunderstanding at a later date, and must comply with any procedures and format which are stipulated in the Contract or the Scheme. The Notice should include sufficient information to satisfy its purpose, which is:

- to inform the recipient Party that the particular dispute is to be referred to Adjudication
- to give any nominating body and potential Adjudicator basic information about the dispute
- to initiate the procedure and move on to the next stage.

The Notice of Adjudication only needs to contain sufficient information for identification and to define the dispute. It should not include a lengthy justification of the referring Party's point of view, or copies of previous correspondence. This information will be submitted at a later stage.

The Adjudicator will then be selected, if not already named in the Contract, and appointed to give a decision on the matter which is defined in the Notice of Adjudication. Neither Party will be permitted to introduce additional issues after the dispute has been defined. If either Party wishes to have some other matter, either an additional claim or a counter-claim, considered then they should issue a separate Notice of Adjudication, unless both Parties and the Adjudicator agree to extend the scope of the Adjudication.

The other Party is then aware of the proposed reference and so can decide whether to wait for the Adjudication to proceed, or take some action which might resolve the dispute, or raise some procedural matter. If the other Party intends to raise any procedural objection it must be raised immediately, or the right to object may have been waived. However, any objection will need to be considered by the Adjudicator and this is obviously not possible until he has been appointed and received the referral.

Some Contracts also require that the Notice of Adjudication includes additional information. This may be the names of potential Adjudicators or further information about the dispute.

Stage 3 – the selection and appointment of the Adjudicator

The Adjudicator must be selected and appointed in order that the Adjudication can commence. A typical sequence of events and points to be checked is shown in Fig. 5.

Irrespective of whether the Adjudicator is appointed at the start of the project or when the dispute has arisen, it is essential to find a suitable person. An Adjudicator must have knowledge and experience of the type of project and be able to understand the issue which is the subject of the dispute. He must have been trained as an Adjudicator, have an adequate knowledge of the particular form of contract and the law, together with the capability to make a judgemental decision.

It is always preferable for the Adjudicator to be selected and agreed by both the Parties to the Contract. Lists of names can be exchanged and discussed. Each side will strike out names which are not acceptable, or with whom there is a potential conflict of interest. The process continues until an Adjudicator is identified who is willing to take on the commission and is acceptable to both sides.

The problem with trying to agree on the Adjudicator after a dispute has arisen is that Adjudication procedures allow only a very

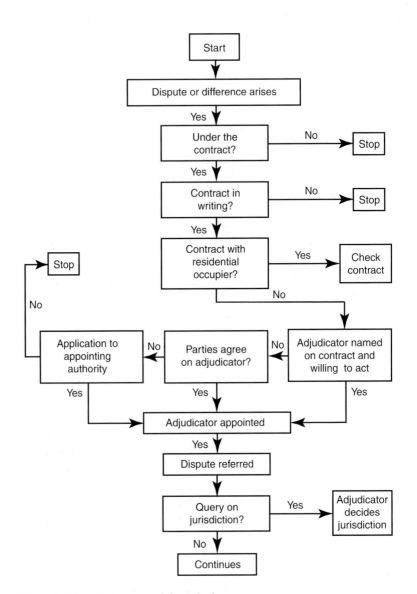

Figure 5. The appointment of the Adjudicator

short time period for the selection and appointment, and some Parties tend to reject any name which has been suggested by the other side.

Consultants and other people within the construction industry build personal files of Adjudicators whom they know are capable of dealing with certain types of dispute. Some organisations, such as the ICE, publish a list of people who have satisfied their criteria and passed the training courses. This list is frequently used as a source of independent professionals, who are not known to either side. Some organisations who train Adjudicators will offer a service for nomination or appointment, but do not publish lists from which the Parties may make their own selection.

In practice, the referring Party does not have to wait until he issues the Notice before starting the selection process. When negotiations are showing signs of failure it may be appropriate for the Parties to discuss the possibility of Adjudication and consider the names of potential Adjudicators.

The appointment of the Adjudicator

The Adjudicator may be appointed at the start of the contract period, or when a dispute has arisen and a Notice of Adjudication has been issued.

Some contracts encourage the appointment of an Adjudicator at tender stage. He is then available to consider any dispute from the start of the contract. However, if an Adjudicator is named in the tender documents he has probably been chosen by the Employer. While this does not mean that the Adjudicator will be biased in favour of the Employer he may be thought to be biased. In particular, if an Employer signs a contract with an organisation to provide Adjudicators they will almost certainly be seen as having lost their independence.

The procedure whereby a tenderer can raise objections to the named Adjudicator does not solve the problem. Tenderers may be reluctant to risk losing the contract by raising objections to an Adjudicator who was chosen by the Employer. They are more likely to accept the named adjudicator but avoid the use of Adjudication. A better procedure is for the Employer to name three or four persons and for the Contractor to select one from the list. Alternatively, the Adjudicator can be selected immediately after the Contract has been signed. He is then available almost from the first day and can be chosen by agreement before hostilities hinder discussion.

Other problems which may arise when the Adjudicator is chosen and appointed at the start of the project are as follows.

- It is necessary to check that the appointed Adjudicator is still available when the dispute actually arises. There may have been changes in his health or circumstances since the appointment. Adjudication requires intensive activity during a short period and he may have other commitments which would prevent him from allocating sufficient time to the Adjudication.
- A possible conflict of interest may have arisen which was not known when he was appointed.
- A particular dispute may require specialised knowledge which is not possessed by this Adjudicator.
- If practising Adjudicators are named in a large number of contracts, or appointed but not used, it becomes impossible for them to plan their availability for other appointments.

In practice, although some of the standard Forms of Contract include provision for the Adjudicator to be named at tender stage, many Employers are not using this facility. The problems of perceived bias, the need for specialist knowledge and possible problems of availability can sometimes result in the decision that the choice will be made when the need arises.

Alternatively, if three or four names are listed in the documents then the Employer has accepted those names. A contractor referring a dispute to Adjudication can select a name from the list when the dispute occurs.

Appointment after the Notice of Adjudication

When the Adjudicator is chosen after the Notice of Adjudication has been issued it is necessary to make a fast selection and appointment. The time available is restricted and the chances of Party agreement are reduced.

When the Parties have not been able to agree on the Adjudicator, the Party who issued the Notice of Adjudication will apply to an Appointing or Nominating Body. This Body may be named in the Contract, chosen by agreement, or chosen unilaterally by the referring Party. Most such bodies have a standard procedure which includes an application form and a fee for making the appointment. The application form may also impose conditions, such as a disclaimer on liability and responsibility for any abortive fees to the Adjudicator if the Adjudication should not proceed. They will require a copy of the Notice of Adjudication together with basic information about the dispute and whether any specialist qualification is required. However the Nominating Body will not normally check the validity of the application. The requirement for a fast appointment does not permit them to spend time considering legal problems or other documentation.

The procedure for the actual appointment can vary and should be studied by both Parties and the Adjudicator in order to safeguard their own interests. An appointment at the start of the project, without the pressure of an immediate referral, gives time for the Parties and the Adjudicator to discuss terms and fees. If the appointment is made after the Notice of Adjudication has been issued there will probably not be time to agree fee rates before referral of the dispute to the Adjudicator. Under most contract procedures, if an appointing body makes the appointment, it will be in accordance with their standard Terms of Agreement between the Parties and the Adjudicator. These procedures and agreements are discussed in later chapters of this book. When the Adjudicator has been appointed, he will be entitled to a reasonable fee. If there is a problem with agreement to his fee rate then it will be determined by the Courts when the Adjudicator sues for his fees.

Stage 4 – referral of the dispute to the Adjudicator

The Act and consequently most Contracts refer to 'appointment and referral', within a stated procedure and time period, as though they are a single operation. In practice, the action of referral will be distinct from the act of appointment, although it should happen immediately after appointment. Referral signals the start of the time period for the Adjudication. It is important that the actual calendar date of referral is clear. If there is any possibility of ambiguity a concerned Party should raise the matter immediately and the Adjudicator will determine the date. In any event, the Adjudicator should confirm the referral date immediately he receives the referral documents.

If the Adjudicator has been appointed, but has not received the necessary information about the dispute, then he cannot start his work and the time period should not commence. This may be because the Adjudicator was appointed before the issue of the Notice of Adjudication, possibly at the start of the project, or it may be that the referring Party has asked for the appointment, but has not yet prepared the necessary papers for referral.

Contracts which follow the provisions of the Act must have a timetable with the object of providing for referral within seven days of the Notice of Adjudication. If referral takes place after this period then a question may arise as to whether there is a valid referral. This will depend on the requirements of the particular procedure. However, if the referring Party is not ready, or for some reason decides not to send the documents to the Adjudicator, then he cannot wait for an indefinite period. The Notice must lapse if the dispute is not referred within a reasonable, and probably very restricted, period. The Adjudicator may have to rule on any objections.

The extent of information which must be provided at referral may be defined in the Adjudication procedure. The referring Party should send the appropriate documents to the Adjudicator, with a copy to the other Party and a clear statement that this is referral. If the Adjudicator considers that the documents submitted are not adequate to constitute referral he will raise the matter with the referring Party.

Subject to any specific requirements in the Contract, the documents which are necessary to constitute referral are the Notice of Adjudication, sufficient information to explain the matter in dispute, the information on which the Referring Party relies and the relief which is being sought.

Jurisdiction

In Adjudication, as with any procedure in which a third person is appointed to determine matters between two contracting Parties, there is the possibility of a challenge to the jurisdiction of that person. The Adjudicator will normally have to rule on his own jurisdiction, either with the support of the procedures under which he has been appointed, or for the practical reason of being able to continue with his work and reach the decision which he has been appointed to make, or to decide to terminate his appointment.

Ultimately, jurisdiction may need to be determined by the Courts but, unless the Parties have agreed on an extension to the Adjudication period, there is no time for a stay to the proceedings in order to consider a matter of jurisdiction. Any final determination by the Courts is likely to be a consequence of proceedings for enforcement, rather than being a reason to delay the Adjudication.

In any event, Adjudication provides an interim decision, which is binding until the dispute is finally determined by legal proceedings, by Arbitration or by agreement. Any problem such as jurisdiction may well be overtaken by a subsequent reference of the dispute itself to Arbitration or legal proceedings.

The mechanics of referral and response

The actual procedure for referral and response varies in different Adjudication procedures, but is based on the following.

- The Adjudicator has been appointed and has a copy of the Notice of Adjudication.

- The referring Party sends the Adjudicator his 'Statement of Case', with a copy to the other Party.
- The responding Party sends the Adjudicator his response, with a copy to the referring Party.

Some procedures, including the Scheme, do not give the responding Party the right to submit a reply to the Statement of Case. The submission of a response may then depend on the Adjudicator asking for further information.

The Statement of Case

While a minimum bundle of documents will enable the Adjudicator to proceed, the referring Party will usually take advantage of the opportunity to provide a detailed explanation of his case. A well-argued presentation, including legal or contractual argument backed by authorities, will inevitably have a persuasive effect on the Adjudicator. The referring Party has the advantage of choosing when to refer the dispute to Adjudication and so of taking as long as he requires to prepare his case. He then has the advantage of being able to submit the first detailed explanation of the problem. The advantages of the first submission are such that a Party who is defending his rejection of a claim may find an advantage in declaring that there is a dispute and becoming the referring Party in the Adjudication.

Some Claimants believe that the greater the number of pages, the more persuasive will be the Statement. This must be a misconception. The Statement should be clear and concise and no Adjudicator will allow himself to be influenced by the mere volume of paper which is presented by one side. Within the limited time period the Adjudicator may even reject an excessive volume of paper and ask for a concise summary of the referring Party's case. Clarity of communication is essential for a procedure within a restricted time period.

The Adjudicator will also be aware that, under the provisions of the Act, the referring Party has been able to choose his time for the issue of the Notice of Adjudication. He has been able to wait for as long as he considers will help his case in order to conduct investigations and research, evaluate the consequences of the initial event, and obtain whatever advice he requires. Under most standard forms of contract the initial notice of a Claim, or of a relevant event, must be given within a fixed time period. The Claimant will give this notice before he is fully aware of all the consequences of the problem and so it may refer to only a limited part of the eventual problem.

The Statement of Case should not be restricted rigidly to one side of the argument. If there has been an exchange of correspondence, discussions, requests for further information and research or investigation, then the complete file should be presented to the Adjudicator. If some information is obviously necessary for the Adjudicator to understand the Claimant's point of view, such as a copy of the question which is being answered, then that information should be included. It is in the best interests of the referring Party that the Adjudicator achieves a clear understanding of the dispute as soon as possible during the Adjudication period.

For a detailed presentation of a major dispute, the Statement of Case may include:

- a brief summary of the dispute and the problem which led to the dispute
- evidence in the form of documents, photographs, witness statements and/or expert opinion to establish the factual basis of the claim
- legal and contractual arguments on which the claim is based with authorities, when available

The referring Party must always bear in mind that someone who makes an allegation must be ready to prove that allegation.

If the referring Party is anxious to prove its case, it will, while preparing its Statement of Case:

- make sure of its legal and contractual position before embarking on the process
- avoid ambiguity so as not to leave any room for doubt

- check and double check all factual matters
- avoid exaggeration and speculative allegations
- look at every point from the opposite point of view and satisfy itself that there are no weaknesses in the arguments or evidence
- take specialist advice where necessary
- make sure that the evidence convincingly supports any allegations or refutations
- have regard to the fact that it is a difficult task to set down unambiguously exactly what happened and how and why the case is justified.

Stage 5 – conduct of the Adjudication

Timetable for the Adjudication

Immediately the Adjudicator has studied the Statement of Case he will prepare the provisional timetable for the Adjudication. A typical programme is shown in Fig. 6. The timetable will show how he proposes to complete his work within the time period which is permitted by the contract procedure, based on his assumptions as to the actions which will be necessary. It will also take into account any requests from the Parties, together with the requirements of his own diary. If the contract procedure does not allow specifically for a response from the responding Party then the Adjudicator may include a suitable provision.

The Adjudicator will revise the initial timetable as the Adjudication proceeds and further information becomes available. The timetable will include a period for the Adjudicator to assess the information which he has received, to reach his decision and to prepare his written decision. If, for whatever reason, the time period becomes unreasonably congested the Adjudicator will ask the Parties for an extension, in accordance with the provisions of the Contract. Should either Party refuse to agree to an extension then the Adjudicator must work within the previous period and take action to accelerate the timetable. He will draw his own conclusions as to why the request was rejected.

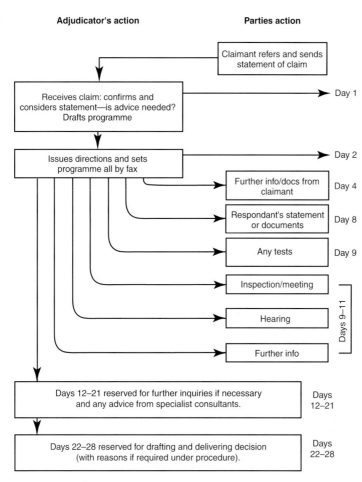

Figure 6. A typical programme

Alternatively, if the Parties agree that they would like to defer the completion of the Adjudication in order to give themselves time for further investigation or negotiation then the Adjudicator may have problems fitting the new dates into his diary.

The response

When the referring Party has sent a Statement of Case to the Adjudicator, the other Party will want to respond. The response may need to be submitted within a certain time period which is stipulated in the contract procedure, or it may follow a direction from the Adjudicator. If no time period for a response has been laid down the responding Party should ask for the opportunity to submit its reply to the Statement of Case. In any event the responding Party may be determined to give its point of view and will send a response to suit its own convenience.

The Adjudicator will want to receive any response as quickly as possible, in order that he can assess both Parties' point of view. The time period may be a number of days which has been fixed in the Contract, or by the Adjudicator, but it will inevitably be a very short period of time. If the Statement of Case is a substantial document, perhaps extending to numerous files, then the Party preparing the response may have severe problems in meeting any stipulated date.

The key to a fast response will be to identify the most critical points and deal with these points first. Consultants who deal with construction contracts will need to develop systems ready to offer fast advice to their clients.

If the Adjudication concerns a dispute which has been discussed and investigated over a considerable period of time then the response should have been developed during the negotiations. The Party preparing the response will know all about the initial problem, have decided to reject the claim and will have made its own investigations as it considered appropriate. However, if the dispute has emerged from a simple request and rejection for lack of justification, the responding Party may have considerable difficulty in preparing a detailed response within the required time period. If the referring Party has deliberately created an ambush situation then the responding Party could be presented with a difficult, or even impossible, task.

In these circumstances the best course of action may be for the Party concerned to write to the Adjudicator, with a copy to the referring Party, explaining the situation. The letter will include a timetable of the development of the dispute and a schedule to show when each item mentioned in the Statement of Case was first notified to the other Party. If the Statement of Case includes allegations and complex evidence which had not previously been notified then there is a clear justification for further time in which to prepare the response.

The Adjudicator, due to the time constraints imposed by the contract procedure, may not be in a position to grant additional time for the preparation of a response to the Statement of Case. He is under an obligation to reach his Decision within a fixed time period. If the referring Party agrees to an extension of the Adjudication period then the other Party can be given more time for the response. If the referring Party refuses to agree to more time then the Adjudicator will draw his own conclusions. The Adjudicator does have considerable discretion to decide what weight to assign to the various arguments and evidence which is put before him. The fact that one Party has deliberately denied the other Party the opportunity to refute important arguments must influence the Adjudicator's assessment of the information which has been presented to him.

The length and detail of the response will depend on the circumstances of the dispute, but it must include a clear denial of any allegation and evidence which is refuted. In the circumstances of Adjudication, an Adjudicator may follow the principle that 'anything not denied is accepted'. It will not be sufficient just to include a blanket rejection of everything stated in the claim. The depth and detail of the discussion and alternative propositions must be at least the equivalent of the evidence which was submitted in the Statement of Case.

The response to a detailed Statement of Case should include:

- a brief summary of the dispute and the problem which led to the dispute, explaining the counter point of view and reasons for rejecting the claim
- legal and contractual counter arguments, with authorities

- evidence in the form of documents, photographs, witnesses and/ or expert opinion to support any counter arguments and allegations.

In its own interests the responding Party will:

- read carefully any claim statement
- deal with the matter thoroughly
- ask for clarification of any ambiguity
- insist that any allegation is supported by evidence, including details of when and where any alleged events are said to have taken place
- make sure that it has dealt with every point made or implied
- point out every factual error and collate evidence which will assist with the Adjudicator's understanding of the case
- consider any contractual or legal point and make sure that everything which can be rebutted is rebutted
- admit those things which are correct but make it clear exactly which points are contested
- make sure the record is complete
- if the Claimant has given only half the story, admit that which is true but explain fully the missing part of the picture, which may put a different complexion on the whole affair.

The Adjudication period

The requirement that the Adjudicator will give a fast decision is an essential feature of Adjudication. The time period which is available will depend on the details of the procedure, but it is always restricted and cannot be unilaterally extended by the Adjudicator. The time period which is desirable for the Adjudicator to establish all the relevant facts and law and reach a good decision is a different matter. This will depend on the details of the dispute and the actions of the Parties. The Adjudication provisions in the Contract or in the Act, by fixing the time period, are telling the Adjudicator to do the best he can, within that time period.

Before the advent of the Act, the Contracts which contained provision for Adjudication incorporated different time periods for the Adjudicator to reach his decision. A period of about three months was generally considered to be reasonable.

Contracts which follow the provisions of the Act must have a basic 28-day period from referral until the Adjudicator reaches his decision. This is a shorter period than would previously have been considered reasonable and means that many adjudicators will find that the period will not give them sufficient time to raise queries, receive further information and allow each Party to review and respond to further evidence which has been provided by the other Party.

The 28-day period can be extended by the Parties, provided the extension is agreed after the dispute has been referred to the Adjudicator. Provision in the Contract for a longer period would not comply with the Act. The Adjudicator may extend the time period, by up to 14 days, with the consent of the referring Party. This provision gives the Party who initiated the Adjudication the unilateral right to veto any extension to the time period.

If the Adjudicator finds that the 28-day period is not sufficient for an adequate review of the dispute then he would ask the Parties to agree to an extension. The referring Party having already had as long as he requires to prepare his Statement of Case, it is more likely to be the preparation of the response that resulted in the need for the extension. Hence the Adjudicator may require the additional time in order to be fair to both sides.

If the referring Party refuses to agree to negotiate an extension and rejects the Adjudicator's request for a 14 day extension then the Adjudicator will allocate the available time in the best way possible, which may well be to the disadvantage of the referring Party.

Actions by the Adjudicator

When the dispute has been referred to the Adjudicator it is for him to take the initiative and decide what actions he is going to take in order to reach his decision.

The first task will usually be to check that the matters to be determined are clearly defined in the Notice of Adjudication. This may have been checked and confirmed at the appointment stage but, if there is any possibility of confusion, the Adjudicator may wish to write to the Parties and confirm his understanding of the situation.

Many of the Adjudication procedures before the publication of the Act were envisaged to be on a 'documents only' basis. Each disputing Party sent a written statement to the Adjudicator. He considered these statements and made his decision based on the information they contained.

The Adjudication procedures which are based on the requirements of the Act enable the Adjudicator to take whatever actions he considers are necessary in order to reach his decision, within wide limitations. The exact powers will depend on the provisions of the particular procedure, but typically will include the power:

- to set the timetable for the Adjudication, within the time period determined by the Contract, or agreed with the Parties
- to take the initiative in ascertaining the facts and the law
- to request further information and clarification of statements and to set a time for reply
- to require Parties to limit the lengths of written or oral submissions
- to meet and question the Parties and other persons who have knowledge of the dispute. Some procedures give the Adjudicator the right to meet the Parties separately. Under other procedures he would try to arrange a joint meeting but could continue with one Party if the other fails to attend the meeting
- to request the production of documents or the attendance of people whom he considers could assist
- to visit the site

- to obtain specialist advice and require tests or investigations
- to set times or deadlines for any of the above
- to continue the Adjudication and reach a decision even if a Party fails to co-operate and comply with a request or direction
- to issue such other directions as he considers to be appropriate.

The extent to which the Adjudicator will choose to exercise these powers will depend on the circumstances of the particular case. The powers are derived from the Contract and have been accepted by the Parties, but he has no power to force a reluctant party to comply or to give directions to third parties.

The first action will be consideration of the programme for the Adjudication. On the calendar, the Adjudicator may have 28 days, with the possibility of an extension. The immediate problem is that Adjudicators lead busy lives, with other engagements in their diaries. The Adjudicator has agreed to take the case and so will have a reasonable amount of time available, but this may be restricted to certain periods or only parts of certain days.

The Adjudicator will study the Statement of Case and set down a framework for his programme. He may decide to ask for an immediate response, together with clarification of certain points from the referring Party. If he decides that a meeting with the Parties, or a site visit, will be necessary then he must immediately contact the Parties to agree on a convenient date. If he wants to question certain people, or consult specialists, then the sooner he decides what he wants, the easier it will be to make the necessary arrangements. He then needs sufficient time to consider the results of any action, instigate possible further action, reconsider the whole case and write up his decision.

Even the most carefully planned programme can be disrupted by some unexpected problem, or by dilatory action by a reluctant or uncooperative Party. An Adjudication period of 28 days can pass very quickly.

The Act requires the period to be extended by extra days for Good Friday, Christmas Day and statutory bank holidays, but not for weekends or days which the industry normally takes as holidays.

Additional information provided by the Parties

The Adjudicator will have received a Statement of Case from the referring Party in order to refer the dispute to him and start the Adjudication. If the Statement of Case does not include sufficient information then he will raise queries and must consider whether the document contains sufficient information to constitute referral. Alternatively, it is possible, but unlikely, that he will decide that the Statement of Case includes sufficient information for him to understand both Parties' point of view and reach his decision. The Adjudicator will generally ask the responding Party to respond to the Statement of Case, even if the procedures do not include a specific requirement for a response.

The Adjudicator will then be able to request either Party to provide additional information. This may be a matter of clarification of a point which is not clear, authorities and arguments to support a statement, or the need for specific information which has been omitted from the previous submissions. In the extreme he may have to tell the Parties that he cannot understand the case from the information which they have provided. A request for further information will not be an opportunity for either Party to develop new ideas or submit additional claims, counter-claims or set-off against the claim which is in dispute. The scope of the dispute has been determined by the Notice of Adjudication.

When the Adjudicator asks for additional information he should make a specific request and give the date by which he requires an answer.

Meetings with the Adjudicator

The Adjudication procedures which follow the Act generally give the Adjudicator the right to meet with the Parties. This is an important provision in that it enables the Adjudicator to discuss the case with the Parties if he feels that this would assist him in his task.

The Adjudicator will decide whether he requires a meeting. There is no automatic right for either Party to demand the opportunity to explain its case in person, or to submit oral evidence from witnesses, although any requests would be considered by the Adjudicator.

The reasons for a meeting may include:

- to resolve any queries on jurisdiction, the interpretation of the Notice of Adjudication or other preliminary matters
- to clarify any points in the Statement of Claim or response
- to visit the site and to inspect any particular part of the Works; to arrange for tests or opening up of the work and inspect the results
- to hear oral evidence
- to discuss queries and resolve any problems which can be sorted out quicker by discussion than by correspondence.

Within a limited time period it may be difficult to arrange a convenient date for the meeting so, while it is preferable for the Adjudicator to meet the Parties together, it may be necessary for him to arrange separate meetings. The Adjudicator will need to arrange any meeting on a date to suit his timetable for the Adjudication. If one Party is unable to attend on that date, and it is impossible to fix a mutually acceptable date, then the Adjudicator will hold the meeting with just one Party present.

The Adjudicator should try to give all Parties the opportunity to attend every meeting. Even if he has the specific power to meet them separately he should try to arrange for joint meetings and should keep the other Party informed of what transpires at a meeting.

If the documents are complete and appear to give him all the information he requires then the Adjudicator may decide that a meeting is not necessary. Meetings are expensive and time consuming and a meeting would only be arranged if it will serve a useful purpose.

If the Adjudicator decides to hold a meeting then it should be arranged as early as possible during the Adjudication period. If there is a good reason to hold a meeting, then there may be further action needed to follow up any problems after the meeting. The Adjudicator will want to resolve any problems as quickly as possible and avoid the pressure of unanswered questions towards the end of the Adjudication period.

A meeting with the Parties will frequently be the easiest way for the Adjudicator to clarify any points which arise from his study of the initial submissions. A face to face question and answer session can resolve problems which would otherwise require a lengthy sequence of correspondence. A serious problem of jurisdiction or interpretation of the Notice of Adjudication may require a special meeting at the start of the Adjudication period.

An Adjudication meeting will generally be more informal than an Arbitration hearing, but more formal than a site meeting. The Parties may be represented by their technical or legal advisers. However, it is the Parties themselves who are in dispute and should take the leading role before the Adjudicator. The Architect or Engineer for the Contract may be involved in the subject matter of the dispute and will be present to assist the Employer, not to administer the Adjudication. The Adjudicator may ask for other people to be present in order to clarify particular points. The Adjudicator has no power to require the presence of any particular person but any failure to co-operate by either Party will tend to weaken their case.

While most Adjudication meetings will be discussions to assist the Adjudicator it is always desirable for the meeting to have a formal agenda. The Adjudicator must be prepared for a Party to be uncooperative or aggressive and must be ready to impose his authority and control the meeting. He may even need to adjourn a meeting in order to allow the Parties to cool down. If the Adjudicator decides that oral presentations by the Parties, followed by evidence from witnesses, would help him to reach his decision then he would issue appropriate directions to the Parties. The Parties do not have the right to present witnesses, or to cross-examine opposing witnesses, and can only do so with the permission of the Adjudicator. When the Adjudicator decides to question witnesses himself he must prepare his questions in advance in order to gain the maximum benefit from the interrogation. If the written submissions include conflicting statements, or allegations which impinge on the integrity of individuals, then the Adjudicator may want to question the person concerned. Also, the person concerned may want the opportunity to state their side of the argument and clear their name of the allegations. In some circumstances the Adjudicator or the witness may ask for the evidence to be given on oath.

The problem will always be the time period. It will always be difficult to organise a series of meetings, or the presence of witnesses, within a 28-day period. If the Parties agree to an appropriate extension to this period then the Adjudicator is more likely to be able to agree to any requests for additional meetings.

Site visits

Construction Adjudication will, by definition, involve construction problems. While there is a very wide range of disputes which can be referred to Adjudication, many disputes will involve quality of workmanship, or something that happened on a construction site. The type of disputes which are best suited to Adjudication are often those for which a site visit will enable the Adjudicator to observe the problem himself. Site visits are therefore an important feature of many Adjudications and may include inspection of disputed work or a direction by the Adjudicator to open up work or conduct tests.

The decision as to whether a site visit is necessary must be a matter for the Adjudicator. However, he will need the agreement of the Party who controls the site and their co-operation in making the necessary arrangements. Before deciding to ask for a site visit, the Adjudicator must consider what he will gain from a visit. A site visit needs to be planned in advance. It costs money and takes up valuable time, so should not be required without proper considera-tion of the benefits.

Normally the site will be under the control of one of the Parties, so the Adjudicator will ask that Party to make the necessary arrangements. However, it may be necessary to obtain permission from another party.

The Adjudicator should tell the Parties, before the visit, what he wants to see and what benefit he hopes to derive from the visit. This will enable the Parties to make the arrangements and to decide what level of representation they should provide at the visit. The Adjudicator must avoid the situation in which one Party takes advantage of the visit by trying to influence him with new arguments and evidence which has not been given to the other Party.

There will generally be an advantage in combining the site visit with an Adjudication meeting. If this is the intention then the Adjudicator should tell the Parties beforehand, so that they can plan their representation and submissions.

Taking the initiative in ascertaining the facts and the law

The Act requires that a compliant Contract shall enable the Adjudicator to take the initiative in ascertaining the facts and the law. The Adjudicator has the power to act on his own initiative, but is not under any obligation to try to ascertain all the facts and law. This would not normally be possible in the restricted time period.

For the same reason the Adjudicator is not obliged to conduct a detailed forensic investigation into the problem which led to the dispute. For example, to take samples and conduct tests may require more than 28 days.

In practice, any Adjudicator should exercise some caution in using his initiative in this way. A Party cannot rely on the Adjudicator to make good deficiencies in the presentation of its case. An Adjudicator who investigates and identifies facts which could have been submitted by the Party who benefits, will be open to the accusation that he is not impartial.

It can also be argued that to give a decision on a dispute is a matter of assessing the views of the disputants, rather than finding the correct solution to the underlying problem. In Adjudication the Parties should make their own investigations and tests and not rely on guidance and directions by the Adjudicator.

The power to take the initiative enables the Adjudicator to make his own enquiries and test the opinions and evidence which have been submitted to him. Enquiries may be made through the Parties, or direct to an outside source if he considers that this will help him to reach his decision.

The use of specialist advice

A natural consequence of the power to take the initiative in ascertaining the facts and the law is the power to consult another person or organisation for specialist advice. Most Adjudication rules and procedures allow the Adjudicator to consult a specialist adviser. The procedures vary and he may need to obtain specific approval for the cost, or just notify the Parties of his intentions. However, if the Parties are relying on the Adjudicator to give a decision which they are obliged to implement, they should also trust him to consult wisely and with due regard to the cost. The Adjudicator must remember that, when he consults a specialist, he will be liable to the specialist for his fees and will have to recover the cost from the Parties.

When the Adjudicator consults a specialist, he can only use the report for advice. The decision must be made by the Adjudicator himself and not be delegated to the specialist.

The type of specialist, technical or legal, will depend on the subject of the dispute and the expertise of the Adjudicator. For a dispute which involves a particular technical subject there is an obvious value in using an Adjudicator with specialist knowledge of that subject.

It will always be important for the Adjudicator to send copies of any specialist reports to the Parties. They will pay for the report so they will want to see what they are getting for their money. The report may be useful to help them to understand the cause of the problem which led to the dispute. Whenever possible they should be given the opportunity of seeing and commenting on the specialist report before the Adjudicator reaches his decision. Some Parties will expect to see any reports as a matter of 'natural justice' before the

Adjudicator's name (*an individual*)

Reference: 176/JT/Q   *Address*

Date: 12th Oct 1998   *Telephone*

By fax & by post   *Fax*

Case 176   AB Contractors Ltd v ZQ Dev Ltd

Contract: *Of ces at Blogg Street, Smith Town*

Adjudicator's Direction No. 1:

1. *Send representative to attend Adjudicator's inspection on site at 10.00 hours on Monday 19th Oct 1998.*

   Adjudicator will report to foreman on arrival.

Adjudicator's signature _____

Please acknowledge receipt of this communication

Sent to:

AB Contractors Ltd	and to	*ZQ Dev Ltd*
Hope House		*Big Town House*
Hope Street		*Small Street*
Smith Town		*Small Town*
Ref. 1989/JD/BT		*Ref. 7/21616/DR*

Figure 7. The Adjudicator's Direction

Adjudicator reaches his decision. In reality there will rarely be time for alternative reports, unless the Parties agree to an extension of the Adjudication period. In any event, the Parties had their opportunity to investigate and commission their own reports before the dispute was referred to Adjudication.

Actions and directions from the Adjudicator

The Adjudicator is in charge of the Adjudication. He has been appointed to make a decision and is entitled to receive the co-operation of the Parties. In order to achieve the result that they want, each Party should endeavour to provide the Adjudicator with all the information and assistance which he requires.

The Adjudicator must follow efficient management procedures. He must treat both Parties fairly and with an equal opportunity to present their case and answer the allegations which have been made against them. All documents must be copied to both sides and the substance of oral information should be confirmed to the other side if they were not present to hear the evidence.

The Adjudicator must also work within the constraints of the rules and procedures under which he has been appointed. Different contracts and different procedures impose different restrictions on the Parties and the Adjudicator.

For the Adjudicator to complete his work within the permitted time period he will need to issue Directions to inform the Parties of his requirements. A typical form for an Adjudicator's Direction is shown in Fig. 7. These Directions will have the authority of the contract under which he was appointed, but he has no practical means of enforcement. If a Party considers that a particular Direction is unreasonable, or outside his authority, then the Adjudicator must deal with the objection. If either Party fails to comply with a Direction, the Adjudicator must continue in the best way possible. Any such failure will be likely to act against the interests of the Party who failed to comply.

The completion of the Adjudication

The Adjudicator has a contract with the Parties under which he has an obligation to reach a decision on the dispute within a fixed time period. As discussed earlier, the time period is normally 28 days from the date on which the dispute was referred to him, unless that period has been extended.

The Adjudicator will need to allow himself several days for the action of reaching and writing his decision. Hence his programme will show that all information from the Parties must have been received by him by perhaps between five and seven days before the completion date.

If the Adjudicator receives, or discovers, information after his stipulated closing date then he must decide whether to make use of that information. If it seems to him that the information is significant then he may ask the Parties to agree to an extension of time. If this is refused then he has no option but to reach his decision within the stipulated period.

When the Adjudicator has reached and delivered his decision he has completed his task. Some procedures allow him to correct clerical errors, but he has no authority to consider additional evidence or change his decision. If either Party is not satisfied with the decision then he must refer the dispute to Arbitration or Litigation, or take any action which is permitted under the law. There is no point in trying to persuade the Adjudicator to reopen the Adjudication, unless both Parties agree to some further procedure and reach a new agreement with the Adjudicator.

4

The Adjudicator's decision

Reaching the decision

The wording of the Act requires that the Adjudicator 'reaches' his decision within the 28 day, or extended, time period. The need to inform the Parties of his decision can be considered as a separate subject. To 'reach' the decision seems to imply that he must have signed and dated his written decision within the stated period. However, whether a decision which is reached within his mind, but not actually typed, would comply with the Rules must be open to doubt.

Other questions which may arise are whether the Adjudicator can hold on to his decision until his fees have been paid and what happens if the decision is late. These matters will be discussed in later chapters in relation to the specific wording of the Scheme and the various Adjudication rules and procedures.

The reference to reaching his decision emphasises the importance of the process by which the Adjudicator makes up his mind and reaches his decision.

When an adjudicator receives a Statement of Case he will ask himself the question: 'Has the Claimant proved his claim?'. If the referring Party fails to include a reasonable level of proof in his Statement of Case then there was really no point in his submitting the dispute to Adjudication. The same question is asked by an Architect or Engineer when a contractor submits a claim, but the Adjudicator may be looking for a different level of proof. If the

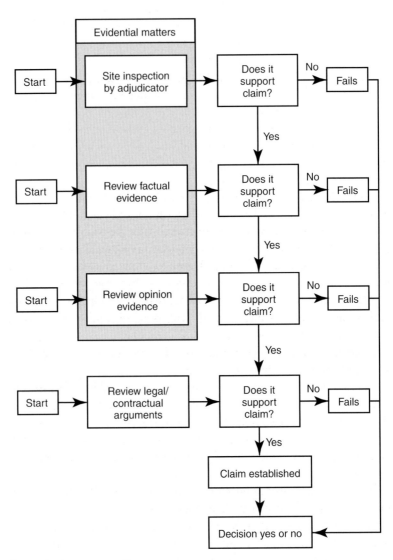

Figure 8. Assessment of case

Architect or Engineer is not satisfied with a claim, he will probably ask the contractor to provide further information 'to prove your claim'. However, a question in general terms, without specifying the information which is required, may result in the contractor deciding to refer the problem to Adjudication.

However, when the Adjudicator reaches a decision on a dispute, he is not just looking at evidence from the claimant. He is looking at evidence from both sides to the dispute and may work on the principle of the 'balance of probabilities'. If the referring Party has submitted and justified a reasonable case, but the respondent has not put forward any logical argument or evidence to refute that case, then the referring Party will win.

The Adjudicator will analyse the details of the dispute, the points which are at issue, the allegations which have been made and the evidence which supports or refutes each allegation. On the basis that the person who makes an allegation must prove that allegation, the Adjudicator will come to a decision on each point which is at issue.

The Adjudicator will identify and schedule all the issues of fact and of law which are disputed. He will then decide the matters of fact, decide the matters of law, and apply the decided law to the decided facts. He will then reach his decision on the dispute by a sequence similar to that shown in Fig. 8.

In practice, the process of reaching a decision will be complex and require considerable study and thought. The process of analysis of the provisions of the contract in relation to the decided facts will not be easy. Many contracts are complex and may not mesh coherently with the Adjudication process. Other contracts may be so vague that it will be difficult to interpret them properly. The Adjudicator may also need to consider the notion of terms which may be implied into the Contract. For example, a claim for acceleration costs may rely on an implied term. A decision on quantum may need to be calculated on a *quantum meruit* basis.

Most adjudicators start the process of formulating their decision at a very early stage in the Adjudication. By listing the various points and building up a logical framework of information on each item he will move towards a logical decision. During this process his thoughts may incline towards one side or the other and the anticipated 'bottom line' may change several times before he reaches his final decision. This is a common feature of any judicial process and illustrates the danger of indicating any particular direction without knowing all the evidence.

The sequence of points to be considered can be summarised:

- reach conclusions on the factual matters
- decide on the merits of any matters of opinion
- reach a conclusion on contractual issues
- apply the contractual conclusions to the decided facts and favoured opinions to give the decision on liability
- repeat the process if it is necessary to settle matters of quantum
- review the logic in order to confirm the conclusion.

The Adjudicator's decision

The aim of Adjudication is for the Parties to receive an impartial decision on their dispute, within a fixed time period. The written decision, which is sometimes known as the 'Adjudication' is the product of the Adjudicator's work. It is what the Parties receive in exchange for paying his fees.

The Adjudicator's decision is not an arbitral award and will normally be shorter than an award on a comparable dispute. There is no standard format or generally agreed list of contents for a Decision. The Act refers to written contracts and so it is reasonable to suppose that the Adjudicator's decision will be a written decision. A skeleton decision is given at the end of this chapter.

The extent of detail in the decision will be decided by the Adjudicator, subject to any requirements which are imposed by the applicable procedures. There are numerous items and details which might be included in a decision and the Adjudicator will decide how much detail is appropriate for the particular dispute.

A requirement for the decision to include reasons, or other information, may be included in the Contract, or the Rules or

Procedures which apply to the Adjudication, or they may have been agreed by the Parties and the Adjudicator. During the Adjudication either Party might ask the Adjudicator for explanations or calculations concerning a particular aspect of the dispute. Provided the subject is within the scope of the Adjudication then the Adjudicator would consider the request.

An Adjudicator's decision can be compared to a technical or expert report. It must be well written, in clear and concise English, so as to express the meaning which is intended by the Adjudicator and enable the Parties to understand that intention. The final decision must be a logical consequence of the preceding arguments and the logic must flow consistently through the document. Facts, opinions and decisions must be clearly differentiated. Liability will normally be dealt with first, as a separate issue, followed by quantum.

The purpose of the decision

The decision must be drafted to serve the purpose for which it is intended. The Adjudicator's decision may be used for several different purposes: for immediate use on the project, or for longer term use, possibly including action in the courts.

The possible uses to which the decision may be put will start with a requirement for immediate implementation. Whether it will become involved in future legal action cannot be anticipated, least of all by the Adjudicator. The Adjudicator cannot anticipate every possible future problem, but the written decision should include the basic information which would be required if certain situations should develop.

The possible purposes and future situations can be summarised as below.

For immediate use on the project:

- implementation by the Parties
- to assist in resolving future claims and disputes
- to assist with future payment certificates and the final account.

Use for legal reasons:

- enforcement if either party fails to implement
- an application to the Courts for the decision to be set aside
- any future Arbitration or Litigation
- any third-party liability of the Adjudicator.

The legal aspects and potential problems which may arise in these situations will be considered in more detail later.

The essential decisions which will have to be made by the Adjudicator can be separated into matters of liability and quantum.

Decisions on liability

The aim of Adjudication is to obtain a fast decision on a dispute, which will then be implemented. The decision must be clear as to what must be done and by whom.

The bottom line, which is what the Parties want, will often be a matter of quantum. However, in order to decide the quantum, the Adjudicator must first decide liability. It can be argued that there is no need for an Adjudicator to state his decision on liability, but just to state the bottom line. In practice, for the Parties to understand the decision, and in the event of the occurrence of any of the situations listed above, a clear decision on liability will be desirable.

In order to reach his decision on liability the Adjudicator will follow the procedure which has already been described, for his analysis of the factual and legal situations. For clarity in his own mind he will need to set down his process of logic and the application of the law to the facts. He will then decide how much of this information he will include in his written decision for the Parties.

In some cases the Adjudicator may only be asked to decide liability. The Parties will then negotiate quantum. In other cases he may consider it desirable to issue his decision in parts, starting with the decision on liability. However, unless a decision in parts is permitted by the procedure, it would require the prior agreement of the Parties. In any event, it may not be a practical proposition unless the parties agree to a time extension for the final part of the decision.

A problem arises if a responding Party dismissed liability and did not respond on quantum. If the Adjudicator then decides the liability in favour of the referring Party, he only has one Party's version of the quantum. If a Claimant's calculations appear reasonable and have not been reviewed by the other Party then they will probably be accepted. With the need for a decision on all matters raised in the Notice of Adjudication, within the time period, there is no time for a second response on items which were not properly covered in the initial response.

Decisions on time

Most contracts include a requirement that any claims for an extension of the contract period shall be submitted and determined quickly after the delay event. When the Adjudicator is asked to decide on a claim for an extension of time, the construction will probably not be complete. Hence, although he will give a definitive and final decision on that particular issue, it may only be a partial decision in terms of the Contractor's final entitlement for an extension of time.

The Adjudicator can only consider the dispute which is before him, which probably relates to a single delay issue. An Architect or Engineer may have considered the same issue, but as one part of a number of delay issues, some of which are the liability of the Employer and some are the liability of the Contractor. Hence, in order to implement the Adjudicator's decision, the Architect or Engineer may need to combine it with other decisions which he has made himself. If the Contractor is not satisfied with the result then there could be another Adjudication.

When making a decision on a delay dispute, the Adjudicator must be careful to state exactly what he is deciding and the basis for his decision. If a contractor demonstrates to the satisfaction of the Adjudicator that he is entitled to additional time of, say 10 days, because a particular item of work was delayed by a particular event, then the decision must state this entitlement and no more. To extend an entitlement due to a particular event into an extension of the contract period may require additional information, which the Adjudicator has not been given. There may be other delays, which are not part of the dispute. Delay events may even occur during the Adjudication.

There may also be problems when the contract allows the contract administrator to make an interim decision and review that decision later in the light of subsequent knowledge. The Adjudicator does not have the power to revise his own decision on a dispute, but would have the power to consider the new dispute which might arise from another decision by the contract administrator.

An Adjudicator's decision cannot be reopened and revised either by the same Adjudicator, or by a different Adjudicator. However, the dispute could be referred to Arbitration. The decision must be precise and carefully worded. If the initial dispute is only on the entitlement to an extension and not on the amount of that extension then this must be clearly stated in the Notice of Adjudication. Subsequent submissions cannot change the scope of the matters in the Notice, without the agreement of all Parties and the Adjudicator.

Even if the Adjudicator is satisfied that he has all the information necessary to calculate an extension to the contract period he may not be able to determine a new calendar date for completion. There may be other delays being considered elsewhere which mean that his calculated calendar date is superseded before he issues his decision. A decision which gives a definite date for the end of the contract period may result in problems later. If the Adjudicator states his decision precisely then the Parties can work out how it relates to the current completion requirements. If this calculation results in another dispute then they can refer that dispute to the Adjudicator and ask him to make a separate decision.

When an Adjudicator has considered and reached a decision on a delay dispute then there are obvious advantages for the Parties to agree to appoint the same adjudicator for any subsequent delay disputes.

Decisions on money

Decisions on quantum will generally be a matter of 'A shall pay B the sum of £x' by a stated date.

The extent of calculations which should be given will depend on the circumstances. If the sum relates to an item, or items, in the Bill of Quantities, then it will be necessary to explain the relationship between the Adjudicator's decision and the Bill items, with calculations as appropriate. This will enable the Parties to establish what part of the Bill items have been paid and what remains to be accounted for in the future.

Even if the sum is quite separate from the Bill it may still be necessary to provide an explanation and calculations. It is possible that a similar problem will arise again later and knowing how the Adjudicator arrived at his figure will enable the Parties to avoid another Adjudication by agreeing to apply the same principles to the new problem. Also, for the Parties to know the Adjudicator's decision on each part of a dispute may help them to accept his decision and avoid future disputes.

In this situation, the referring Party may ask that the Adjudicator includes the appropriate details in his decision.

The Act states that the Adjudicator's decision is binding until the dispute is finally determined. Hence, any financial decision must be paid and any directions for the time or procedure for payment must be followed. Some contracts and procedures state that a sum determined must be paid 'forthwith' and give requirements for the mechanism by which the payment should be incorporated into the contract certification procedure. These requirements are discussed in the appropriate chapters of this book.

The Adjudicator may also be asked to award interest in his decision. Adjudication is intended to be a procedure for the fast determination of disputes, so any entitlement to interest is likely to be much less than with a longer, more drawn out dispute resolution process. The Adjudicator does not have a statutory right to award interest, but some procedures enable him to award either simple or compound interest, at the rate and for the period which he considers appropriate.

Decisions on other matters

An adjudicator should not give decisions on subjects such as design requirements or whether a particular item of work should remain on site or be removed and replaced. The Employer's Representative will give an instruction which, if it is in accordance with the contract, must be obeyed by the Contractor. The Adjudicator's decision will concern the financial consequences of that instruction. The problems which will arise if a dispute on this type of problem is referred to Adjudication are considered elsewhere in this book.

When, for whatever reason, an adjudicator does give a declaratory or non-monetary decision the Parties have an obligation to implement that decision. If one party does not comply then the other Party may want a monetary alternative. The Adjudicator may have given this in his decision or it may become the subject of a new dispute.

The content and form of the decision

The length and content of the written decision will depend on the details of the dispute. However, certain basic information should always be included and the layout of the written decision should follow a logical sequence.

The preparation of a logical written decision will also help the Adjudicator to reach a logical conclusion. Some adjudicators start to prepare their written decision at an early stage during the Adjudication. This helps them to keep the events in perspective and to identify any problems. The final conclusion will gradually emerge during the process of writing the decision. However, if the Adjudicator changes his opinion during this process it is essential that he checks to ensure that the final decision is a logical consequence of the earlier parts of the written decision.

The written decision should include reference to:

1. the contract between the Parties under which the Adjudication takes place
2. the contract between the Parties and the Adjudicator
3. the scope of the issues which are included in the Adjudication

4. the events which led up to the Adjudication
5. the actions taken by the Adjudicator
6. the information upon which the Adjudicator's decision was based
7. conclusions on conflicts or allegations, of fact, liability, interpretation or law
8. calculations
9. the Decision
10. the date for implementation.

It is not normally necessary for copies of other documents to be appended to the decision. The decision is written for the Parties, who will already have copies of the relevant documents. If any problem is referred to legal proceedings then the Party concerned will provide copies as necessary.

The contract between the Parties

The Adjudicator's decision should start with a reference to the contract between the Parties. It is not necessary to include a copy of the contract, just the title and date, any reference and the names of the Parties.

It must be stated whether the reference to Adjudication is under a clause of the contract, or under the Scheme. Details of the Adjudication clause should be given, together with reference to any applicable Rules or Procedures.

The Adjudicator's Contract

Reference should also be made to the contract between the Parties and the Adjudicator. The circumstances of the appointment of the Adjudicator should be described.

The scope of the issues

A problem which may arise with the enforcement of an Adjudicator's decision is that he has failed to address the correct issues. He may have omitted one of the issues from his decision, or given a decision on an issue which had not been referred to him.

The issues to be decided should have been stated clearly in the Notice of Adjudication. This was the starting point of the Adjudication and everything which happened afterwards should have derived from that Notice. The issues will normally be listed in the decision, copied from the Notice, so that there can be no misunderstanding.

If the extent of the issues has been modified then the details and circumstances must be clearly explained. The modifications may be attributable to the following.

- The Notice was not clear and the Adjudicator, or the other Party, required clarification. Any such clarification must have been agreed with the Referring Party. If the Adjudicator has not been able to obtain this agreement then he would give his interpretation of the Notice.
- The particular Rules or Procedures allow the Adjudicator to extend the scope of the dispute in the Notice, with or without the agreement of the Parties. The details and references to any relevant documents should be clearly stated in the decision.

The reference to the Notice of Adjudication will also enable the reader to identify this particular Adjudication. Any one contract may lead to several Adjudications, possibly on similar subjects with different adjudicators.

The events which led up to the Adjudication

A short summary of the sequence of events which led to the Adjudication, together a reference to the Statement of Case, will give readers the background and enable them to understand how the dispute arose. It may also be necessary to demonstrate that the Parties have followed any necessary procedures before the reference to Adjudication. The summary will also help to show that the Adjudicator has understood the essential points in the dispute.

The actions taken by the Adjudicator

The decision should give the complete story of the actions taken by the Adjudicator, including:

- any objections, to jurisdiction or anything else, showing how the objection was handled
- requests for additional submissions and information, together with references to the Parties' response
- meetings with the Parties, naming the people present and any requests for meetings and agreements that he should meet with the Parties separately, or with other people
- investigations and tests which he has made and advice which he has sought, whether he had the specific agreement of the Parties, the result of the investigations and whether he has followed the advice
- visits to the site, with details of people present and areas visited
- any other actions that he has taken.

It is not normally necessary to include copies of the various documents, or fully detailed reports on every action taken. It is sufficient to show what has been done during the Adjudication, which will demonstrate that the Adjudication has been properly conducted, in accordance with the provisions of any applicable Rules or Procedures.

The parties will normally have been given copies of any investigation reports or specialist advice as soon as they available during the Adjudication. If, for any reason, they were not distributed then copies should be sent with the decision.

Information on which the decision was based

The documents which provided the information on which the decision was based should be listed. This may just be a matter of referring to the enclosures with the Statement of Case and documents received in response to requests for further information. However the Adjudicator may have received additional information from other sources.

A short but comprehensive summary of the information which has been received will help to demonstrate to the Parties that the Adjudicator has understood and taken into account their various submissions and arguments.

Conclusions on points of dispute

Any dispute may include allegations and conflict on matters of fact, liability and interpretation. The Adjudicator will have to reach a decision on every significant difference which has emerged during the Adjudication. The extent to which he states these intermediate decisions, together with the basis on which he reached each decision will depend on the circumstances.

Facts, opinions and conclusions must be kept separate and may need to be written as separate sections of the decision. The supporting information and any explanations must be clear as to whether each statement is something which has been stated by someone else and is either accepted or disputed, is the Adjudicator's opinion, or is the Adjudicator's conclusion on a matter of fact or law.

Reasons

If the contract or the Rules requires the Adjudicator to give reasons with his decision, or enables a Party to request reasons, then the Adjudicator must comply with the requirement and consider any request. If the Rules say that the Adjudicator is not obliged to give reasons then he must decide how much information to incorporate into the decision. However, for ease of understanding the decision, if reasons are given they should be incorporated into the decision itself and not written as a separate document.

The argument in favour of giving reasons is that the losing Party is more likely to accept the decision if he is told why he lost and can see that the decision was reached in a fair and logical manner. On the other hand, if the losing Party wishes to avoid having to comply with the decision then the reasons may give him the basis for an application to the Courts.

There is also an argument that reasons are essential as a matter of justice and this position is discussed in Chapter 12.

From a practical point of view, some explanation and calculation is essential in order that the decision can be understood and incorporated into the project administration. A statement such as 'A shall pay B the sum of £x' is unlikely to be sufficient. It is reasonable that A should know why he is being instructed to pay the money. This will require a simple statement referring to the logic behind the decision and not a detailed analysis of the merits of the arguments from both sides and exactly why the submission by one side was preferred.

The Adjudicator must always avoid the temptation to include lengthy dialogue, under the guise of reasons, in order to demonstrate that his own astuteness and skills are superior to those of the Parties who failed to resolve their dispute.

On balance, the Adjudicator is employed to make a decision and, provided the decision is clear, there should be no need to justify that decision by explaining in detail how it was reached. However, while explanations should be kept to a minimum, the Parties must be able to understand and implement the decision.

Calculations

The practical argument in favour of the Adjudicator including his calculations is stronger than that for giving his reasons. Decisions on matters of money or time will frequently have to be incorporated into later valuations or extensions of time. It is therefore essential that the Adjudicator includes sufficient explanation and calculations to enable the party representatives to incorporate his figures into their later calculations.

Either Party may have asked the Adjudicator to include specific calculations in relation to his acceptance, or part acceptance, of a particular item or calculation of any time extension or quantum.

The Decision

The final conclusion must be clearly stated to be the decision on the dispute which was referred to the Adjudicator and must be capable of being implemented by the Parties. Sums of money are normally stated in figures, followed by the sum in words.

Every issue which has been referred to the Adjudicator must be dealt with as a separate decision. While decisions on particular issues will have been given in the earlier sections it is useful to give a summary in the final section. If the Notice of Adjudication or Statement of Case includes a list of issues which are to be decided then the summary should incorporate the same list of issues.

The 'bottom line' must be clear, must be consistent with earlier conclusions and must be a logical consequence of the development of the earlier sections of the Decision.

The Decision must be signed and dated, but it is not normally necessary for the signature to be witnessed.

After the Decision

The Act states, in Section 108(3), that the Adjudicator's decision shall be binding until the dispute is finally determined by legal proceedings, Arbitration or agreement. This does not permit the Adjudicator to reopen the case or change his decision. If he makes a mistake, then the Parties have to live with that mistake until it is changed by one of the other procedures.

Some procedures allow the Adjudicator to correct typing or clerical errors. The extent of the corrections which are permitted, together with time limits for the change and whether they must be requested by a party or can be at the Adjudicator's initiative, vary in different procedures.

The subject of enforcement of the decision is considered in Chapter 5.

Chapter 4. Appendix: skeleton for Adjudicator's decision (below and overleaf)

Parties in dispute: **Ref:**
    Referring party   *name and address*

    Responding party   *name and address*

<u>Contract</u>:   *brief description:*

<u>Date</u>:   . . . .

<u>Notice of adjudication reference</u>:   . . . .

<u>Dated</u>:   . . . .

<u>Appointment</u>:   . . . .

<u>Agreement dated</u>:   . . . .

<u>Adjudication conducted under</u>:   . . . .

<u>Referral dated</u>:   . . . .

<u>Referral statement</u>:   . . . .

Appendix – continued

Quote document received

Quote remedy required

The issues

1. ### The claim
   Quote from document supplied

2. ### The Response
   Quote from document supplied

Appendix – continued

3. *Brief description of actions taken and further information received by Adjudicator:*
   Set out summary

Having considered all that has been put before me and all matters revealed in my investigation and having considered all these matters carefully I have reached the

DECISION IN THIS CASE AS FOLLOWS:

1. Directions on substantive matters of liability, quantum, conclusions, interest (if applicable), and implementation.
2. Reasons, calculation or explanation (if any).
3. Any directions on payment of Adjudicator's fee.
4. 'Bottom line' statement of decision.

Signed   . . . .
Name and qualifications

Date

5

The Act

Government orders for the Act, the Scheme, the Scheme for Scotland and the exemption orders for public finance initiative (PFI) were brought into force on 1 May 1998. The relevant part of the Act, namely Part II, is reproduced in full in Appendix 1.

The part of the Housing Grants Construction and Regeneration Act 1996 dealing with Adjudication is Part II Construction Contracts and consists of only eight pages covering Sections 104–107 inclusive. While common law may have effectively implied various terms into contracts, as for example, that the Parties will co-operate with each other to achieve the objectives of the contract, the Act represents a further stage of Government interference in business contracts. The actual Adjudication arrangements are dealt with only in Section 108 which is less than one page, and most of the provisions were eventually amplified within the 'Scheme', which was published later. It is made clear that either the contract shall provide for arrangements for Adjudication in accordance with the Act or, alternatively, if the contract between the Parties fails to comply with the Act, in respect of Adjudication arrangements, Adjudication will be governed by procedures set out in the 'Scheme'. The detailed provisions are not absolutely synonymous in the Act and Scheme. As the provisions of the Act or Scheme are mandatory they must be the primary source of reference for Architects, Engineers and Adjudicators.

Section 104 defines a construction contract, 105 defines the meaning of 'Construction Operations' and 106 makes it clear that Adjudication does not apply to a contract with a residential occupier as defined in that section. Subsequently, PFI contracts or the relevant parts of contracts, were excluded.

Section 107 makes it clear that provisions are only applicable to Agreements in Writing: Section 108 covers Adjudication; Sections 109–113 are payment provisions and the remaining sections 114–117 are Supplementary Provisions permitting the Minister to make regulations for the 'Scheme'. It also sets out arrangements for the service of Notices, reckoning periods of time and the application of the arrangements to the Crown.

Section 104: Construction Contracts

1. The definition of Construction Contracts is very wide and includes:
   (*a*) the carrying out of construction operations
   (*b*) arranging for the carrying out of construction operations by others under a subcontract
   (*c*) the provision of labour for construction operations.
2. Under the same section it is made clear that references to a Construction Contract include an agreement to do:
   (*a*) architectural, design, or surveying work
   (*b*) to provide advice on building, engineering, interior or exterior decoration, or on the laying out of landscape, in relation to construction operations. Hence it will be seen that consultant's contracts are covered.
3. A contract of employment is not a construction contract.
4. Where an agreement relates to construction operations and other matters, this part of the Act applies only to the construction operations.
5. The Act covers construction operations in England, Wales and Scotland and has since been extended to include Northern Ireland. This applies only to contracts entered into after the commencement of this Part of the Act. This was 1 May 1998.

Section 105: the meaning of 'Construction Operations'

1. The definition of construction operations covers:
    (*a*) construction, alteration, repair, maintenance, extension, demolition or dismantling of buildings or structures forming, or to form, part of the land (whether permanent or not)
    (*b*) construction, alteration, repair, maintenance, extension, demolition or dismantling of any works forming, or to form, part of the land, including walls, roadworks, power lines, telecommunication apparatus, aircraft runways, docks and harbours, railways, inland waterways, pipelines, reservoirs, water mains, wells, sewers, industrial plant and the installations for the purposes of land drainage, coast protection or defence
    (*c*) building services installations generally
    (*d*) external or internal cleaning of buildings and structures, so far as carried out in the course of their construction, alteration, repair extension or restoration
    (*e*) preparation and site works including excavation, tunnelling and boring, etc. and landscaping
    (*f*) painting or decoration.
2. Under this there are *exclusions* for:
    (*a*) drilling for oil and gas
    (*b*) extraction of minerals
    (*c*) assembly, installation or demolition of plant and machinery, nuclear processing and power generation, water and effluent treatment and the production and processing for bulk storage of chemicals, pharmaceuticals, oil, gas, steel or food and drink
    (*d*) the manufacture or delivery of engineering components or equipment, services installations except where a contract also provides for their installation
    (*e*) the making and installation of artistic works.

Despite the definitions there are likely to be situations where the position is not clear. As an example, is the building of a cake factory a construction contract or is it excluded as an installation for processing food? It is not clear whether stained glass windows are artistic works or not. The Act applies to individual contracts so that a subcontract may be included although the main contract is excluded.

Section 106: residential occupiers

It is made clear that the provisions do not apply to a contract with a residential occupier. It should be clear, however, that residential properties constructed by Housing Associations, or Local Authorities or part of a building which will not be in owner occupation, will be included. The result of all this is that a multi-million pound residence for a millionaire is excluded from the statutory requirement for Adjudication, but a subcontract between the contractor for such a project and a subcontractor is included within the scope of the provisions.

Section 107: agreements in writing

1. The construction contract is covered by the Act if it is in writing, but the definition of what constitutes 'in writing' is extremely wide! It applies:
   (*a*) whether or not it is signed by the Parties
   (*b*) or if the agreement is made by exchange of communications in writing
   (*c*) if the agreement is evidenced in writing.
2. Where the Parties agree otherwise than in writing by reference to terms which are in writing, they make an agreement in writing.
3. Alternatively an agreement may be recorded by one of the Parties or by a third Party.
4. An exchange of written submissions in Adjudication, in which one Party alleges the existence of agreement not in writing but not denied by the other Party, constitutes an agreement in writing. This is a most unusual arrangement.

5. 'In writing' includes being recorded by any other means and includes, therefore, E-mail and fax.

These are all important provisions affecting the validity of the reference to Adjudication. An Adjudicator will need to ensure that his or her appointment, for example, relates to a written contract as defined by the Act. It may be that the Adjudicator will have to see if either Party has an objection to his continuing because of some valid challenge to his jurisdiction.

Section 108: Adjudication

This is the most important section so far as the subject of this book is concerned. It sets out the right of either Party to a construction contract to refer disputes to Adjudication. A dispute includes any differences *arising under the contract*.

1. Unless the 'Scheme' is to come into operation the contract has to cover various requirements set out under (2) below. Either Party has the right to give notice of the intention to refer a dispute to Adjudication *at any time*.

2. (*a*) Disputes may be referred to Adjudication before the project commences on site, since contracts for professional services are covered by the Act.

   (*b*) The contract must also provide a timetable with the object of securing the appointment of the Adjudicator and the referral of the dispute within seven days of such notice.

   Appointing or nominating authorities will accept a considerable burden of responsibility on appointing Adjudicators, and will have to be efficient in making appointments.

   (*c*) The contract must require that the Adjudicator reaches a decision within 28 days of referral, or such longer period as is agreed by the Parties after the dispute has been referred.

   The whole construction industry will have to come to terms with short, simple referral of disputes, rather than allowing them to fester.

(d) The contract should allow the Adjudicator to extend the period of 28 days by up to 14 days with the consent of the Party by whom the dispute was referred.

(e) It must also impose a duty on the Adjudicator to act impartially which implies that an Adjudicator would not accept an appointment if he or she had a connection with either Party, or knowledge of the subject matter of the dispute.

(f) The contract must enable the Adjudicator to take the initiative in ascertaining the facts and the Law.

3. The contract also has to provide that the Adjudicator's decision shall be binding until the dispute is finally determined by legal proceedings or by Arbitration, if the contract provides for Arbitration or the Parties otherwise agree to Arbitration. The Parties may, however, agree to accept the Adjudicator's decision as final and binding.

4. The Act requires the contract to give the Adjudicator immunity as the contract must provide that the Adjudicator is not liable for anything done or not done in the discharge of his or her duties unless the act or omission is in bad faith. An agent or employee of the Adjudicator is similarly protected. The immunity does not extend to claims from third Parties.

5. Unless the contract makes provision for all the above minimum requirements, the 'the Scheme for Construction Contracts' applies.

Sections 109–113 deal with payment provisions in Construction Contracts.

Supplementary provisions

Section 114 covers arrangements to be made in respect of 'the Scheme for Construction Contracts'.

4. Where any provisions of the Scheme ... apply by virtue of this part in default of contractual provision agreed by the Parties, they have effect as implied terms of the contract concerned.

That is to say, the contract has to be construed as if they were written into it.

Section 115: service of notices
1.   The Parties are free to agree the manner of service of any notice or other documents required or authorised to be served. In the absence of agreement, a notice or other document may be served on a person by any effective means.

Section 116: time periods

This confirms that time periods are to commence from a specified date and they shall begin immediately after that date. Christmas Day, Good Friday and Bank Holiday extend time periods. Other days which are normally taken as holidays within the industry, together with weekends, do not extend the time period stated as 28 days and could substantially reduce the number of working days available within the 28-day period to a smaller number of working days. There is a special note regarding the equivalent of Bank Holidays for the Banking and Financial Dealings Act 1971 in Scotland.

Section 117: Crown application
Contracts entered into or on behalf of the Crown are covered by the Act.

Enforcement
Provisions for enforcement are not particularly well covered in the Act, except to say that the contract shall provide that the decision of the Adjudicator is binding until the dispute is finally determined by legal proceedings, by Arbitration or by agreement.

There is also a reference to an application of the provisions of the Arbitration Act 1996. The latter eventually emerged in the Scheme utilising an adaptation of Section 42 of the Arbitration Act in a rather complex way to provide enforcement of an Adjudicator's decision appointed under the Scheme. This particular aspect seems to have all the hallmarks of a lawyer's bonanza.

What happens when there is only partial compliance?

The Act requires that the Scheme applies if the contract is in default of provisions required by the Act. What is not clear is what the position is if the contract is, say, in default of only one of the provisions and if the missing provision can be imported from the Scheme or whether the Scheme as a whole has to be used. Presumably, if both Parties agree on the importation of the missing item, then that might be the best way forward.

The question also arises as to how an Adjudicator can best ensure that his fees are going to be paid. One answer might be to incorporate the amount and allocation of his fees as part of his Decision, thus if the Decision can be enforced on behalf of one of the Parties, then the same machinery would also ensure that his fees could be paid.

Comments on non-conforming situations and witness examination

Dispute resolution often operates on the borderline between the chaotic world of real events and the orderly, systematic world of contracts and systems. The Parties in the cases will be immensely variable in their approach, in the problems which they have to deal with, in their understanding of the basic contractual relationships and in their understanding of actual events, the facts relating to the matter in dispute. There may be errors in the applications for appointment, in the appointments and sadly, since we are all human, in the decisions which Adjudicators make. Nevertheless, the overriding aim must be to understand what really happened in any given situation and to bring it into conformity with the contract or the legal situation. It would be easy to deal with these matters if they all ran according to the theoretical process but life is more complicated than that. This part of the chapter seeks to identify some strategic lines which the Adjudicator may choose to follow. It will cover:

- appointments
- obfuscation
- delay and time wasting
- investigations or examination technique
- fraud and allegations of fraud.

Appointments

Nominating or appointing bodies will not normally have the appropriate staff or they will not necessarily have the necessary time to check applications which are made to ensure that they conform to all the requirements of the Act, Scheme or contract. The applications themselves may not necessarily be fully coherent or may be deliberately designed to confuse or create misunderstanding. One would like to hope that everything will be done in good faith but this will not necessarily be the case. If there is an obvious lack of jurisdiction then there will be little point in the Adjudicator proceeding. The Adjudicator can require the referring Party to demonstrate how he, the Adjudicator, has jurisdiction and an inspection of the works will often help to resolve the absence of clarity in the documentation provided.

There have been suggestions that the Architect or Engineer named in the contract could also be the Adjudicator because nothing in the Act prohibits this. The authors disagree with the suggestion since quite obviously the Adjudicator may be looking at situations where the contract administrator's decisions may be included in the substance of the reference or there may even be suggestions that a decision of the contract administrator has been influenced by matters where a poor professional performance is at the root of the dispute. If this latter point is true and the contract administrator also acted as Adjudicator and his decision was again influenced by improper conduct, his limited immunity as Adjudicator would be in jeopardy. This could lead to a position where, while acting as contract administrator, he would have no duty of care to the contractor, as Adjudicator he might be found guilty of bad faith and the limited degree of immunity would disappear.

Obfuscation

The key point so far as the Adjudicator is concerned is that the referring Party has the onus of proof and if the Claimant or referring Party cannot establish its case and uphold it against all questions, arguments and conflicting information, then the case will be lost. A practical problem may be, at its worst, fraud or otherwise misrepresentation, intentional or unintentional. There may be no contract even as alleged by the Claimant, there may be various misrepresentations of the contract's conditions and there be erroneous or misleading representations of the legal position or presentations or allegedly expert opinion or there may be a deliberate smoke screen of obfuscation expressed so as to divert the Adjudicator's attention into a series of blind alleys. If the Adjudicator is not clear in his mind, it may be that it would be helpful for the Adjudicator to take legal advice in these situations as to the validity of any matter arising.

Experts may need to be asked if their reports or assertions represent the whole truth of the matters referred to. Watch the response very intently and carefully and probe any signs of weakness.

Delay and time wasting

One process which is occasionally resorted to is to endeavour to delay or upset the whole proceedings, to seek extensions of time or promise later delivery which does not materialise and to add general confusion to the proceedings. The Adjudicator's response to these situations must be to endeavour to forestall them, to emphasise time limits from the first communication and to emphasise the fact that his period of time in which to deal with the matter is limited by statute and default of delivery will mean that he has to proceed in the absence of any Parties response. From the responding Parties' point of view its interests are best served by delivering its best defence at the earlier stage and it may help them to understand that to neglect to do so is likely to be counter productive to their case and their interests.

Investigations and examinations

Examination and cross examination of witnesses is a highly skilled task. What is often deceptive is that to watch a skilled Advocate conduct an examination or cross examination gives an impression of simple, smooth flowing and effortless progress. This is usually the end result of intensive preparation. The preparation of a skeleton with alternative lines of questions, according to the response to the earlier questions will help. One Barrister has suggested that for each hour of cross-examination of a witness he needs two hours of preparation time beforehand: it will certainly not be wise to plunge into investigative situations without considerable preparation beforehand. Adjudication will not necessarily be conducted with the formality of Arbitration or legal proceedings anyway. Where one has an Adjudicator and he does examine a witness with legal representation present, the examination may become more formal. Except for non-controversial facts, like the name or address of the witness, leading questions should not be asked (that is to say questions which suggest the answer required). This all becomes more important if the two Parties' lawyers are not present to voice any objection to the manner in which the examination takes place otherwise the Adjudicator may find himself accused of bias. Opposing witnesses should be accorded broadly similar treatment. The purpose of the process is not to make the Adjudicator look clever – it is to find the relevant facts regarding the case. An Adjudicator will need to take time to carefully note the answers or he may get carried away asking the questions without having a note of what has finally transpired with the witnesses answer. Slow progress is better than superficial but ineffective progress.

On no account should more than one person be allowed to speak at one time.

If in fact the Parties are represented by lawyers conducting examination of witnesses, the authors take the view that the Adjudicator may make it clear if necessary that excessively aggressive or flamboyant questioning is undesirable and should be discouraged. The aim again, is to obtain the evidence of a witness and not to browbeat him into submission. Some witnesses may be very evasive and it may be helpful for the Adjudicator to emphasise that it will assist the Adjudicator to hear the answer to the questions if the witness actually knows them. A hearing in an Adjudication should not be allowed to descend into a 'Court or star chamber'.

If a session threatens to become disorderly the Adjudicator should adjourn and state that he will reconvene when all those concerned behave in an orderly fashion.

However the examination is carried out, the witness may lie and if there is conflicting evidence the Adjudicator will have to decide which evidence he prefers. It is at that point that evasive or doubtfully reliable evidence will be rejected. A liar also needs to have a good memory and careful comparison of the whole of the evidence may be illuminating.

Fraud and allegations of fraud

Fraud and allegations of fraud are not a suitable subject for Adjudicators to deal with. Fraudulent behaviour on the part of an Adjudicator would constitute 'bad faith' under Section 108(4) of the Act and the Adjudicator would no longer have the protection from the limited immunity given in Section 108(4).

6

The scheme

The Scheme for Construction Contracts will only apply where there are no compliant arrangements in the contract. The Scheme is reproduced in full as Appendix 2.

Notice of intention to seek Adjudication

A Party to a construction contract may give written Notice of intention to refer the dispute arising *under the contract* to Adjudication. It also has to give notice to every other Party to the contract. The Notice has to set out briefly:

- description of dispute and the Parties involved
- where and when it has arisen
- nature of redress sought
- names and addresses of Parties to contract including addresses (or addresses specified for the giving of Notices).

Following that:

(a) the Adjudicator may be agreed by Parties or
(b) the Party giving notice then requests the person written into the contract to act as the Adjudicator or if he has indicated that he is unable or unwilling to act, or
(c) requests the nominating body listed in the contract to select a person as Adjudicator, or
(d) where neither of those options applies, goes to a body holding itself out as a nominating body to select an Adjudicator. This has to be accompanied by a copy of the Notice.

A person requested to act as Adjudicator under (*b*) above has to indicate within two days of receiving the request if he will act.

The request referred to must be accompanied by a copy of the Notice of dispute.

Any person asked to act as Adjudicator has to be a natural person, not a partnership, firm or body corporate and acts in his personal capacity. A Party dealing with the matter as Adjudicator must not have any personal interest in the matter nor be employed by either of the Parties and must declare any interest (financial or otherwise) in any matter.

A nominating body or the nominating body referred to as a fallback situation must appoint within five days of receipt the request to select a person. The referring Party may agree with the other Party to appoint another person or request another body in the list of nominators to select an Adjudicator.

Where an Adjudicator named is named in the contract and indicates the Party is unable or unwilling to act, there are fallback arrangements to obtain another Adjudicator. Responses have to be within two days!

Where an Adjudicator has been selected in accordance with the earlier procedure the referring Party must, not later than seven days from the date of the Notice of dispute, refer the dispute in writing to the Adjudicator. A referral Notice may be accompanied by copies of or extracts from the contract and such documents as may be relevant.

The referring Party must not later than seven days from the date of the Notice send a copy of the referral Notice together with the name and address of the person who is to act as Adjudicator to every other Party to the dispute.

There are then arrangements explaining how related disputes can be dealt with. The Parties may agree extended time limits.

Where an Adjudicator ceases to act, the arrangements for the fees incurred so far are set out.

An Adjudicator may resign at any time on giving notice to the Parties.

Where an Adjudicator ceases to act in the circumstances above, then there are arrangements for a fresh Notice and a fresh Adjudicator.

The Adjudicator must resign if he thinks he is not competent to decide the newly defined dispute or if he thinks the dispute is the same or substantially similar to one which has previously referred to Adjudication and a decision given. An Adjudicator may resign because there has been a decision or the dispute varies significantly from what was contained in the referral Notice and for that reason he is not competent to decide. He is entitled to reasonable payment. An Adjudicator may act in other contracts in related disputes and more than one dispute between the Parties with the consent of the Parties.

Where the Party to the dispute objects to the appointment of a particular Adjudicator, the objection does not invalidate the Adjudicators appointment.

The Parties to the dispute may agree at any time to revoke the appointment of the Adjudicator but they have to meet reasonable expenses unless the Adjudicator has defaulted or misconducted himself. In the absence of such an agreement the Parties are jointly and severally liable for the costs of the Adjudicator.

Powers of the Adjudicator

The Adjudicator must act impartially and needs to reach his decision in accordance with the contract and the applicable law and avoid incurring unnecessary expense.

The Adjudicator in the Scheme, may take the initiative in ascertaining facts and law and he may:

- decide the procedure to be followed
- request any Party to the contract to supply him with such documents as he may reasonably require and any written statement from a Party
- decide a language or languages and whether or not a translation is required

- meet and question any of the Parties to the contract and their representatives
- subject to obtaining necessary consents from Third Party, make visits and inspections whether accompanied by the Parties or not
- subject to obtaining necessary consents from the Third Party or Parties, carry out tests or experiments
- obtain and consider representations or submissions as he requires; provided that he has notified the Parties of the intention, appoint experts, assessors or legal advisers
- give Directions as to the time-table for any deadlines or limits to the length of written documents or oral representations
- issue such other Directions as he considers appropriate.

The Parties have to comply with requests or Directions from the Adjudicator.

If a Party fails to comply, the Adjudicator may:

- continue in the absence of the Party or the document or written statement
- draw such adverse inferences from failure to comply as he thinks are justified
- make a decision on the basis of the information submitted to him attaching such weight to evidence submitted outside any period he has requested.

Subject to agreement between the Parties to the contrary, any Party in the dispute may be assisted by or represented by Advisers or representatives whether legally qualified or not.

Where the Adjudicator is considering oral evidence, a Party may be represented by more than one person unless all Parties agree to the contrary.

An Adjudicator may consider any relevant information submitted to him by any Party in dispute and shall make available to them any information to be taken into account in reaching his decision.

The Adjudicator and any Party to the dispute shall not disclose any information to any other person if it is indicated as being confidential, except to the extent that it is necessary for the purposes of the Adjudication.

The Adjudicator has to give his decision not later than 28 days or 42 days with the agreement of the referring Party, or such period exceeding 28 days as both Parties agree.

Where the Adjudicator fails to deliver his decision within time limits, any of the Parties may serve a fresh Notice and start again.

Adjudicator's Decision

In his decision, the Adjudicator may order peremptory compliance with the decision or part of it.

The Adjudicator has to decide the matters in dispute. He may take into account any other matters which the Parties agree should be within the scope, including:

(a) review and revise any decision taken or any certificate given by any person referred to in the contract, UNLESS THE CONTRACT STATES THAT THE DECISION OR CERTIFICATE IS FINAL OR CONCLUSIVE

(b) decide that any of the Parties to the dispute is liable to make a payment under the contract and when it is due and the final date for payment

(c) decide the circumstances in which interest (simple or compound) for what periods and at what rate it should be paid.

In the absence of directions by the Adjudicator relating to the time for performance of his decision the Parties must comply immediately on the delivery of the decision.

If requested by any of the Parties to the dispute the Adjudicator is required to provide reasons.

This requirement is not incorporated in the Act and is not incorporated in some standard contract provisions.

Effects of Decision

In his decision the Adjudicator may order compliance peremptorily with his decision or any part of it.

The decision of the Adjudicator is binding until such time as the matter is determined by legal proceedings, Arbitration or agreement.

There are references to the 1996 Arbitration Act under Section 42, the effect of which is to treat the Adjudicator's decision in the same way as a peremptory order from an Arbitrator which, under Section 42, can be enforced by the courts. It appears that it is intended to make an Adjudicator's decision enforceable in this way.

The drafting of the Scheme makes the position far from clear, but if one of the Parties requests a Decision to be marked 'PEREMPTORY', then the Adjudicator can add this word at the top of the decision.

The Parties to the dispute and the Adjudicator may agree over the amount of and method of determining the Adjudicator's fees and expenses in default of agreement. On that the Adjudicator should be entitled to payment of a reasonable amount and the Adjudicator may decide in what proportion the Adjudicator's fees are paid by each Party but they are jointly and severally liable.

The Adjudicator is not liable to either of the Parties in respect of any act or omission unless it is done in bad faith and the same applies for his agent.

Comments

The effect of (*a*) above means that the detailed form of the contract becomes even more important than is usually the case, since if a large number of matters are subject to the decision or certificate as final or conclusive, few, if any, matters of importance could remain open for Adjudication.

The Scheme for Scotland is essentially similar to the Scheme for England and Wales, though there are minor differences in the wording.

It should also be noted that the detailed provisions of the Scheme and the detailed provisions of the Act are not necessarily the same in each case and an Adjudicator may be working to different provisions under the Act and, therefore, under a compliant contract, or under the Scheme.

In the interests of securing the Adjudicator's fees, and if the enforcement system actually works, it may be a good thing if the Adjudicator includes the Statement of the Requirement of his fees as part of the Decision. Thus if the Decision is enforced, then his requirement for fees can be enforced with it.

7

The ICE Conditions of Contract

Introduction

This chapter considers the amendments which have been published to the ICE Conditions of Contract in order to take into account the requirements of the Act.

The chapter is divided into four sections:

- The application of Adjudication to the ICE Contracts.
- The Adjudication provisions in the ICE Contracts.
- The ICE Adjudication Procedure (1997).
- The 'Blue Form' of Subcontract.

The application of Adjudication to the ICE Contracts

The ICE family of Conditions of Contract includes:

- The ICE Conditions of Contract for use in connection with Works of Civil Engineering Construction, 6th Edition. The 5th Edition is still in use and the 7th Edition is currently being prepared.
- The ICE Conditions of Contract for Minor Works, 2nd Edition.
- The ICE Design and Construct Conditions of Contract.

The related Subcontract is:

- The Form of Subcontract for use with the ICE Conditions of Contract 6th Edition, which is known as the 'Blue Form'.

- Versions of the 'Blue Form' are also published for use with the 5th Edition and the Design and Construct Conditions.

The ICE Agreement for Consultancy Work in Respect of Domestic or Small Works was published in 1997.

The ICE also publish the Engineering and Construction Contract and the NEC family of Contracts. The Adjudication provisions in these contracts are reviewed in Chapter 8.

The ICE Conditions of Contract 5th and 6th editions (ICE 5 and 6) and the Minor Works Contract are traditional contracts, between Employer and Contractor, with the design of the project being carried out by a Consultant. The Employer appoints the Engineer, who administers the contract by carrying out the duties which are specified in the contract, including the issue of additional drawings and variations, the certification of payments and being a first point of referral for claims.

In the Design and Construct Contract the design is carried out by the Contractor; there is no Engineer but the Employer's Representative has certain powers and the authority to issue instructions and approvals.

In any construction contract it is the Employer who has initiated the project, tells the Contractor what he wants, pays for the work and finally has to live with the completed project. In the ICE Contracts the Employer passes his requirements to the Contractor through the Engineer or the Employer's Representative.

The precise duties and authority of the Engineer and Employer's Representative are stated in the contract but among other tasks he will:

- conduct the day to day administration of the project
- issue instructions for variations and give the Employer's requirements for the completed project, either as the detailed design or as a design brief
- certify payments and extensions to the contract period
- check and consent to, approve or reject the programmes, materials, workmanship and other matters as provided by the Contract.

The ICE Contracts have an established procedure for dealing with problems and claims, based on administration by the Engineer or Engineer's Representative. When an independent adjudicator is imposed on to the project organisation it is inevitable that he will interfere with the smooth running of the project and the Engineer or Employer's Representative will need to absorb and co-ordinate the Adjudicator's decisions with the project administration.

Efficient project administration, absorbing the Adjudicator's decisions, is essential not only for the completion of the project, but also because the Adjudicator's decision may only have a temporary effect. It may be reversed later, by agreement or by an arbitrator. This may result in a need for dual records, with and without the Adjudicator's decision.

The problem situations which may arise as a consequence of Adjudication have already been considered in other chapters. Some of these typical situations can be reviewed in relation to the relevant clauses in the ICE Contracts. For simplicity the following notes refer to clause numbers in ICE 6. Similar principles can be applied to the relevant clauses in the other ICE Contracts.

Clause 5 requires the Engineer to explain and adjust any ambiguities or discrepancies in the drawings and other contract documents and issue appropriate instructions under Clause 13. While the Clause does not seem to give scope for a dispute on the meaning of the document, there is certainly scope for disputes on the consequences of the Clause 13 instruction, which could be considered by the Adjudicator.

By explaining the discrepancy the Engineer may have unwittingly made the Employer liable for an additional payment and exposed himself to criticism from his Client.

Clause 12 concerning adverse physical conditions and artificial obstructions will certainly give scope for disputes and Adjudication. The situation that the Adjudicator reaches a different decision to the Engineer and consequently the Contractor may become entitled to an additional payment is relatively straightforward. The Employer pays and decides whether to refer the dispute to Arbitration. However, if the dispute as referred to the Adjudicator concerns the

Engineer's instruction or other action under sub-clause (4) then any contradiction of the Engineer's instruction by the Adjudicator would have extremely serious consequences, ranging from collapse of the project to confusion on the site. Hopefully, although the Adjudicator has the power to 'open up, review and revise any decision, opinion, instruction, direction, certificate or valuation', he will restrict himself to making decisions on the time and money consequences. If the Adjudicator did venture into the realms of sub-clause (4) the Engineer would be bound to intervene. The Engineer may invoke Clause 13(1) that the Contractor shall take instructions only from the Engineer, or issue a variation under Clause 51. The Engineer must retain the last word for engineering instructions.

If the Adjudicator decides a Clause 12 dispute in favour of the Contractor then the Engineer will be obliged to certify the payment of a sum of money. If a similar problem occurs later in the same contract the Contractor will wish to use the previous decision as a precedent. If the Engineer has decided to accept the Adjudicator's decision then he may agree to this. However, if the Engineer believes that the Adjudicator was wrong, then he will maintain his previous point of view and reject the new claim. If the Employer has given notice to refer the original dispute to Arbitration then the Engineer will certainly oppose the new claim. This may result in a new Adjudication, possibly with a different Adjudicator and a different decision.

Clause 13 includes the all-important requirements that the Contractor shall work 'in strict accordance with the contract to the satisfaction of the Engineer', 'shall comply with and adhere strictly to the Engineer's instructions' and 'shall take instructions only from the Engineer'.

Whatever situations may arise as a result of badly worded referrals and rogue adjudicators, these requirements should enable the Engineer to keep control of the quality and form of the finished project. It is clearly essential that Engineers are prepared to act and issue instructions as appropriate. It is also essential that Employers recognise the additional administration, changes to cash flow and potential for additional arbitrations which may result from these situations.

Clause 39, which gives the Engineer the power to order the removal of materials or workmanship which are, in his opinion, not in accordance with the contract, is also a potential source of disputes.

The Adjudicator cannot change the opinion of the Engineer. An opinion is a personal matter and only the person concerned can change his own opinion. The Adjudicator can 'open up, review and revise' and substitute his own opinion. However, it is suggested that, taking all factors into consideration, the Contractor should still remove the rejected materials or workmanship, but would be entitled to payment for the work.

Clause 44 gives the procedures under which the Engineer can grant the Contractor an extension of the time for completion of the Works. The procedure includes, at sub-clause (3) the right to grant an interim extension, at sub-clause (4) the duty to consider all the circumstances known at the due date or extended date for completion of the Works and, at sub-clause (5) the duty to review all the circumstances at the issue of the Certificate of Substantial Completion and determine the final extension.

When a dispute concerning extension of time has been referred to an adjudicator he will make his decision, probably after the Engineer's interim extension and before the Engineer's final extension. Clearly the Engineer cannot change the Adjudicator's decision but there could be a further dispute as to whether the Engineer's final extension should be increased by the amount of the Adjudicator's decision. The answer will depend on the circumstances but clarity of records, analysis and reasons will be essential.

Virtually any clause in the contract can result in problems, additional costs and claims from the Contractor. The general procedure is given at Clause 52(4) and any dispute which arises under the contract should have gone through the Clause 52(4) procedure. Sub-clauses 52(4)(e) and (f) restrict the Contractor's entitlement to payment if he has failed to follow the correct procedures and these restrictions should also apply to any assessment by an adjudicator.

Most Adjudications will involve a request for payment, for which the decision may be either zero or a sum of money. Any payment then needs to be integrated into the contract payment procedure. This will almost inevitably result in administrative problems. The Employer is obliged to pay and the Engineer is obliged to incorporate the payment into the Clause 60 Payment Certificate. How the Adjudicator's decision fits into the payment procedures will depend on the circumstances but, if the Employer intends to refer the dispute to Arbitration it will be important to ensure that this payment can easily be extracted from the other payments.

If the Engineer strongly disagrees with the Adjudicator's decision then he may wish to keep the payment separate, so as to keep his disagreement on record.

Any dispute which follows a notice of determination under Clause 63 would require very careful consideration. The Adjudicator can 'open up, revise and review', but whether he can reinstate must be open to question. Before giving notice of Adjudication the referring Party would need to consider his position and decide what is the best way to resolve the situation. When the Employer has already entered the site and expelled the Contractor under Clause 63(1), Adjudication is clearly not the appropriate procedure.

However, the Clause 63 procedure requires a sequence of events before and after the Employer enters the site. A dispute concerning a specific stage in the process could well be suitable for Adjudication.

The Adjudication provisions in the ICE Contracts

Following the publication of the Act, the ICE Conditions of Contract Joint Standing Committee (CCSJC) had to decide whether to publish amendments to the Conditions of Contract, or whether to retain the previous dispute resolution procedures. If the contracts did not incorporate the requirements of Section 108 then a party wishing to refer a dispute to Adjudication would use the

Scheme. CCSJC decided to publish amendments and also to publish a separate ICE Adjudication Procedure, which would be incorporated into the Contracts by reference.

Amendments to each of the ICE Contracts were published in March 1998 to incorporate the payment and Adjudication requirements of the Act. The amendments are effectively the same, with different clause numbers to suit the different contracts. A copy of the amendment to ICE 6 is included as an Appendix.

The ICE Conditions of Contract 6th Edition

The dispute procedure in ICE 6 is given at Clause 66 and the procedure before the amendment can be summarised as follows.

- The submission of claims is dealt with separately and a dispute arises only when a Party serves on the Engineer a Notice of Dispute.
- The Engineer gives a written decision on the dispute.
- After the Engineer's decision either Party may request the other Party to agree to refer the dispute to conciliation.
- After the Engineer's decision either Party may refer the dispute to Arbitration.

The March 1998 amendment includes changes to the Clause 60 payment provisions, to take into account the payment requirements of the Act, and it also provides for disputes to be referred to Adjudication. The payment and Adjudication provisions are intended to comply with the requirements of the Act and so to avoid the possible imposition of the Scheme for Construction Contracts.

The amended dispute procedure at Clause 66 can be summarised as follows.

- Either Party is dissatisfied with some action of the Engineer, or with any other matter.
- The matter of dissatisfaction is referred to the Engineer who gives a decision.
- If the decision is unacceptable or is not implemented, the Employer or the Contractor serves a Notice of Dispute.

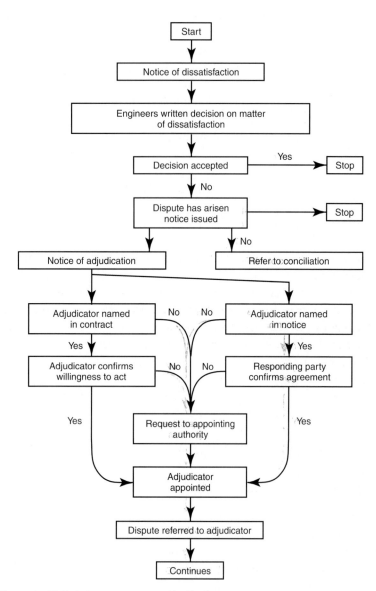

Figure 9. ICE 6 Commencement of Adjudication

- Either Party may refer the dispute to conciliation, with the agreement of the other Party.
- Either Party may refer the dispute to Adjudication at any time.
- Either Party may refer the dispute to Arbitration.

The previous Clause 2(7) which provided for the Contractor to refer to the Engineer any matter of dissatisfaction with any act or instruction by the Engineer's Representative has been deleted, as this procedure is now covered by the revised Clause 66(2)(a).

Clause 66: avoidance and settlement of disputes

The original ICE 6 Clause 66 did not include the Adjudication provisions which are listed in Section 108 of the Act. Hence, if the unamended ICE 6 is used for contracts after 1 May 1998 then any Adjudication would be conducted in accordance with the Scheme. The amendment to Clause 66 introduces provision for Adjudication and also revises the overall disputes procedures. The amendment requires that any Adjudication will be conducted under the ICE Adjudication Procedure. The procedures that precede the commencement of adjudication are summarised in Fig. 9.

The new dispute procedure is an essential pre-condition for reference to Arbitration, Adjudication or conciliation. Each of the stages must be followed if either Party wishes to pursue a claim through the procedures for the settlement of disputes.

Clause 66(1) is a statement that the procedure applies for the avoidance and settlement of disputes. The statement adds nothing to the procedure but seems to be included in order to demonstrate compliance with the assumed intention of the Act.

Clause 66(2) concerns 'matters of dissatisfaction'. Any matter of dissatisfaction must be referred to the Engineer for a decision. This reference replaces two of the original referral procedures. The original Clause 2(7) is replaced by 66(2)(a), although an entitlement has become a requirement. This Clause only applies when the Contractor is dissatisfied with an action or instruction of the Engineer's Representative or any other person responsible to the Engineer.

Clause 66(2)(b) replaces the previous reference for an Engineer's decision when the Contractor was not satisfied with an action by the Engineer. In order to avoid confusion with the requirements of the Act, the reference to the Engineer now relates to a 'matter of dissatisfaction' rather than a 'dispute'. This procedure can be used by the Employer as well as the Contractor and applies to 'any other matter arising under or in connection with the contract or the carrying out of the Works' as well as to actions of the Engineer. If the Employer or the Contractor has a problem which he wishes to refer to a third person procedure then he must first refer it to the Engineer for a decision under Clause 66(2).

This requirement has been criticised as a delaying tactic and an attempt to circumvent the requirement of the Act that a 'dispute' can be referred to Adjudication 'at any time'. While it introduces a procedure before a claim can become a dispute and be referred to Adjudication it will certainly assist in the speedy and efficient resolution of claims. Not only will it bring the opportunity for the Contractor to obtain a fully considered and impartial decision from the Engineer but it will help to ensure that a matter which is referred to Adjudication has been properly delineated and that both sides are aware of the dispute and the logic behind the other side's point of view.

Clause 66(3) concerns the definition of a dispute. The Clause starts and finishes with statements that a 'dispute' can only exist when these procedures have been followed. The statutory right to refer a dispute to Adjudication can therefore only be exercised after the procedures have been followed and a dispute exists.

Clause 66(3)(a) gives the general requirement that, when a matter of dissatisfaction has been referred to the Engineer and either the time for him to give a decision has expired, the decision is unacceptable or has not been implemented, then either the Employer or the Contractor can serve on each other and on the Engineer a Notice of Dispute.

In the situation that the Engineer rejects the request from the Party who referred the matter to him, the procedure is straightforward. The referring Party may be dissatisfied with the rejection and issue a Notice of Dispute under Clause 66(3).

If the Engineer gives a decision which accepts the submission by the referring Party, then the other Party can issue a Notice of Dispute. Alternatively, if the losing Party simply fails to implement the Engineer's decision, then the referring Party can still issue a Notice of Dispute. No time is stated for the decision to be implemented but this will become apparent from the next monthly payment certificate.

In the situation that the Engineer decides in favour of the Contractor, but the Employer refuses to pay, the Employer must take care to observe the new payment procedures as the amended Clause 60(10). The Engineer will include the consequences of his decision in the next payment certificate and the Employer will then need to issue a Notice of Intention to Withhold Payment, not less than one day before the final date for payment. Failure to issue this Notice could result in the Contractor being entitled to suspend performance of his obligations under the contract in accordance with Section 112 of the Act.

If the Engineer fails to give a decision on the matter of dissatisfaction by the due date then either Party can issue a Notice of Dispute.

Clause 66(3)(b) refers only to the special situation when an Adjudicator's decision has been given, but was not implemented. The Employer or Contractor can then issue a Notice of Dispute, without the need to refer the matter of dissatisfaction to the Engineer. This provision is related to amended Clause 66(9)(a) and enables a dispute concerning implementation to be referred to the Courts, without the need to refer to Adjudication or Arbitration.

The Notice of Dispute having been issued, Clause 66(4)(a) requires that the Employer and the Contractor shall continue to perform their obligations.

Clause 66(4)(b) requires the Employer and the Contractor to give effect forthwith to every decision of the Engineer and the Adjudicator, unless and until it is revised either by agreement or pursuant to this Clause 66. This confirms a very important principle of Adjudication. The Adjudicator's decision must be implemented, as an obligation under the contract, even if the dispute is going to be considered elsewhere. If the decision is later revised then the implementation may have to be reversed. The implications of a possible reversal of the implementation could be considerable and should be considered during the Adjudication.

Clause 66(5) enables either the Employer or the Contractor to refer a dispute to conciliation under the ICE Conciliation Procedure. This is virtually unchanged from the previous Clause 66, with the additional provision that the Conciliator's recommendation would not become binding if the dispute is referred to Adjudication.

The ICE Conciliation Procedure has been retained, although the number of alternative procedures has increased. When considering which procedure to use the Parties must consider the advantages of conciliation. Disputes which are partly due to a misunderstanding or communications problem, or where there is still a possibility of a negotiated settlement, should be referred to conciliation.

Clauses 66(6), (7) and (8) are the Adjudication clauses. They repeat the wording of Section 108 of the Act and ensure that the contract complies with the requirements of the Act. Clause 66(6)(a) refers to the ICE Adjudication Procedure. This Procedure also repeats and amplifies the other requirements and is reviewed later in this chapter.

Clause 66(9) enables either Party to refer a dispute to Arbitration and is similar to the previous Clause 66. Clause 66(9)(a) includes the provision that a dispute arising from failure to give effect to an Adjudicator's decision cannot be referred to Arbitration. This enables the concerned Party to refer the matter direct to the Courts. However, it will still be necessary to declare the failure to implement as a dispute, under Clause 66(3)(b).

Clause 66(9)(b) stipulates that if no Notice to Refer is served within three months of an Adjudicator's decision given under Clause 66(6) then the decision becomes final as well as binding. The failure to serve the Notice to Refer would be effectively an agreement that the Adjudicator's decision has finally determined the dispute, as Section 108(3) of the Act.

Application to Scotland and Northern Ireland

Clause 67 has also been amended and incorporates provision for enforcement of the Adjudicator's decision in Scotland.

A new Clause 67(2)(e) has been added and requires the other Party to consent and take the appropriate action when either the Employer or the Contractor wishes to register the Adjudicator's decision in the Books of Council and Session.

When using the amended Conditions of Contract in Northern Ireland it must be remembered that the order for Northern Ireland uses different Section numbers to the Act. The Construction Contracts (Northern Ireland) Order 1997 covers only Part II of the Act, so Section 108 becomes Section 7.

The ICE Conditions of Contract 5th Edition

An amendment has also been issued for the ICE 5th Edition.

The new Clause 66 and addition to Clause 67 is the same as for the 6th Edition. The amendment includes the provision for conciliation, which is new to the 5th Edition and could be an unexpected bonus from the incorporation of Adjudication.

The ICE Design and Construct Conditions of Contract

An amendment has also been issued to the ICE Design and Construct Conditions of Contract.

The new Clause 66 and addition to Clause 67 is the same as for the 6th Edition, except that the Engineer is replaced by the Employer's Representative, following the procedures in the Design and Construct Contract.

The ICE Conditions of Contract for Minor Works, 2nd Edition

An amendment has also been issued to the Minor Works Contract, 2nd Edition.

The existing Clauses 11.2–11.7 are deleted and replaced by a new Addendum A.1–A.12. The Addendum is the same as the new Clause 66 for the ICE 6th Edition, with the appropriate changes to clause numbers. The addition to Clause 12 is the same as the addition to Clause 67 in the 6th Edition.

The ICE Agreement for Consultancy Work in Respect of Domestic or Small Works

The dispute procedure is given at the final paragraph of Section E – Payment and other provisions and states: 'If any dispute or difference arises between the Client and the Consultant in connection with or out of this contract, it shall be settled in accordance with the Institution of Civil Engineers' Adjudication Procedure (1997) ...'.

Followed by: 'The adjudicator's decision shall be final and binding upon both the Client and the Consultant.'

The incorporation by reference of the ICE Adjudication Procedure will comply with the requirements of Section 108 of the Act and so avoid the Scheme.

This contract allows disputes 'in connection with or out of' the contract to be referred to Adjudication which is a wider scope than is permitted in the ICE Procedure. Hence it is necessary to expand the scope of the Procedure and this has been provided for at paragraph 9.1 of the Procedure.

However, the requirement that the adjudicator's decision shall be final and binding may cause problems with the Consultant's PI Insurers and this point should be checked before signing this Agreement.

The ICE Adjudication Procedure (1997)

Introduction
The ICE Adjudication Procedure has been prepared principally for use with the ICE family of Conditions of Contract. That is, the ICE Conditions of Contract for use in connection with Works of Civil

Engineering Construction, 6th edition, the 5th edition where it is still used, the Design and Construct and the Minor Works Conditions of Contract.

The amendments to the 'Blue Form' of Subcontract also incorporate the ICE Procedure, but require a change to the procedure to enable the Contractor to require a Subcontract dispute to be referred to the same Adjudicator as a connected main Contract dispute.

If the ICE Procedure is used with other Conditions of Contract it is necessary to check that the Contract and Procedure are compatible.

A copy of The ICE Adjudication Procedure (1997) is included as an Appendix to this book. The Procedure is divided into nine sections, which follow the same general sequence as an Adjudication.

Section 1: general principles

Paragraphs 1.1–1.6 give the important principles which control the Adjudication.

Paragraph 1.1 is a general statement to confirm that the Adjudication shall be conducted in accordance with the edition of the ICE Adjudication Procedure which is current at the date of issue of the Notice of Adjudication and that the Adjudicator shall be appointed under the Adjudicator's Agreement which forms a part of the Procedure. The use of the ICE Adjudicator's Agreement as the Form of Contract between the Adjudicator and the Parties is important to safeguard the interests of the Parties and the Adjudicator and to ensure that their Agreement is consistent with the Procedure.

Paragraph 1.1 also stipulates that, if a conflict arises between the Procedure and the Contract then the Procedure shall prevail. If the Procedure is used with an amended ICE, or a non-ICE Contract, then the Procedure must prevail over any conflicting requirements in the Contract to ensure that the Adjudication provisions comply with the requirements of the Act. Hence, if the Parties wish to change any part of the Procedure the amendment must be carefully worded to prevent the change being overruled by paragraph 1.1.

There is no generally accepted definition of Adjudication but paragraph 1.2 lays down the guiding principle of Adjudication by requiring the Parties and the Adjudicator to interpret the Procedure with the object of reaching a 'fair, rapid and inexpensive determination' of the dispute.

The matters that can be referred to Adjudication are restricted to disputes 'under' the Contract, as in the Act. This is not consistent with the Engineer's decision procedure. The Engineer can consider a much wider range of claims in connection with, as well as under, the Contract. This could result in a problem if the responding Party alleges that the particular dispute being referred to Adjudication was not under, but only in connection with, the Contract. The Adjudicator would then have to decide whether the particular dispute could be referred to him. The decision as to whether a dispute is under or only in connection with a Contract could raise legal issues which are not appropriate for consideration in a limited time period.

Adjudication procedures do not allow any time for the consideration of preliminary issues before the start of the period for the Adjudicator to reach his decision. The ICE Procedure does not specifically empower the Adjudicator to rule on his own jurisdiction. However, if a point of jurisdiction is raised the Adjudicator has to decide whether to continue or to stop, so he is, in effect, ruling on his own jurisdiction. While the Adjudicator cannot resign, he could make a decision that he does not have jurisdiction on this particular issue.

Paragraph 1.3 requires the Adjudicator to act impartially, which follows the Act and the principles of any judicial decision. The Adjudicator is not specifically required to be 'independent' of the Parties. However, any possible conflict of interest or connection with the Parties must always be declared before the appointment, in order to avoid possible accusations, at a later date, of lack of impartially. The Adjudicator must be very careful not to do anything which could give an appearance of bias.

The Adjudicator must also be a 'named individual'. This prevents the appointment of a company as Adjudicator. A fast decision requires an individual who will administer the Adjudication and make the decision. When the Parties appoint a named person they know who they are appointing and who will make the decision. To appoint a company would mean that the company, not the Parties, would decide who actually makes the decision. It has been suggested that a complex dispute, or a series of different disputes arising from the same Contract, might require a greater range of specialist knowledge than would be possible for a single person. However, the Parties are not obliged to appoint the same Adjudicator for every dispute and the Adjudicator can obtain specialist advice if he considers it necessary.

For a very large project it might be appropriate to appoint a dispute board or panel of Adjudicators, but this would be a different process, with a different contract procedure. The current procedures for the appointment of Dispute Boards do not comply with the requirements of the Act. However, Dispute Board procedures, which do comply with the Act, are likely to be developed very soon.

Paragraph 1.4 follows the Act and enables the Adjudicator to take the initiative in ascertaining the facts and the law. This gives the Adjudicator considerable powers, not only to ask questions, but also to conduct his own research and investigations if he considers this to be desirable. The use of the word 'may', as the word 'enable' in the Act, gives the Adjudicator the power to decide to what extent it is necessary and practical to exercise this power, particularly in view of the limited time period within which he must make his decision. The imposed time period and the requirement for a rapid and inexpensive determination of the dispute means that there will always be a limit to the extent to which the Adjudicator, in practice, can ascertain the facts and the law.

The second sentence of paragraph 1.4 enables the Adjudicator to use his own expert knowledge and expertise. The fact of his particular knowledge is one of the reasons why he was chosen for the appointment. Adjudication is also stated to be neither an expert determination nor an Arbitration, so the Adjudicator is free from the constraints which apply to those procedures.

Paragraph 1.5 repeats the requirement of the Act that the Adjudicator's decision shall be binding until the dispute is finally determined by agreement, Arbitration or Litigation.

Paragraph 1.6 requires the Parties to implement the decision without delay even if the dispute is referred to Arbitration or Litigation. If the Adjudicator decides in favour of a Party who is claiming money then the money moves to that Party during the period before the dispute is finally determined. This means that, for example, the Employer would have to refer the Contractor's claim to Arbitration if he wants to recover money which has been paid as a consequence of an Adjudicator's decision.

Paragraph 1.6 also requires payment to be made in accordance with the payment provisions in the Contract, unless otherwise directed by the Adjudicator. Under the ICE Contracts the payment will be included in the next certificate, although a problem may arise for a certificate which is being processed when the decision is issued. If, for whatever reason, either Party wishes to request any different procedure they must submit a proposal to the Adjudicator.

The exception to this procedure arises when the dispute concerns payment of a sum which has been withheld under Section 111 of the Act. Section 111(4) of the Act requires that, if the Adjudicator decides that the sum must be paid then payment must be made not later than seven days from the date of the decision, or the date which apart from the notice would have been the date for payment, whichever is the later.

It will generally be necessary for any decision for payment of a sum of money to be integrated with the valuation of other payments under the Contract. It may also be desirable for the Adjudication payment to be highlighted in the payment certificate. If the dispute is later referred to Arbitration then this would help the Arbitrator if he decides to revise or cancel the payment in his Award.

By following this procedure the payment ordered by the Adjudicator may become subject to retention as Clause 60(5).

Section 2: the Notice of Adjudication

Paragraph 2.1 follows the requirement of the Act and the Contract that any Party may give notice at any time of its intention to refer a dispute to Adjudication.

The Notice of Adjudication is prepared by the Party who has decided to refer the dispute to Adjudication and should include sufficient information to enable the other Party to identify the dispute which is being referred.

The Notice of Adjudication must include the details of the Contract between the Parties, the issues which the Adjudicator is being asked to decide and the nature and extent of the redress which is being sought. The ICE has published a standard form for the Notice of Adjudication.

The referring Party may also include with the Notice the names and addresses of one or more people, who have agreed to act as Adjudicator and any one of whom would be acceptable to the referring Party. These names are then available for selection by the other Party, in accordance with paragraph 3.2.

The Notice will establish the scope of the Adjudication and enable potential Adjudicators to decide whether they are willing to accept the appointment. If a potential Adjudicator feels that the Notice includes a number of separate issues, which it will be impossible to deal with in the fixed 28 day period, then he could raise an objection before agreeing to accept the appointment. The referring Party may then decide to reissue the Notice for a single issue. After the Notice has been issued the scope of the matter in the Adjudication cannot be changed without the agreement of the Parties and the Adjudicator, as paragraph 5.2.

The scope of the Adjudication is determined by the Notice of Adjudication, but this must be consistent with the Notice of Dispute and the original Notice of Dissatisfaction. If the responding Party believes that the dispute which is being referred to Adjudication is a different matter to that which was raised with the Engineer then he should raise the objection as soon as he receives the Notice of Adjudication. If the referring Party persists with the referral then the objection should be raised with the

Adjudicator. The Adjudicator will decide whether he is able to continue with the Adjudication.

Section 3: the appointment of the Adjudicator

Paragraph 3 gives the different procedures which may be used for the appointment of the Adjudicator. All these procedures work under very restricted time periods. To meet the requirements of Section 108(2)(b) of the Act the Contract must provide a timetable with the object of securing the appointment of the Adjudicator and referral of the dispute to him within seven days of the issue of the Notice. For practical reasons it is also necessary to provide a fallback procedure in case, for whatever reason, this object is not achieved.

Paragraph 3.1 covers the situations when the Adjudicator has either been named in the Contract or agreed prior to the issue of the Notice of Adjudication. When the referring Party issues the Notice he must send a copy to the named Adjudicator. The Adjudicator can then confirm that he is available and willing to act for this dispute. The requirement that the decision must be issued within 28 days imposes a strict discipline on the Adjudicator and it is essential that anyone who has already been appointed, perhaps some years earlier, should check their commitments and confirm their availability. Also, a particular dispute may be very specialised and the Adjudicator may suggest that a different area of expertise is required, or his personal circumstances may have changed and so he is no longer able to act. If the Adjudicator is able and willing he must confirm his acceptance within four days of the date of issue of the Notice. If he is not available or does not reply within the four days then the referring Party must follow an alternative procedure. If the named Adjudicator has a problem with the 28 day period then the referring Party can agree to extend the period by 14 days, as paragraph 5.1. The referring Party can extend his options during the seven-day period for appointment and referral by checking with a named Adjudicator before issuing the Notice of Adjudication.

Paragraph 3.2 gives the procedure when the Adjudicator has not already been appointed but the referring Party has included with the

Notice the names and addresses of one or more potential Adjudicators. The other Party can select a name and notify the referring Party and the selected Adjudicator within four days of the issue of the Notice. If he does not confirm his selection within this period then the referring Party must move to the procedure in paragraph 3.3.

Paragraph 3.3 gives the fallback procedure if the previously appointed Adjudicator is not available or the Parties have failed to agree on the selection or an Adjudicator who was selected has failed to confirm his acceptance. Either Party may then ask an appointing authority to make the appointment. The request must be made within a further three days from the four day periods in paragraphs 3.1 or 3.2. The sequence of four days and three days means that the Parties would have completed their actions within the seven day period which is stipulated in the Act. No time limit is stated for the appointment by the appointing authority, which is outside the control of the Parties. This would normally be within a further five days.

The appointing authority may be named in the Contract or, if no name is given, will be The Institution of Civil Engineers. The request must be made on the appropriate form and be accompanied by a copy of the Notice of Adjudication and the appropriate fee. A copy of the ICE application form is provided with the Procedure. The information required is basically the same as is given in the Notice. The appointing authority should make the appointment within a few days and will not check the validity of the request. The Party making the application is required to confirm that it has performed any actions which the Contract requires to be taken before the appointment is requested and that it will meet any reasonable cost incurred by the appointed person if it is not entitled to make the application. Any problems or queries will be dealt with by the Adjudicator after his appointment.

When the ICE have selected the Adjudicator, who will have confirmed his availability, willingness to act and absence of any conflict of interest, the applicant is informed, by means of the appropriate page of the application form, with copies to the other Party and the Adjudicator.

Paragraph 3.4 states that the Adjudicator shall be appointed on the terms and conditions set out in the attached Adjudicator's Agreement and Schedule. The Parties are required to sign the Agreement within seven days of being requested to do so. The Adjudicator has already been appointed, by the Parties or the appointing authority, and so has an obligation to act and proceed with the Adjudication. Under the first sentence of paragraph 3.4 he is entitled to be paid a reasonable fee together with his expenses. Hence, if either Party fails to sign the Agreement, the Adjudicator's entitlement to a reasonable fee has been established. The actual figure for the hourly rate, together with certain other provisions, will be confirmed in the Agreement.

Paragraph 3.5 gives the procedure if the appointed Adjudicator is unable to act, or fails to complete the Adjudication. Either Party may apply to the appointing authority to appoint a replacement Adjudicator in accordance with the procedure in paragraph 3.3. If the situation arises due to non-delivery of the decision then the procedures in paragraph 6.3 will also apply.

Section 4 : referral

Section 108(2)(b) of the Act requires the Contract to provide for appointment and referral of the dispute to the Adjudicator within the seven day period following the Notice. This is achieved by the referring Party sending to the Adjudicator, within two days of confirmation under 3.1, or notification under 3.2, a full statement of his case. If the appointment is to be made by an appointing authority, after the failure of the normal procedure, then the Statement of Case is to be sent within two days of the appointment. A copy of the Statement of Case will be sent to the other Party.

The restriction to a two day time period is necessary not only to comply with the Act but to ensure that the referring Party, having started the process, does not delay the referral to the Adjudicator. The Adjudicator has confirmed that he has the time available to deal with the matter within the restricted period for the Adjudication and any delay in referral could move the Adjudication into a period when he is not available. To comply with the timetable, the referring Party must have prepared his Statement of Case before issuing the Notice of Adjudication.

Paragraph 4.1 requires the Statement of Case to include a copy of the Notice of Adjudication, the Adjudication provision in the Contract and the information on which the referring Party relies, including supporting documents. This is the basic information which is necessary to enable the Adjudicator to start his work.

Paragraph 4.2 fixes the date of referral. This is the date which starts the 28 day, or extended, period for the Adjudication. Unless provided otherwise in the Contract it will be the date on which the Adjudicator receives the documents referred to in paragraph 4.1. The Adjudicator must confirm having received these documents, so the date of referral will be established and known to the Parties.

The Adjudicator should also calculate and confirm to the Parties the calendar date for the end of the 28-day period, taking into account any additional days for Good Friday, Christmas Day and any Bank Holidays as stated at Section 116 of the Act.

Section 5 : conduct of the Adjudication

Section 5 stipulates the obligations of the Adjudicator and gives him the powers which are necessary in order to meet these obligations. The requirements of the Act form the basis of these obligations and powers and are amplified as necessary to establish a practical procedure.

Paragraph 5.1 sets the time limits for the Adjudicator to reach his decision and follows Section 108(2) of the Act.

Paragraph 5.2 restricts the matters which can be determined by the Adjudicator. He is obliged to determine the matters set out in the Notice of Adjudication and these can only be expanded with the agreement of the Parties and the Adjudicator. If the Adjudicator realises that the Statement of Case, or other submissions, include matters which are outside the scope of the

Notice of Adjudication then he must either decide not to determine those matters or obtain the agreement of all Parties to expand the scope of the Adjudication.

If the responding Party considers that any part of the Statement of Case is outside the scope of the Notice, or any part of the Notice is not subject to Adjudication then it must state the objection at the very beginning of the Adjudication or risk losing the right to object. The Procedure does not give the Adjudicator the specific power to decide on his own jurisdiction, or the power to adjourn consideration of the main dispute while considering a question of jurisdiction. The Adjudicator will have to tackle any question or problem as best he can. The power to reach a decision on a particular aspect of the dispute before deciding the main dispute, under paragraph 6.1, could be useful.

Paragraph 5.3 deals with the powers which are necessary to enable the Adjudicator to change previous decisions in order to determine the dispute. The problems which could arise if an Adjudicator changes the design have been discussed elsewhere in this book. The final sentence in paragraph 5.3 emphasises that the Parties retain their powers to vary the contract or the Engineer to vary the Works in accordance with the Contract. If the Parties have been clear in their submissions then there should not be any problem but if, for example, the Engineer considers that the Adjudicator's interpretation of the Contract would result in the final works being different to his requirements then he can issue a variation to ensure that the Works are to his satisfaction. The consequences of the variation can then be valued in accordance with contract procedures.

Paragraph 5.3 also makes it clear that the Adjudicator cannot change the decision of another Adjudicator, which is repeated at paragraph 6.7. If either Party is not satisfied with an Adjudicator's decision it must refer the dispute to Arbitration and not try another Adjudication in the hope of achieving a different result. Obviously the Adjudicator himself will not know if the same dispute has previously been referred to another Adjudicator. The Party who objects to the dispute being reconsidered will need to make a submission to the Adjudicator. Failure to draw the Adjudicator's attention to the problem would, in effect, be an agreement to allow the Adjudicator to reconsider a previously adjudicated dispute.

Paragraph 5.4 entitles the non-referring Party to submit a response to the Statement of Case. The response must be submitted within 14 days of referral, unless this period has been extended by agreement between the Parties and the Adjudicator. The clear entitlement to submit a response is essential in order to maintain a fair balance between the Parties.

The period for this response may be half the total period for the Adjudication. However the Adjudicator will not sit back and wait for the response. A properly prepared Statement of Case will enable him to establish the timetable and plan the actions which may be appropriate as listed in paragraph 5.5, or for legal or technical advice under paragraph 5.6, or for joinder under paragraph 5.7.

Paragraph 5.5 gives the Adjudicator complete discretion as to how to conduct the Adjudication. The powers which are noted and listed are extremely wide, but are not exhaustive. The complete generality of the powers are subject to any limitation in the Contract or the Act.

Paragraph 5.6 requires the Adjudicator to notify the Parties before he obtains legal or technical advice. This gives the Parties the opportunity to make alternative proposals if they are concerned about the value or cost of the Adjudicator's intention.

Section 6 : the decision

Paragraph 6.1 requires the Adjudicator to reach his decision within 28 days, or the period which has been established in accordance with paragraph 5.1. Having reached his decision he then notifies the Parties, subject to the lien procedure at paragraph 6.6.

The Adjudicator may reach a decision on different aspects of the dispute at different times. This power will be useful if the Adjudicator has been asked to decide on a preliminary issue of the jurisdiction or scope of the Adjudication. Also, the Parties may ask for an initial decision on liability. They could then try to agree the quantum and refer it to the Adjudicator if they fail to reach agreement.

Paragraph 6.1 also states that the question of whether to give reasons with the decision is a matter to be decided by the Adjudicator. The Parties may request, but not require, reasons. However, for the decision to be effective, the Adjudicator will need to include a certain amount of explanation as to how it was reached and relates to the contract administration procedures.

Paragraph 6.2 entitles the Adjudicator to direct the payment of interest as he considers appropriate. The inclusion of compound as well as simple interest gives the Adjudicator wide powers. However, the power is only likely to be exercised if a Claimant has asked for interest and justified his request.

The procedures to be followed if the Adjudicator fails to reach his decision and notify the Parties in due time are given at paragraphs 6.3 and 6.4. If a decision is given before the dispute is referred to a replacement Adjudicator then it will still be effective. This does not give the Adjudicator an automatic right to extend the period. He will be in breach of his agreement with the Parties. It is a practical procedure to avoid the need to repeat the whole Adjudication due to an accidental overrun. If the decision is so late that the dispute has been referred to the replacement then the original Adjudicator will not be entitled to any fees. However, if a legal or technical advisor has been appointed under paragraph 5.6 and the Parties have received that advice, then the Parties will be responsible for the fees and expenses of the advisor. This enables the advisor to be paid and the Parties to make use of the advice in the subsequent Adjudication.

Paragraph 6.5 deals with the payment of fees and expenses. The Adjudicator does not have the power to direct that either Party shall pay the costs and expenses of the other Party. This is an important provision. For either Party to enter an Adjudication thinking that they could recover legal costs would encourage legal analysis and argument, in contradiction to the principle that Adjudication should be 'fair rapid and inexpensive', as paragraph 1.2.

The Adjudicator's fees and expenses will be paid in equal shares by each Party, unless the Adjudicator directs otherwise.

As noted above, paragraph 6.6 gives the Adjudicator the right to a lien on his decision, pending payment of his fees and expenses. In order to exercise this right he must give notice to the Parties prior to seven days before he is due to reach his decision. If the Adjudicator is concerned that his fees may not be paid then this is an important provision. It is for the Adjudicator to decide whether to exercise this right and whether to discuss the matter with the Parties prior to exercising the right.

Paragraph 6.7 deals with the enforcement of the decision and states that the parties are entitled to seek summary enforcement of the decision. This should be considered in conjunction with the Clause 66(9) provision that a dispute concerning implementation of an adjudicator's decision cannot be referred to Arbitration.

Paragraph 6.8 confirms that the Adjudicator's decision shall not inhibit a Court or arbitrator from determining the Parties rights and obligations anew. This is consistent with Section 108(3) of the Act which requires that the decision is binding until the dispute is finally determined. There is nothing to prevent the Parties from agreeing to accept the decision as finally determining the dispute, as the second part of Section 108(3) of the Act.

Paragraph 6.9 enables the Adjudicator to correct the decision, within the stated time periods, so as to remove any clerical mistake, error or ambiguity. This power to correct only refers to clerical problems and would not enable the Adjudicator to change his mind, or to correct any other error. If the Parties agree that the Adjudicator has made a mistake then they could agree to change the decision in a final determination of the dispute under paragraph 1.5.

Section 7: miscellaneous provisions
Paragraph 7.1 prevents the Adjudicator from being appointed as arbitrator in any subsequent Arbitration between the Parties under this Contract, unless the Parties agree. For the same person to serve

as Adjudicator and arbitrator will generally be unsatisfactory. He would have preconceived ideas about the case and might be reluctant to change his previous decision even if additional evidence showed it to be mistaken. However, there could be circumstances when the Parties agree to appoint the Adjudicator as arbitrator.

An arbitral appointment by agreement would already have the agreement of the Parties. However, an appointing authority might appoint as arbitrator someone who had previously served as Adjudicator, without being aware of the previous appointment, so it would be incumbent on the person concerned to refuse the appointment as arbitrator, or to obtain the agreement of the Parties.

Paragraph 7.2 repeats the requirement of Section 108(4) of the Act for Adjudicator immunity. The second sentence gives the Adjudicator additional protection by making the Parties jointly and severally responsible to save harmless and indemnify him against claims from third parties. In this context the 'third party' is a separate person, not a 'Third Party' who has been joined under paragraph 5.7.

While this provision would seem to give protection to the Adjudicator it would be difficult to apply in practice. If a third party chooses to take action against the Adjudicator then the Adjudicator himself will need to find a way to claim from the Parties who have given him the indemnity. It may be necessary for the Adjudicator to instigate legal proceedings against the parties. The Adjudicator will certainly incur legal costs even if the indemnity enables him to recover these costs. However, it would also be very difficult for a third party to prove a case for damages against the Adjudicator.

Paragraph 7.3 gives immunity to The Institution of Civil Engineers, its servants and agents.

Paragraph 7.4 requires Notices by recorded delivery to the address given in the Contract and any agreement to be in writing.

Paragraph 7.5 states that the Procedure shall be interpreted in accordance with the law of the Contract.

Section 8: definitions

Section 8 gives the definitions of the terms used with capital letters in the Procedure.

Section 9: application to particular contracts

Section 9 says that when the Procedure is used with the ICE small works consultancy agreement the Adjudicator can determine disputes in connection with or arising out of the Contract. This qualification is necessary to avoid conflict with this Contract.

If the Parties to a particular contract want the scope of Adjudication increased to include the other disputes which could be considered by the Engineer under Clause 66(2) of ICE 6 then a similar paragraph could be added to Section 9.

Similarly, if the Procedure is to be used with a non-ICE Contract, it may be necessary to introduce additional Clauses into Section 9.

Adjudicator's Agreement

The ICE Adjudicator's Agreement forms a part of the Adjudication Procedure, as paragraph 1.1 of the Procedure, and should always be used when an Adjudicator is appointed under this Procedure. The Agreement can be used with other rules and procedures, or when the Adjudication procedures are given in the Contract, but it should be checked for compatibility with the requirements of the Contract. If any Party, or the Adjudicator, wants to change any of the requirements in the Agreement then the change would require the agreement of all Parties and the Adjudicator. The Adjudicator must be told of any such changes before he is asked to act as Adjudicator.

The numbered items 1–3 confirm the rights and obligations of the Parties and the Adjudicator as in the Procedure. Item 4 is the confidentiality rule. Complete confidentiality is not always possible, particularly in the event of enforcement problems, but any Party is required to obtain the consent of the other Parties, but not of the Adjudicator, before breaching confidentiality.

Item 5 covers the question of how long the Adjudicator should retain the documents after the completion of the Adjudication and requires that the Adjudicator shall inform the Parties before he destroys the documents which have been sent to him in relation to the Adjudication. Hence, if a Party envisages using the same Adjudicator for another dispute under the same Contract, or some exceptional circumstance has arisen, then they have the opportunity to ask the Adjudicator to retain the documents for a further period.

The Agreement is to be signed by all the Parties and the Adjudicator. If for some reason any Party refuses to sign the Agreement, which would be a breach of paragraph 3.4 of the Procedure, that Party will still be jointly and severally liable to pay the Adjudicator a reasonable fee and expenses, in accordance with paragraphs 3.4, 6.5 and 6.6.

The Schedule to the Adjudicator's Agreement will be completed by the Adjudicator inserting his hourly rate, any appointment fee and whether he is registered for VAT, before the Agreement is sent to the Parties for signature.

The provision for an appointment fee is appropriate if the Adjudicator is appointed at the start of the project. However, if he is required to spend any time for the project before the start of the Adjudication it is important that time spent is recorded as chargeable time, in order to avoid it being negated in the final statement.

When the Adjudicator is appointed after the dispute has arisen then the appointment fee will not be due for payment until half way through the Adjudication and the Adjudicator will be obliged to complete his task, even if the fee is not paid.

The 'Blue Form' of Subcontract

Revisions to current subcontracts
The following amendments have been published by The Civil Engineering Contractors Association (CECA):

- Amendments to 'Blue Form' of Subcontract 1991. (For use with the ICE 6th Edition.)

- Amendments to 'Blue Form' of Subcontract 1984. (For use with the ICE 5th Edition.)
- Amendments to 'Blue Form' of Subcontract 1994. (For use with the ICE Design and Construct.)

These amendments follow the same principles, adjusted to suit the particular version of the subcontract. The following notes refer to the amendments to the 1991 Subcontract, for use with the ICE 6th Edition. Reference should be made to the actual amendments for the full details of each revised clause.

The amendments relate to Clauses 1, 10, 15 and 18.

Clause 1: definitions

A new sub-clause 19(1)(h) has been added to define 'insolvent'. This is necessary to follow Section 113 of the Act, which bans 'pay-when-paid' clauses except when the person who is due to pay the Contractor becomes insolvent. The definition follows the principles defined in the Act.

Clause 10: notices and claims

The existing sub-clause 10(2) is deleted and a new sub-clause inserted. The amendment is necessary because 'pay-when-paid' clauses have been banned by Section 113 of the Act.

New sub-clause 10(2)(a) follows the first part of the existing sub-clause for the Subcontractor to provide information to the Contractor in support of any claim from the Contractor to the Employer on account of adverse physical conditions or artificial obstructions.

New sub-clause 10(2)(b) requires the Contractor to determine and notify to the Subcontractor, within 28 days of notification from the Engineer, the proportion which is due to the Subcontractor of any sum due to the Contractor. Payment will not be due if the Employer is insolvent and has failed to make payment to the Contractor.

New sub-clause 10(2)(c) requires the Contractor to determine a fair and reasonable proportion of any extension of time.

New sub-clause 10(2)(d) follows the final part of the existing sub-clause.

Clause 15: payment

The existing clause 15 is deleted and a new clause inserted. The amendment is necessary to comply with the payment requirements in Sections 109–113 of the Act. The layout and many of the provisions remain the same as in the existing clause, with modifications to comply with the requirements of the Act.

Clause 17: Subcontractor's default

The list of reasons for which the Contractor may determine the Subcontractor's employment is extended by the Subcontractor being in breach of the Subcontract in suspending performance of his obligations under the Subcontract.

Clause 18: disputes

Sub-clause 18(1) follows the existing one and requires any dispute or difference in connection with the Subcontract Works, only excluding a dispute concerning VAT, to be settled in accordance with these provisions. This covers a wider range of disputes than those 'under the Contract' which are covered by the Act.

Disputes concerning VAT should presumably be referred to the Customs and Excise.

Sub-clause 18(2) introduces an important new procedure, as a precondition to the existence of a dispute.

Sub-clause 18(2)(a) requires the Subcontractor to notify the Contractor when he is not satisfied with the amount of a payment or with virtually anything done by the Contractor. The notification must be in sufficient detail for the Contractor to understand and consider the Subcontractor's submission.

Sub-clause 18(2)(b) requires the Contractor to notify the Subcontractor, as soon as possible, when, in the Contractor's opinion, any such submission gives rise to a matter of dissatisfaction under the Main Contract. The Contractor will then pursue the matter of dissatisfaction, with the co-operation of the Subcontractor. The Sub-clause then states that the Contractor and Subcontractor agree that no such submission shall constitute or give rise to a dispute until the matter of dissatisfaction procedure has been completed.

Sub-clause 18(3) enables either Party to refer the dispute to conciliation under the ICE Conciliation Procedure.

Sub-clause 18(4)(a) enables either Party to refer the dispute to Adjudication under the ICE Adjudication Procedure, which is to be modified as stated at Sub-clause 18(10)(b).

Sub-clauses 18(4)(b)–(f), 18(5) and (6) repeat the requirements of the Act.

Sub-clauses 18(7), (8) and (9) give the procedure for referring a dispute to Arbitration.

Sub-clause 18(7)(a) excludes from Arbitration a dispute concerning failure to give effect to an Adjudicator's decision. This exclusion enables either Party to apply to the Courts for an Order to enforce the decision.

Sub-clause 18(10) gives new procedures for co-operation and connection of Subcontract disputes with Main Contract disputes.

Sub-clauses 18(10)(a) and (b) refer to conciliation or Adjudication of a Main Contract dispute if the dispute has any connection with the Subcontract Works. Under 18(10)(a) the Contractor can require the Subcontractor to provide information and attend meetings.

Under 18(10)(b) the Contractor can require the Subcontract dispute to be referred to the same Conciliator or Adjudicator as the Main Contract dispute. The use of the same Conciliator or Adjudicator should ensure that the decisions on the connected disputes are consistent, but depends on the Conciliator or Adjudicator accepting the Subcontract appointment. The main

Contract Conciliator or Adjudicator would not necessarily be aware of this provision in the Subcontract.

The disputes would be dealt with separately unless the Employer agreed to them being joined. For Adjudication, such joinder would require agreement to extend the time period for the Main Contract Adjudication. However, the joint dissatisfaction procedure should help to gain the co-operation of all the different people concerned.

Sub-clauses 18(10)(c) and (d) give similar provisions for Arbitration.

Sub-clause 18(10)(11) is a without prejudice provision for conciliation.

The Second and Third Schedules are amended to suit the new clauses.

8

The Engineering and Construction Contract and other NEC Contracts

Introduction

This chapter considers the Adjudication procedures in the Engineering and Construction Contract and the other standard forms which comprise the NEC Family of Contracts. These contracts include the NEC preferred Adjudication procedures in the Core Clauses, together with optional procedures which take into account the requirements of the Act.

The chapter is divided into five sections:

- The application of Adjudication to the NEC Contracts.
- The amended Adjudication clauses in the Engineering and Construction Contract.
- The Engineering and Construction Subcontract.
- The Professional Services Contract.
- The Adjudicator's Contract.

The application of Adjudication to the NEC Contracts

The first edition of the Engineering and Construction Contract was published in 1993 and was called the New Engineering Contract (NEC). However, the prefix 'new' cannot be used indefinitely and for the second edition the name was changed to the Engineering and Construction Contract (ECC). The ECC and its associated contracts are known as the NEC family of contracts and includes:

- The Engineering and Construction Contract, second edition 1995.
- The Engineering and Construction Subcontract, second edition 1995.
- The Professional Services Contract, second edition 1998.
- The Adjudicator's Contract, second edition 1998.

The NEC contracts have always been intended to be non-adversarial, with the aim of resolving the causes of disputes before the problem escalates. However, in case any disputes should arise, the contracts include provision for immediate Adjudication as the primary dispute resolution procedure. However, although the NEC Adjudication procedures complied with the recommendations of the Latham Report they do not comply with the requirements of Section 108 of the Act.

The NEC first edition included the procedures for the settlement of disputes at Section 9. The Contractor could ask the Adjudicator to settle a dispute which arose from an action, or failure to act, by the Project Manager or Supervisor. In the second edition the disputes which could be referred to the Adjudicator were extended to allow either Party to refer a dispute about 'any other matter'. NEC Adjudication was based on the principle that any problem should be identified and resolved as quickly as possible. The contract required that the Contractor must notify the Project Manager within four weeks of becoming aware of the action or inaction which is disputed. The dispute could then be submitted to the Adjudicator between two and four weeks after the notification to the Project Manager. Further information can be submitted within the next four weeks and the Adjudicator would notify his decision within a further four weeks. In general terms the NEC procedure required about three months rather than the 28 day period stipulated in the Act. The NEC contracts also include provision for an 'early warning meeting', at which the Project Manager and the Contractor try to find the best technical solution to any problem before it escalates into a dispute.

The original NEC Adjudication procedures do not comply with the 'at any time' requirement at Section 108(2)(a) or the '28-day' requirement at Section 108(2)(c) of the Act.

Also, the NEC Adjudication procedures do not specifically enable the adjudicator to take the initiative in ascertaining the facts and the law, as required by Section 108(2)(f) of the Act. While some inquisitorial powers might be implied from the requirement that he acts as an independent adjudicator and not as an arbitrator, the Guidance Notes to the NEC first edition suggested that he is not permitted to ascertain additional facts. The Guidance Note to Clause 90.2 included:

> It is important that the Adjudicator has all the relevant information, to enable him to put himself in the position of the Project Manager or Supervisor when taking the action which is disputed. Information which has become available after the disputed action was taken is not admissible.

The Guidance Note to the ECC second edition omits this requirement but, at Clause 91.1 emphasises the importance of the Parties providing full information to the Adjudicator. The Contract does not specifically allow the Adjudicator to adopt an inquisitorial role.

The other contracts in the NEC family have always included similar provisions for Adjudication. While these procedures do not comply with the requirements of the Act they must, together with the non-adversarial attitude which is encouraged by the NEC, offer a better chance of avoiding delays and excessive costs than do the procedures of Section 108.

The amended Adjudication clauses in the Engineering and Construction Contract

Following the publication of the Act and the Scheme the NEC drafting committee decided:

- that the Adjudication procedure in the ECC second edition is the preferred procedure and should be retained for international use; hence, the Core Clauses remain unchanged
- that for contracts which are subject to the Act, the ECC should incorporate an option which includes the requirements of Section 108, in order to avoid the Scheme
- that all the necessary provisions should be incorporated into the contract, rather than by reference to a separate Adjudication procedure.

The addendum to the ECC was published in April 1998 as Option Y(UK)2: The Housing Grants, Construction and Regeneration Act 1996. The addendum includes amendments to comply with the payment and Adjudication provisions in the Act. Because the amendments are published as an Option it is necessary to state in the Contract Data that this Option is to be used. The printed Core Clauses remain unchanged and Option Y(UK)2 introduces a new Clause 90 and changes to Clauses 91 and 92. Hence, for NEC contracts in the UK it will be necessary to 'cut and paste', with the risk of confusion and mistakes.

The Notes for Guidance in Option Y(UK)2 state that the option is prepared solely for use when the contract is subject to the Act and that 'The option should not be used in other circumstances'. However, as has been discussed in earlier chapters of this book, Section 105(2) of the Act excludes certain work from the definition of what is a construction operation. If the Employer decides that a particular contract is covered by an exclusion and hence does not incorporate Option Y(UK)2 he could face problems if the Contractor, or a Subcontractor, believes that the exclusion does not apply. The Contractor or Subcontractor might refer a dispute to Adjudication under the Scheme. Also, the Employer would not have the benefit of the matter of dissatisfaction procedure.

If there is any doubt about whether the Act applies, and reliance on Section 105(2) exclusions must always by questionable, then the Employer should incorporate Option Y(UK)2 into the Contract Documents.

Option Y(UK)2 includes the amended Adjudication provisions at Clauses Y2.5–2.7. Clause Y2.5 gives a new Clause 90: Avoidance and settlement of disputes. The new Clause 90 repeats the requirements of Section 108 with, in addition, a dissatisfaction procedure which must be followed before a problem can become a dispute.

Clause 90.1 is a general statement that the Parties and the Project Manager follow this procedure for the avoidance and settlement of disputes.

The reference to the avoidance of disputes emphasises the principles of the NEC contracts. The matter of dissatisfaction requirement provides a procedure for settling problems before they become formal disputes.

Clause 90.2 requires that if the Contractor is dissatisfied with an action or failure take action by the Project Manager he must notify the Project Manager within four weeks of becoming aware of the action or failure to act. The Contractor and the Project Manager will then meet, within two weeks of the notification, in order to discuss and seek to resolve the matter.

This matter of dissatisfaction meeting is a different requirement to the early warning meeting which is described at Clause 16. However, as both meetings concern procedures for resolving problems, one could follow from the other, or in some circumstances they might even be combined. It is therefore important that a party giving notice of dissatisfaction ensures that the notice is clear and unequivocal.

This Clause follows the NEC principle that any problem must be notified and discussed within a fixed time period from the time the Contractor becomes aware of the problem. The Clause refers to situations when the Contractor is dissatisfied with an action or failure to act by the Project Manager, which covers most of the day-to-day technical and financial problems which arise during a project.

Clause 90.3 requires that if either Party is dissatisfied with any other matter he must notify the Project Manager and the other Party within four weeks of becoming aware of the matter. Again, within two weeks of the notification, the Project Manager and both Parties will meet in order to discuss and seek to resolve the matter.

This clause extends the dissatisfaction procedure to cover any problem which may arise. Unlike the Act, there is no restriction to problems which are 'under' rather than 'in connection with' the Contract.

Clauses 90.2 and 90.3 require the dissatisfaction to be notified within four weeks of the Party becoming aware of the problem. While immediate notification is often desirable in order that a potential problem can be identified and resolved there will be situations when, for whatever reason, the Party fails to give notice within this time period. Confusion may arise when the Project Manager and the Contractor have exchanged several letters and it is doubtful whether it is the first letter, or a later letter, which constitutes the action with which the Contractor is dissatisfied. However, while a late notification may be a breach of Clause 90.2 or 90.3 and the consequences of the breach will be noted, it seems unlikely that the notifying Party would lose the right to instigate the dispute procedure under Clause 90.4.

Clause 90.4 is a clear statement that:

> The Parties agree that no matter shall be a dispute unless a notice of dissatisfaction has been given and the matter has not been resolved within four weeks. The word dispute (which includes a difference) has that meaning.

This clause marks the point when a problem or claim becomes a 'dispute'. No notice is required to confirm that a Party is not satisfied with the result of the meeting or subsequent correspondence but, four weeks after the notice of dissatisfaction, either Party can decide that the matter has become a dispute. In practice, the Project Manager should ascertain whether the matter has been resolved or whether a query, possibly concerning the financial consequences of the original problem, is still open to be raised as a dispute at some future date.

The matter of dissatisfaction procedure has been criticised as causing a four week delay to the start of any Adjudication. It is similar to the dissatisfaction procedure in the ICE Contracts except that NEC endeavours to resolve the matter by discussion rather than by the Engineer giving a decision. If the procedure has a good chance of resolving the problem, or at least ensuring that both sides are prepared, and the Adjudicator has a better chance of reaching a good logical decision, then a delay of four weeks should not be significant.

Whatever might be said about the dissatisfaction procedure, both Parties entered into the Contract knowing that it contained this procedure and that the contract procedure is intended to comply with the requirements of the Act. For a claimant Party then to try and avoid the dissatisfaction procedure by requiring immediate Adjudication under the Scheme would seem to be, at the very least, an attempt to circumvent the procedure which was agreed when they entered into the contract.

A more serious potential problem is that failure to follow the dissatisfaction procedure could result in the loss of the right to refer a claim to the tribunal, which may be Arbitration or the Courts. The ECC Core Clause 93 states that a matter cannot be referred to the tribunal unless it has first been referred to the Adjudicator and, as has been discussed, reference to the Adjudicator depends on having followed the dissatisfaction procedure.

Clause 90.5 repeats Section 108(2)(a) and (b) of the Act, that either Party may give notice to the other Party at any time of his intention to refer a dispute to Adjudication and the dispute must be referred to the Adjudicator within seven days of the notice.

The removal of any time period for the notice of Adjudication is a consequence of the requirements of the Act and is in direct conflict with one of the primary principles of NEC that any problem should be tackled and resolved as quickly as possible.

As with the matter of dissatisfaction, the reference to Adjudication is not restricted to disputes which arise under the contract.

The NEC contracts require that the Adjudicator is named in the contract between the Parties and is appointed under the NEC Adjudicator's Contract as soon as the Parties enter into their own contract. The Adjudication clauses do not therefore need to include provision for the selection and appointment of the Adjudicator. While there is no requirement that the referring Party should check that the Adjudicator is still available and willing to act, this is obviously necessary to ensure that the Adjudicator accepts the referral and completes the Adjudication within the time limits imposed by the Act.

While the Adjudicator's Contract requires the Adjudicator to notify the Parties if he becomes aware that he is unable to act as Adjudicator, there is a distinction between being permanently unable to act and not being available for a significant part of a particular 28-day period. It would clearly be prudent for the referring Party to check the Adjudicator's availability before issuing the notice of Adjudication, perhaps raising a query during the matter of dissatisfaction period. As the Adjudicator has already been appointed it would be logical to defer or extend the 28-day period to suit his availability.

If, for any reason, the Adjudicator is not named in the Contract then the Contract Data should include a requirement that the Clause 92.2 procedure will be used for the appointment of the original Adjudicator as well as any replacement Adjudicator.

Clause 90.6 requires the referring Party to include with his submission 'information to be considered by the Adjudicator'. Any further information which either Party wishes to have considered by the Adjudicator must be submitted within fourteen days of referral.

These procedures rely on co-operation by the Parties. If, for example, the referring Party only submitted minimum information with the referral and submitted further information on day 13, the responding Party would be placed at a severe disadvantage. The Adjudicator could presumably ask for further information under Clause 90.8.

Clause 90.7 requires both Parties and the Project Manager to proceed as though the matter had not been disputed until the Adjudicator has given his decision.

If the dispute concerns an instruction by the Project Manager then the instruction must be obeyed and the Adjudicator will be considering the consequences, rather than the implementation, of the instruction.

Clause 90.8 repeats Sections 108(2)(e) and (f) of the Act requiring the adjudicator to act impartially and enabling him to take the initiative in ascertaining the facts and the law.

Unlike other procedures the ECC does not give the Adjudicator specific powers to take particular actions. Presumably this overall power would enable the Adjudicator to ask for further information, to visit the site, to call a meeting and to proceed in the absence of co-operation from either party. However, as the Adjudicator may need to wait for 14 days in order to receive basic information from the Parties he will have a very limited time period in which to take these actions.

If the matter in dispute was discussed by the Parties and the Project Manager at the dissatisfaction meeting under Clause 90.2 or 90.3 then any disagreement about the relevant facts and law should have been identified at that time and so there should be less need for the Adjudicator to take the initiative.

Clause 90.9 repeats Sections 108(2)(c) and (d) concerning the 28-day period for the Adjudication, with possible extensions.

Clause 90.10 requires the Adjudicator to provide reasons with his decision.

The question of whether or not the Adjudicator should give reasons is discussed elsewhere in this book. The ECC is unequivocal on this point and the Adjudicator is obliged to give reasons with his decision.

The Adjudicator's decision is considered at Section 90.2 of the Guidance Notes to the ECC second edition. The Adjudicator must include background information, which is basically the same as was considered in Chapter 4 of this book, and reasons are referred to at the fifth paragraph which states:

> Where contradictory facts are submitted by the parties, the Adjudicator should state his findings. He should summarise the arguments submitted to him, and then state his decision clearly. The Adjudicator is also required to state the reasons

for his decision. These should show how they led to the decision reached.

The application of these principles to particular situations still leaves the details to the discretion of the Adjudicator. It is suggested that the reasons should be clear but concise, in order to avoid argument and possible disputes as to the validity of the decision.

Clause 90.11 repeats Section 108(3) of the Act that the Adjudicator's decision is binding until the dispute is finally settled. The ECC allows for final determination of a dispute by the tribunal, which may be Arbitration or the Courts, whichever is stated in the Contract Data.

Clause 90.12 repeats Section 108(4) of the Act concerning the Adjudicator's liability. This requirement is repeated at Section 4 of the Adjudicator's Contract and extended to indemnify the Adjudicator against third party claims.

When Option Y(UK)2 is used, Clause Y2.6 introduces amendments to Clause 91 and changes the side heading to 'Combining procedures'. The old Clause 91.1 is deleted because it referred to the submission of information to the Adjudicator, which is now covered at Clause 90.6.

The new Clause 91.1 allows a subcontractor to attend the dissatisfaction meeting if the same matter has caused dissatisfaction under or in connection with the subcontract. When a problem arises from a subcontract as well as the main contract there will always be practical difficulties in joining the disputes. For the disputes under both contracts to be discussed at the same meeting is a good way to resolve the problem or co-ordinate the potential disputes.

The use of the phrase 'under or in connection with' confirms the wider range of disputes which can be referred to Adjudication under the ECC, which is an improvement on the basic requirements of the Act.

Clause 91.2 is amended to replace 'settles' with 'gives his decision on'. The change in wording is necessary because, under the Act, the Adjudicator does not settle the dispute. He gives a decision which may, or may not, be agreed as the final settlement of the dispute.

Clause 91.2 also enables the Contractor to submit a subcontract dispute to the Adjudicator at the same time as a main contract dispute on the same matter. The Adjudicator will then give his decision on the two disputes at the same time.

Similarly, if the subcontractor acts first with a claim which he decides to refer to Adjudication then, if the Contractor has a claim against the Employer on the same matter, he will wish to have it dealt with in the same Adjudication. As the Adjudicator is appointed at the start of the contract the same person can be appointed for the main contract and all subcontracts. By discussing the problem at the dissatisfaction meeting it is possible to agree that the Adjudicator can be asked to deal with both disputes at the same time.

Clause Y2.7 amends Clause 92 by replacing 'settles' with 'gives his decision on', as for Clause 91.2.

Clause 92.1 gives general requirements for the Adjudication, which have not been changed by the addendum:

- The Adjudicator acts as an independent adjudicator, not as an arbitrator.

Action as an 'independent adjudicator' presumably means 'in accordance with the contract provisions for Adjudication'. The separation from Arbitration is repeated in the next point that the decision is not an arbitral award.

- The Adjudicator's decision is enforceable as a matter of contractual obligation and not as an arbitral award.

The procedure for enforcement as a matter of contractual obligation is not clear. Failure to meet the contractual obligation to pay money would become a matter of dissatisfaction, which merely repeats the Adjudication process. Clause 93.1 does not include failure to implement the Adjudicator's decision as a matter which can be referred direct to the tribunal. However, if the Adjudicator failed to give a decision on the implementation dispute then it could be referred to the tribunal.

- The Adjudicator's powers include the power to review and revise any action or inaction of the Project Manager or Supervisor related to the dispute.
- Any communication between a Party and the Adjudicator is communicated also to the other Party.
- If the Adjudicator's decision includes assessment of additional cost or delay caused to the Contractor, he makes his assessment in the same way as a compensation event is assessed.

This requires the Adjudicator to follow the procedures of Clause 63: Assessing compensation events.

Clause 92.2 gives the procedure for the appointment of a replacement Adjudicator if the first Adjudicator resigns or is unable to act. The procedure requires the Parties either to choose the new Adjudicator jointly, or to accept the choice of the person named in the Contract Data.

Clause 93 gives the procedures if either Party is not satisfied with the Adjudicator's decision, or the Adjudicator fails to give a decision within the time provided by the Contract.

Clause 93.1 enables either party to give notice of his intention to refer the dispute to the tribunal, which may be either Arbitration or the Courts, whichever is stated in the Contract Data. The notice must be given within four weeks of the earlier of the date of notification of the Adjudicator's decision, or the date when the period for such notification expired.

A dispute cannot be referred to the tribunal unless it has first been referred to the Adjudicator.

The Employer is required to include the name and address of the Adjudicator in the Contract Data. In practice, some Employers include several names in the Tender Documents from which the Contractor will choose the Adjudicator, or the choice may be deferred until names can be discussed with the successful tenderer.

While these alternative procedures ensure the independence and acceptability of the Adjudicator, the practice of asking several potential Adjudicators if they are available results in uncertainty among practising adjudicators as to whether they will be appointed. Those who are not selected should be informed as soon as possible.

The Engineering and Construction Subcontract

The Adjudication provisions in the Engineering and Construction Subcontract follow the same pattern as for the main contract. The procedure at Section 9 of the second edition is retained for international use and Option Y(UK)2 has been published as an Addendum, incorporating the requirements of the Act, for use in the UK.

The details of the subcontract Adjudication procedure are similar to the ECC procedure but have been modified to suit the requirements of the subcontract. There is no Project Manager in the subcontract so all references to Project Manager are omitted and the procedure refers only to 'the Parties'.

Clause 91 has been amended in the same way as for the main contract. The new Clause 91.1 provides for a sub-subcontractor to attend the meeting to discuss a matter of dissatisfaction if the matter also causes dissatisfaction under or in connection with the sub-subcontract.

The new Clause 91.3 requires the Subcontractor to attend a meeting concerning a main contract matter of dissatisfaction if it also concerns the subcontract.

Clause 91.3 of the second edition now becomes 91.4. This clause enables the Contractor to submit a subcontract dispute to the main contract Adjudicator when the same matter is in dispute under both contracts. The main contract Adjudicator then gives his decision on the two disputes together. The main contract Adjudicator had presumably seen the conditions of the main contract before he accepted the position and so was aware that he might be required to act for subcontract disputes in this way.

For the combining procedure to work in practice it is important that the different notices are co-ordinated during the matter of dissatisfaction period.

The Contractor is required to include the names and addresses of both the subcontract Adjudicator and the main contract Adjudicator in the Subcontract Data. The Contractor can name the same person for both contracts.

The Professional Services Contract

The second edition of the Professional Services Contract (PSC) was published in July 1998 and Option Y(UK)2 is included in the printed document. The PSC can be used either as the contract between Employer and Consultant or as a subcontract between Consultant and Subconsultant.

The Adjudication provisions in the Core Clauses, for international use, and in Option Y(UK)2, for use in contracts which are subject to the Act, are the same as in the other NEC contracts.

When the PSC is used in the UK, which must be the majority of the projects for which the contract is used, it will be necessary to incorporate Clauses 90, 91.1 and 91.3 from the Option with Causes 91.2, 91.4 renumbered from 91.3 and 92 from the Core Clauses. Care will be needed to avoid confusion and mistakes.

The PSC does not have a Project Manager, so the Adjudication clauses follow the Subcontract provisions.

As for the ECC, the Employer is required to include the name and address of the Adjudicator in the Contract Data. If the contract is a subcontract and the main contract provides for joint Adjudication of disputes then the name and address of the main contract Adjudicator must also be included in the Contract Data.

The PSC includes at Clause 81.1 a requirement that the Consultant shall provide insurance against: 'Liability of the Consultant for claims made against him arising out of his failure to use the skill and care normally used by professionals providing services similar to the services.'

The requirement for insurance cover means that any claim for failure of skill and care will be dealt with by the insurer. This must inevitably result in delay in dealing with the claim and will probably result in a lengthy investigation and negotiation.

In these circumstances the requirement for a dissatisfaction meeting, followed by an open time period for referral to Adjudication, as in Option Y(UK)2 seems preferable to the restricted times for referral to Adjudication under the Core Clauses.

The Adjudicator's Contract

The second edition of the NEC Adjudicator's Contract was published in June 1998 and so incorporates any changes which were necessary as a consequence of the Act and the publication of Option Y(UK)2. The same contract and Form of Agreement are used for the appointment of the Adjudicator for the main contract, subcontract and professional services contract, using either the Core Clauses or Option Y(UK)2. The Adjudicator's Contract could also be used for the appointment of an adjudicator under other forms of contract.

The Form of Agreement is intended to be signed by the Parties and the Adjudicator at the commencement of the contract between the Parties and refers to the attached conditions of contract. If the Adjudicator's Contract is used when the Adjudicator is appointed after the dispute has arisen then the Adjudicator should insist, when he accepts the appointment, that his acceptance is subject to appointment under this Contract.

A separate Form of Agreement is provided for appointments under the Scheme. This can used whether or not the Parties are using an NEC contract. In order to comply with the Scheme any reference to the contract between the Parties is extended to include a reference to the Scheme. Also the Adjudicator is given the power to apportion payment of his fees and expenses in order to follow the provision in the Scheme

The use of an Adjudicator's Contract under the Scheme could cause problems, but does have advantages. The Scheme does not refer to any form of agreement and does not allow the time or opportunity for the Adjudicator to send his contract to the Parties for signature before he receives the referral. The procedures for payment are dealt with in the Scheme, but the Adjudicator will need to tell the Parties the figure for his hourly rate. There are other details which are not dealt with in the Scheme, such as the indemnity against third-party claims at Clause 4.2 of the Adjudicator's Contract.

The Conditions of Contract use the same style and phraseology as the other NEC Documents and comprise five Sections, followed by the Contract Data:

- general
- adjudication
- payment
- risks
- termination
- contract data.

Clause 1.1 requires the Adjudicator to act impartially and the Parties and the Adjudicator to act as stated in this contract and in the contract between the Parties. The Adjudicator has therefore agreed to follow the Adjudication procedures which are given in the contract between the Parties or the Scheme.

Clause 1.2 requires the Adjudicator to notify the Parties as soon as he becomes aware of any potential conflict of interest or that he is unable to act. Under Clauses 5.1 and 5.2 this notification could enable the Parties by agreement, or the Adjudicator, to terminate his appointment.

The notification that he is unable to act is important when an adjudicator has been appointed for the project and presumably refers to his being permanently unable to act. This could be followed by termination and the appointment of a replacement Adjudicator. It would not be practical for the Adjudicator to notify the parties every time he is not available for a period of, say, two or three weeks, although this might render him unable to act in a 28-day Adjudication. The Adjudicator would probably not even realise that he was unable to act until he received the notice and dates for the particular Adjudication.

Clause 1.3 gives definitions and Clause 1.4 lists the items which are included in the Adjudicator's expenses. In addition to the usual communication and travel costs the list includes 'charges for help in an Adjudication'.

The word 'help', which is repeated at Clause 2.2, implies a wider range of assistance than the 'specialist advice' which is used in other Adjudication procedures. The Adjudicator could delegate work to assistants and charge for their services. The Adjudicator is not required to notify the Parties when he obtains help, but this would be a reasonable procedure in order to alert the Parties to the future expenses.

Clause 1.5 is the usual singular/plural clause and 1.6 states that this contract is governed by the law of the contract. The applicable law is stated in the Contract Data.

Clause 1.7 states that in the event of conflict between this contract and the contract between the Parties then this contract prevails. When the contract between the Parties is an NEC contract then conflict should not arise, but this priority could be important when the contract is used with other forms of contract between the Parties.

Clause 1.8 confirms that the word 'Parties' includes an additional Party who has become a Party to the dispute and is important when the main contract Adjudicator is also dealing with a dispute from a Subcontract.

Clause 1.9 effectively requires communications to be in writing in the language of this contract, which is stated in the Contract Data. The clause also confirms that communications become effective when received, which can be important when the contract stipulates time periods for certain actions.

Under Section 2:

- the Adjudicator is required to reach a decision
- the Adjudicator may obtain help from others
- the decision and information are kept confidential
- the Adjudicator keeps the documents until termination.

The first three points are normal for any Adjudication but the fourth point makes it clear that the Adjudicator only needs to keep the documents until the termination date stated in the Contract Data.

Section 3 gives the provisions for payment to the Adjudicator. As he is appointed for the period of the contract between the Parties the Adjudicator will send an invoice after each decision on a dispute has been communicated to the Parties. The Parties will pay the fees and expenses in equal shares and the Adjudicator does not have the power to impose an unequal division unless the Parties have agreed. The invoice must be paid, in the currency stated in the Contract Data, within three weeks, unless a different period is stated in the Contract Data. Late payment will attract interest, at the rate stated in the Contract Data.

Clause 3.5 is effectively a joint and several liability clause. This avoids the need for the Adjudicator to take legal action against a Party who fails to pay his fees. Any such action could compromise the position of the Adjudicator for any future dispute.

Section 4 repeats the requirement of the Act that the Adjudicator is not liable to the parties except in bad faith. Clause 4.2 requires the Parties to indemnify the Adjudicator against claims from third Parties.

Section 5 gives the provisions for the termination of this contract. The Parties can only terminate the appointment of the Adjudicator by agreement, which prevents a dissatisfied Party from changing the Adjudicator.

The Adjudicator, as mentioned already, can terminate his appointment if he foresees a conflict of interest, or is unable to act. No explanation or limitation is given as to the reason why he may be unable to act.

The Adjudicator may also terminate his appointment if he has not been paid a sum due within five weeks of the date by which the payment should have been made. As he will presumably have already asked both parties to pay any outstanding amount he then has no other option but to take legal action to recover his fees and so can resign before taking such action. This five weeks, plus the three weeks in Clause 3.4 gives a period of eight weeks from the invoice, which is not a very long period, but presumably he will have assessed the overall situation before deciding to terminate his employment.

Clause 5.3 states that unless previously terminated, the appointment terminates at the date stated in the Contract Data. The Guidance Notes to the Adjudicator's Contract recommends a date which is one year after the completion of the work in the contract between the Parties.

The Contract Data give the facts and figures as required in the contract and which must be agreed between the Parties and the Adjudicator.

The Adjudicator's Contract envisages that the Adjudicator is appointed as soon as the contract between the Parties is agreed and that he deals with all disputes which arise from that contract. However, no provision is made for an appointment fee or for any retainer for keeping himself available. The details of any such fee and the services for which it is paid would need to be agreed and added to the contract.

9

JCT Contracts

General introduction to JCT Contracts and Adjudication in JCT 80

The following JCT Contracts are reviewed here in relation to Adjudication where the Rules adopted comply with the Act or the Scheme applies.

- Adjudication in JCT 80
- JCT 80
- Minor Works
- JCT 81 With Contractor's Design
- IFC 84
- For JCT Management Contract 1987, see Chapter 10.

Most of the issues arising on the various contracts are covered in JCT 80. Other points, on particular contracts, are dealt with under each separate contract, but otherwise the generic points are to be found cross-referenced to JCT 80. For the sake of brevity, the clause headings are given for main points only. Reference should be made to the actual contracts for the full text in each case.

Section 108 (1) of the Act gives a Party to a construction contract the right to refer a dispute ARISING UNDER THE CONTRACT for Adjudication. It follows that a dispute about the VALIDITY of the CONTRACT ITSELF is not a matter for Adjudication since it is not a matter *arising under the contract*.

It has to be acknowledged that where the contracts have been formulated on the basis that they will be administered by an impartial Architect or Contract Administrator, the imposition of an additional layer of administrative decision making (by the Adjudicator) turns an already complex process into a cat's-cradle of potentially conflicting decisions, and a subsequent paper-chase of documentation. If the Adjudicator's decision is accepted by all Parties, it can probably be subsumed into subsequent documentation, but if it is not, separate chains of documentation recalling both the Contract Administrator's decisions and the Adjudicator's decisions will be required.

In either case, a reasoned decision or at least a make-up of any figures embodied in the decision from the Adjudicator will be particularly helpful, as it will enable the detailed record of payment under various headings to be allocated and reconciled in a provisional final account pending final resolution by Arbitration or Litigation.

The client will need to decide whether to retain the JCT Adjudication clause or to exclude Adjudication when the contract is prepared if the category of work is excluded by the Act.

Where the contract is excluded from Adjudication by statute, as in the case of a residential occupier, contract documentation will probably be required which does not contain Adjudication provisions or the contract will need laborious amendment to exclude these. Otherwise, Adjudication will have been built into the contract under the terms agreed by the Parties.

Before referring an issue to Adjudication, it is wise to consider whether or not Adjudication is the best way forward.

- What is the issue which we want to resolve?
- Have I made my view clear to the other side? Do they realise that the initial problem has become a dispute?
- Can I prove my case? Would further tests help to identify the case before the clock starts ticking on the Adjudication period?
- Will an impartial decision, within the limited time, be helpful to the project as a whole?

- Would negotiation, mediation or conciliation be preferable?
- Would it be best to go direct to Arbitration and when would this be possible?

Refer to Figure 10.

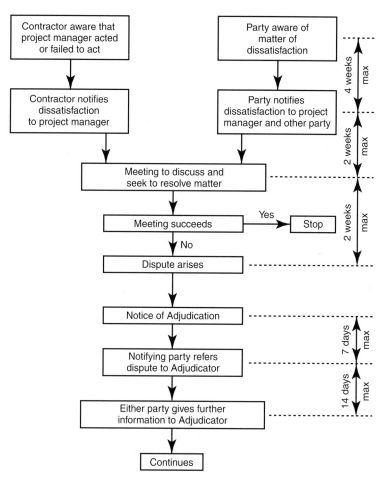

Figure 10. Adjudication under JCT 80

Settlement of disputes – Adjudication – arrangements in JCT 80 (Amendment 18)

The Contract lists bodies available for the nomination of Adjudicators. This list will include the RIBA and the ICE but there are, at the time of writing at least 16 Nominating Bodies.

The Clause in the Contract is number 41A. The first item states that Clause 41 applies where either Party refers any dispute or difference arising under the contract to Adjudication.

The Clause which follows can be summarised as falling into five sections:

- Provisions for settling the identity of the Adjudicator.
- The essential actions of the Parties.
- The conduct of the Adjudicator.
- The Adjudicator's fee and reasonable expenses.
- The effect of the Adjudicator's decision.

Provisions for settling the identity of the Adjudicator

Clause 41A.2 states that the Adjudicator to decide the dispute or difference shall be either an individual agreed by the Parties, or on the application of the Party who is referring the dispute or difference to Adjudication, an individual to be nominated by the nominating body named in the appendix.

In any case, no Adjudicator can be agreed or nominated who is not willing to execute the standard agreement issued by the JCT for the appointment of the Adjudicator issued by the JCT and where the Parties make any other arrangements for the appointment of an Adjudicator the appointment must be made in sufficient time so that the dispute or difference can be referred within seven days of the date of notice to refer. Any application for an Adjudicator to be nominated must be made with the object of securing appointment or referral of the dispute to the Adjudicator within seven days of the intention notice. As soon as agreement is reached by Parties on the appointment of an Adjudicator or when he has been nominated, the

Parties have to execute, with the Adjudicator, the Adjudication agreement.

If death or illness or some other reason prevents the Adjudicator dealing with the matter then a replacement Adjudicator can be agreed or nominated. Figure 10 should be referred to.

• No Adjudicator can be agreed or nominated under Clause 41A.2.2 who would not execute the standard agreement for the appointment of an Adjudicator issued by the JCT with the Parties and

• Where either of the Parties gives notice of their intention to refer a dispute to Adjudication, then any agreement made by the Parties on the appointment of an Adjudicator must be reached and the appointment made in sufficient time so that the dispute or difference can be referred within seven days of the date of notice to refer. Also, any application to the nominator must be made with the *object of securing appointment* and the referral of the dispute or difference to the Adjudicator within seven days of the intention notice. When agreement is reached by the Parties on the appointment of the Adjudicator or when the nominator has named the Adjudicator, the Parties are required to execute with the Adjudicator the Adjudication agreement.

If the Adjudicator is unavailable through death or illness or for some other reason, Parties may either agree a replacement Adjudicator or apply for another one to be nominated. Figure 9 should be referred to. The Parties would then have to execute the JCT Adjudicator Agreement with the replacement Adjudicator.

Essential action by the Parties
Where a matter is to be referred to the Adjudicator then the referring Party is required to give notice to the other Party of his intention to refer the dispute which is briefly identified in the notice within seven days of the notice or the date of execution of the JCT Adjudication Agreement if this is later. The Party giving the Notice of Intention is required to refer the dispute or difference to the

Adjudicator for his decision and is required to include with the referral:

- particulars
- a summary of the contentions to which the matter relates
- a statement of the relief or remedy which is sought
- any material which he requires the Adjudicator to consider.

All this has to be copied, at the same time, to the other Party. This can be done by delivery, by fax, by registered post or by recorded delivery. The normal requirement is that when it is by fax then a copy has to be forwarded by first-class post or delivery and sent by registered post or recorded delivery and unless there is proof to the contrary, it shall be deemed to have reached the other Party within 48 hours of the date of posting (excluding Sundays and public holidays).

The conduct of the Adjudicator

The Adjudicator's first and immediate action on receipt of the referral, etc. is to confirm the receipt to the Parties and the Party not making the referral has seven days from the date of referral to send a written statement of his contentions on which he relies and any material which he wishes the Adjudicator to consider.

This is a very sensible arrangement and it should be noted that neither the Act nor the Scheme provides such positive prompting for the responding Party to put his side of the case. It is not incumbent on the respondent to participate in a response anyway, but it is probably sensible for the Adjudicator to direct the respondent's attention to the matter in any case and stress the urgency of the matter.

It is possible, or even probable, that one of the Parties involved in the Adjudication will be totally ignorant of the whole arrangement and the Adjudicator will need to be patient and seek to explain matters to a Party in the contract who is, so to speak, an uninformed bystander. It will be very important that any explanations which the Adjudicator gives are accurate and it will probably be best if these are given in writing so that there can be no doubt about what is written. Like everything else it should be forwarded to BOTH SIDES. At the same time, the Adjudicator should not actually give any advice to any Party as this might appear to detract from his impartial status. It may help the Adjudicator to develop a series of standard letters, pro formas, acknowledgements, cover sheets, etc. for decisions and so on. Figure 7 gives a suggested format for an Adjudicator's Direction. If the case is reasonably close to the Adjudicator, it may be helpful to hold what an arbitrator would call a 'preliminary meeting' especially if one Party is not a large organisation. This may assist in sorting out any misconceptions. It should not be taken for granted that a large organisation will necessarily be informed about the procedure as they may well delegate the matter to an uninformed person and the result may be pathetic, but that is their problem. Any Party can ask a specialist to represent them and that specialist could be a lawyer, a specialising Architect or specialising Engineer.

The Adjudicator is required within 28 days of his receipt of the referral and accompanying documentation to reach his decision and forthwith send that decision in writing to the Parties. It is confirmed in the JCT Rules that the Adjudicator is NOT acting as an expert or arbitrator. The referring Party may consent to the Adjudicator extending the period of 28 days by up to 14 days, or longer, if both sides agree a longer period in which to reach the decision. If the case is complex, the 28 days may be taken up with increasingly intensive activity. See Figures 6 and 7.

The Adjudicator is not required to give reasons for his decision. It should be noted that this is a different requirement from that included in the Scheme. Even though the Adjudicator may not be required under the terms of the contract to give reasons for his decision it is probably a good idea that he commits these in writing to his own records so that he is confident that he has made a logical decision. The process of drafting the decision TOGETHER WITH THE REASONS helps to ensure that the logical integrity of the process is complete and reliable. The reasons can be extracted, if necessary, from the final document.

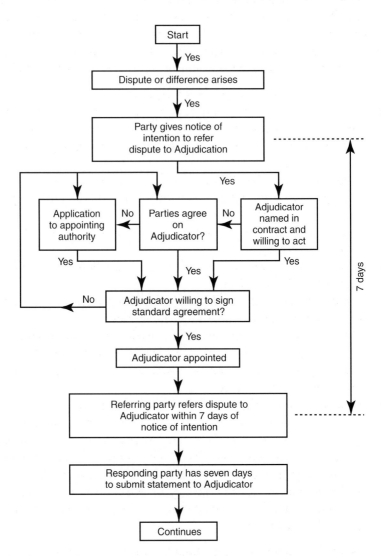

Figure 11. Adjudication under JCT 80 – continued

Clause 41A 5.5 confirms that the Adjudicator is required to act impartially and set down his own procedure at his discretion, but may not prolong the period within which the decision is given and may take the initiative in ascertaining the facts and the law if he considers this necessary in respect of the referral which may include:

- using his own knowledge and/or experience
- opening up, reviewing and revising any certificate, opinion, decision, requirement or notice given or made under the contract as if no such certificate, opinion, decision, requirement or notice had been given
- requiring from the Parties further information than that contained in the notice of referral and its accompanying documentation or in any written statement provided by the Parties including the results of any tests that have been made or of any opening up
- requiring the Parties to carry out tests or additional tests or for further opening up of work
- visiting the site of the works or any workshop where any work is being or has been prepared for the contract
- obtaining such information as he considers necessary from any employee or representative of the Parties provided that before obtaining information from an employee or Party he is given prior notice to that Party
- obtaining from others such information and advice as he considers necessary on technical or legal matters subject to giving prior notice to the Parties together with the statement or estimate of the costs involved. The terms of the contract relating to payment of interest must be taken into consideration and the Adjudicator may have to decide the circumstances in which it is paid, the rate of interest and the period over which it should be calculated.

It should be noted that an Adjudicator acting under JCT 80 is acting under different requirements to those incorporated in the Scheme in that under Section 20(a) an Adjudicator may not re-open a decision or certificate which is stated to be final and conclusive. This arrangement is not incorporated in JCT Provisions which specifically say that he may open up, review and revise *any* certificate, opinion, decision, requirement or notice or made under the contract as if no such certificate, opinion, decision, requirement or notice had been given.

It may be useful to note under what conditions The Scheme would be used for Adjudication where JCT 80 has been used. This will probably arise in many instances at first, where out-of-date contracts have been used. It could also arise where home-made amendments to a current contract invalidate what would otherwise be compliant contracts.

The Adjudicator's fee and reasonable expense

It is important to note that the failure of any Party to enter into JCT Adjudication Agreement or to comply with any requirements of the Adjudicator does not invalidate the decision of the Adjudicator. The Parties are required to meet their own costs of the Adjudication except that the Adjudicator can allocate the costs of any tests or opening up, if required, as he thinks appropriate. The Adjudicator in his decision is required to state how payment of his fee and reasonable expenses are to be apportioned between the Parties and in default of such statement the Parties bear the Adjudicator's fee and reasonable expenses in equal proportions.

The Parties are jointly and severally liable to the Adjudicator for his fee and for all reasonable expenses incurred in dealing with the matter.

The effect of the Adjudicator's decision

The decision of the Adjudicator is binding on the Parties until the dispute or difference is finally determined by Arbitration or legal proceedings or by agreement in writing. The Parties are required 'without prejudice' to their rights under the contract to comply with the decision of the Adjudicator and ensure that the decision is given effect. If either Party fails to comply with the decisions of the Adjudicator the other Party is entitled, pursuant to Article 6 of the contract to take proceedings in the Courts to secure compliance pending any final determination in accordance with Clause 41A.7.1.

The Adjudicator is not liable for anything done or omitted in the discharge or the purported discharge of his functions as Adjudicator (unless in bad faith) and this protection from liability is similarly extended to any employee or agent of the Adjudicator. This does not give immunity from action by any Third Party who may consider that his interest has been damaged by the decision.

Under Article 5 according to reference (f) page 45 of Amendment 18 and guidance notes, the Parties may submit sealed letters to the Adjudicator to be opened after he has reached his decision, if they wish him to consider particular matters before reaching his decision on the apportionment of his fee and reasonable expenses under Clauses 41A.6.1 and 41A.5.7 on payment of the cost of any tests or opening up.

JCT 80 Standard Form of Building Contract (Private with Quantities)

1A. General – *should be referred to by any Adjudicator*
This deals with interpretation and definitions. This should be referred to by the Adjudicator if any matters in a dispute involve interpretation or definition of the Conditions of Contract.

2. *Contractor's obligations*
The Contractor is charged with carrying out and completing the works in compliance with the Contract Documents using materials and workmanship of the quality and standards specified. Where and to what extent the approval of the quality of materials or standards of workmanship is a matter of the opinion of the Architect such quality and standards should be 'TO THE REASONABLE SATISFACTION OF THE Architect'.

The whole area of quality of materials and workmanship is a fertile area for disputes and one which can be quickly referred to Adjudication. It should be noted that while the Adjudicator can be called on to decide if work is to the required standard or not, under the terms of the contract, the decision should be limited to just that and the Adjudicator should not go on to decide if work is to be demolished and replaced or retained. The Architect can still make a decision as to whether demolition is required and re-building is to take place for other reasons, regardless of the Adjudicator's decision, but if the Adjudicator decides that the work which has been executed is in accordance with the contract, then additional payment would be due to the Contractor for the additional work. In such circumstances, for example, the load-bearing capacity of the work may be the subject of complex design and calculation, but these matters are not likely to figure directly in the specification in the contract and the Adjudicator should confine himself to the area over which he has jurisdiction, the resolution of disputes arising under the contract between Employer and Contractor. He should not get involved in design-related decisions, which are outside his jurisdiction and which could have far-reaching ramifications for design responsibility. (See also Condition 8 Work, Materials and Goods.)

3. Contract sum additions or deductions – adjustment – interim certificates

This deals with questions as to when such amounts shall be certified. Disputes arising here are suitable for Adjudication.

4. Architect's instructions

To avoid disputes it is desirable to issue as few Instructions as possible and particularly to avoid Variations. Issues which can arise include:

- Is the Instruction a Variation?
- Is the Instruction in writing?
- Has the Instruction been complied with?

- Is payment to be deducted from the Contractor owing to failure to comply, leaving restitutional work having been paid for which has been carried out by others?
- Does the Contract empower the Architect in the particular case to issue what purports to be an Instruction?

All these points are suitable for Adjudication.

5. Contract documents – other documents – issue of certificates
Architects/Engineers should note that the Standard Method of Measurement 7 calls for certain information to be shown either on location drawings or on further drawings which accompany the Bills of Quantities including, among other things, location and extent of existing structures to be demolished and, for the reinforced concrete, the permissible loads in relating to casting times. The Architect/Engineer should ensure that what is incorporated by the Quantity Surveyor in the Contract documents is acceptable from their points of view.

The custody and provision of certified copies of contract documents would seem to be straightforward. This clause has been a focus for disputes. Recent revisions may assist in clarifying the situation of the Contractor's master programme under 5.3.1.2 and the Architect's duty to provide further drawings and details, etc. The recent revision to 5.4.1 'information release schedule' requires that 'except to the extent that the Architect is prevented by the act or default of the Contractor or any other person for whom the Contractor is responsible, the Architect shall ensure that copies of the information referred to in the information Release Schedule is released at the time stated in the Schedule provided that the Employer and the Contractor may agree, which agreement shall not be unreasonably withheld or delayed, to vary such time.

Section 5.4.2 says that: 'except to the extent included in the Information Release Schedule the Architect as and when from time to time may be necessary without charge to the Contractor shall provide him with two copies of such further drawings or details which are reasonably necessary either to explain and amplify the

Contract Drawings and shall issue such instructions (including both for in regard to the expenditure of Provisional Sums) to enable the Contractor to carry out and complete the Works in accordance with the Conditions ...'.

Contract documents as a whole are essential to define exactly the scope, quantity and quality of the Works. They will be used:

1. By the Contractor to enable him to understand:
   - what he has to do
   - where he has to do it
   - and when it has to be done.
2. By the Contractor to enable him to know how much he can charge and when he is to be paid.
3. By the Surveyor to assist in the measurement and valuation of the works.
4. By the Adjudicator if a dispute arises.
5. By the Arbitrator or Courts if there is subsequent Arbitration or Litigation.

The documents will also define the extent of the site which is to be placed in the possession of the contractor and it is important that any restrictions which will be imposed on the use of the site are made clear.

Architects/Engineers should note that the Standard Method of Measurement 7 calls for certain information to be shown either on location drawings or on further drawings which accompany the Bill of Quantities including, among other things, location and the permissible loads in relation to casting times. Drawings or diagrams may also be included to amplify the information on various other items. The Architect/Engineer should ensure that any drawings and information incorporated by the Quality Survey is acceptable from their point of view.

Further information to be issued at a later date is only used to amplify that which is contained in the Contract Documents. Further information provided by other Consultants, Structural, Mechanical, Electrical or Landscape should be issued and scheduled by the Architect so that there is a full record of what was issued to the Contractor and when it was issued. Key documents from the Consultants should have been incorporated, in any case, with the Contract documents. The Contract does not recognise anyone but the Architect as the issuing Authority in the Contract and if other Parties become involved, lines of communication will become blurred and confusion may result.

Contractor's master programme

Experience shows that the phrase 'the Contractor ... shall provide the Architect ... with two copies of his master programme for the execution of the works ...' is imprecise. If the circumstances are that possession of the site follows fairly closely on the execution of the contract, and there are no special reasons for delay, the master programme is required within a few days of the execution of the contract. If it does not arrive then the Architect should request its delivery. The Architect does not have to 'approve' the programme, and it is probably best if its arrival is acknowledged but no specific approval is noted. It should be noted if the programme complies with the contract period. If it does not, it is clearly not acceptable and the point should be made forthwith.

The progress of the contract should be monitored against the programme and if there are any lapses or shortcomings these should be pointed out *at the time*. These will be useful reference points in any dispute which may subsequently arise over progress or completion. It should be noted that both substantially premature completion, as well as late completion, may have serious implica-tions for the employer. Premature completion may imply an accelerated cash flow and late completion will have obvious problems. Delays in construction projects are notorious areas for dispute. The master programme is then frequently used to support various arguments. The preparation of the master programme may well have been prepared with that sort of scenario in mind. These issues are likely to result in frequent references to Adjudication. If disputes arise, the earliest practical referral is probably the most satisfactory since the cumulative effect of a series of delays or alleged delays make it increasingly difficult to properly assess knock-on effects and resolution becomes increasingly difficult. This is an aspect of construction where the Architect should seize the initiative in pin-pointing culpable behaviour on the part of a dilatory contractor. If the contractor does not agree that his delay is jeopardising the progress of the works and the eventual completion date, the Architect should register his difference of opinion and point out any liquidated and ascertained damages (LAD) provisions in the contract. Subsequently, when the time for Practical Completion arises and the works are incomplete, then the Certificate for Non-completion under Clause 24 should be issued. This enables the employer to deduct LAD from any subsequent certificate issued under Clause 30.

The contentious nature of delay makes the whole subject a suitable subject for Adjudication and early records of the Contractor's culpable behaviour will strengthen the employer's hand, but there would be little point in either side invoking Adjudication before a specific trigger point such as the practical completion date is reached.

Further drawings or details

Clause 5.4 imposes a duty on the Architect 'as and when from time to time may be necessary the Architect ... shall provide [to the contractor] two copies of such further drawings or details as are reasonably necessary, either to explain and amplify the Contract Drawings or enable the Contractor to carry out and complete the Works ...'.

It is the Contractor's duty to programme the work. This will be embodied in the master programme and if it is prepared on a reasonable basis it will give an indication when further drawings or details are likely to be necessary taking into account lead-in times. The Contract will include an 'Information Release Schedule'.

It is often instructive to compare both documents and, where relevant, the state of progress on the site. There is a presumption in law that the Employer will act (and the Architect acting on his behalf will also act) in such a way as to impart business efficiency to the performance of the contract. That is to say that the Architect must be expected to produce information in time for the work to be done, when it should be done, to achieve reasonable and economic production of the work. If the information is not produced on time then the contractor may have proper grounds for an extension to the contract period (Condition 25). In the event of a dispute Adjudication may follow. Again, the sooner this type of issue is dealt with the more efficiently it can be resolved and Adjudication should assist in pinpointing responsibility at an early stage.

6. Statutory obligations, notices, fees and charges
These matters could, at times, become a disputatious area referable to Adjudication.

7. Levels and setting out of the Works
No particular comments, except that it is necessary to ensure that no ambiguities are allowed to confuse the proper setting out. If there are any disputes arising in these matters, early resolution by Adjudication may be helpful to all Parties.

8. Work, materials and goods
The phrase 'reasonable satisfaction of the Architect', occurs more than once and the comments in Clause 2.1 are repeated. It should be noted that the wording is not to the satisfaction of the Architect but to the *reasonable* satisfaction of the Architect and that the term 'reasonable' is a matter capable of interminable debate. It should be noted that the Architect is empowered under Clause 8.4 to issue instructions in regard to the removal from the site of any work, materials or goods which is not in conformity with the contract documents. A bald statement that the work materials or goods is unsatisfactory is *not* the same as an instruction to remove work which is not in conformity with the contract. ICE Contracts seem to

have a more decisive use of language when they refer to an Engineer's 'decision'.

The issue as to whether the Architect's decision in a particular case is reasonable or not, may well be the subject of a reference to Adjudication. Any decision which is made in this area needs to take account of the whole context of the contract, and the general character of the building as shown by the Contract Documents. As an example, in the absence of any other criteria, a bank in the high street of a large city could be expected to have brickwork of high quality as compared with the brick wall of a warehouse on an industrial estate. The type of brick, in one case expensively hand-made and in the other case a cheap common brick, would also indicate a reasonable expectation of the finished standard. The jointing would be expected to be uniform in its general effect in both cases – but with the hand-made brick it might well be variable with the brick, but still present a general consistency in effect when viewed from a distance. The necessity for the prior construction of a sample panel would be more critical for the high street bank than the other example. The consistency of the mortar colour would be important in both cases. Aesthetic judgements would probably be involved, and these may appear to be subjective unless judged against an approved sample.

If a dispute arose regarding the standard of the facing brickwork, the professional qualifications of the Adjudicator could influence the way in which the Parties presented their case to the Adjudicator. If the Adjudicator was an Architect, it would be reasonable to expect that he could use his own expertise to assess the quality of facing brickwork. On the other hand, if the Adjudicator was a quantity surveyor it might be considered unlikely that he would have the training and background to assess the quality particularly the visual quality, of the work personally, and at least one of the Parties might think it necessary to obtain an independent and suitably qualified expert to report.

If a dispute arose because the Contractor had laid the bricks frog-down in contravention of the contract documents, and the Architect condemned the work, and Adjudication was involved, the arguments that the work would be sufficient for the purpose would be irrelevant, and the Adjudicator should decide the issue on the basis of the contractual position, does the work comply with the Contract or not?

Implied obligations

If the contract Bills do not describe the standards of materials or goods fully, they should be supplied by the contractor in accordance with the standards implied by law, that is to say the materials or goods should be of satisfactory quality. Section 1 of Sale and Supply of Goods Act 1979 applies. This term of satisfactory quality can mean fitness for all the purposes for which such goods are commonly supplied, appearance and finish, safety and durability. However, the Court of Appeal in *Rotherham Metropolitan Borough Council and Frank Haslam Milan & Co Ltd. and M J Gleeson (Northern) Ltd.* [1997] decided that, on the facts of that case, Rotherham did not rely on the judgment of the contractor in selecting suitable material, that the Architect had believed that the material specified and supplied would fulfil the design requirement, and a warranty was not implied. The more closely the standard of the work can be defined in the contract documents, the less scope will be available for disputes to arise, but the possibilities for disputes to arise seems endless!

If Architect's decisions on standards of work are referred to the decision of an Adjudicator, it may be quite important to establish early testing arrangements to ensure that the Adjudicator is acquainted with the results of any necessary tests quickly so that a decision can be reached within the very limited time scales allowed where an Architect's decision is being questioned through Adjudication. The only way in which the necessary evidence may be available in time is if the Architect, in conjunction with the employer, organises immediate tests on the item in question, and it might be necessary to do this before the Adjudication procedure is invoked.

9. Royalties and patent rights

No particular comments.

10. Person in charge

No particular comments.

11. Access for Architect to the Works

No particular comments.

12. Clerk of Works

No particular comments.

13. Variation Instruction – Contractor's quotation in compliance with the instruction

As pointed out earlier it is in the interest of dispute avoidance to restrict and, wherever possible, to avoid variations. Nevertheless, disputes over these matters would be suitable for Adjudication.

14. Contract sum

This sets out how the figure can be adjusted in accordance with the contract. Disputes may arise here and such disputes could be adjudicated.

15. Value Added Tax

The Adjudicator has no role in relation to VAT authorities. There may be issues which could be adjudicated but not matters involved in the VAT arrangements themselves.

16. Materials and goods unfixed or off-site

Some issues under this heading could be adjudicated.

17. Practical completion and defects liability

Clause 17.1 states that where in the opinion of the Architect Practical Completion of the works is achieved and, if relevant, the Contractor complies with Clause 5.9 (supply of as-built drawings, etc. – performance-certified work), he shall forthwith issue a certificate to that effect. Before issuing a certificate of Practical Completion an Architect has to be satisfied that the work has been properly and fully completed in all but minimal respects. JCT 80 requires that under, Clause 6.1 the Contractor shall comply with any regulation or by-law of any Local Authority, so that it is unlikely that Practical Completion can be achieved if the building fails to comply with Building Regulations (see *Antino* v. *Epping Forest District Council [1997]* QBD 53BLR.56). Adjudication concerning practical completion is likely to be very complicated, and the matter may be better suited to Arbitration. The question as to what constitutes practical completion in any particular building would have to take account of:

- the requirements incorporated in the contract documents
- the nature of the building
- how it was to be used
- the standard of finish
- the operation of any mechanical electrical, safety or security installations
- the condition of external works and seasonal aspects of landscaping
- the removal of any Contractor's temporary accommodation
- making good snagging lists, though there is no obligation on the Architect to produce these
- damaged work.

Defects liability

Defects, shrinkage and other faults are covered in Clause 17.2 and it should be noted that defects, shrinkages and other faults which are covered have to be due to materials or workmanship not in accordance with the contract or to frost occurring before practical completion of the works.

Disputes as to a Contractor's Liability in these areas are a subject which could well be a matter for Adjudication together with Architect's Instructions related to same. In such cases the Architect's dated site notes could be crucial as would dated photographs.

These are all matters which could be referred to Adjudication.

18. Partial possession by Employer
The practical effects of a partial handover and associated matters of defects and LAD could all lead to Adjudication. A reference of such matters at the time might have advantages over any delayed Arbitration.

19. Assignment and subcontracts
Disputes arising here could be appropriate for Adjudications.

20. Injury to persons and property and indemnity to the Employer
The Contractor has clear-cut liabilities spelt out.

21. Insurance against injury to persons or property
The consequences of default in these areas are potentially so serious that it is in the mutual interest of both Employer and Contractor to ensure that the necessary insurance cover is effected. Contractors of any standing are likely to have serial policies in force and the most effective way of ensuring that compliance is covered is for the Employer's Insurance Broker to meet the Contractor's Insurance Broker and sort the matters out to their mutual satisfaction, having regard to the particular clauses in the Contract.

There is also the associated insurance under sub-clause 21.2 for which the Architect may need to issue instructions.

Any disputes arising under these clauses may be heavily involved in legal arguments and specialist knowledge and are not necessarily suited to the truncated time-scale of Adjudication.

22. Insurance of the Works

Any disputes arising under the clause may be very heavily involved in legal arguments and specialist knowledge and are not necessarily suited to the truncated time scale of Adjudication.

23. Date of possession, completion and postponement

One central concept in JCT Contracts regarding the time for completion etc. centres on the dates for commencement and completion and the arrangements for extension of time and consequent effects affecting the Employer's option to deduct Liquidated Damages. In order that the Liquidated Damages Clause may remain intact, even though variations and so on are given which extend the time needed to complete the work, there are arrangements embodied in Clause 25 to extend the Contract period to take account of instructions which are issued and which under the terms of the Contract qualify for additional time. While the Clause is often regarded as a Clause which principally benefits the Contractor, it may also be viewed as an advantageous arrangement so far as the Employer is concerned because it enables him to retain the Liquidated Damages arrangements despite variations or changes in the scope of the work. Liquidated Damages should be a genuine pre-estimate of the actual damages which are likely to be suffered by the Employer in the event of work not being completed by the time stipulated in the Contract and are normally expressed in terms of cost per day or per week. The alternative to Liquidated Damages is to leave the Clause blank (*not* entered as nil) and the employer will have the option of claiming damages at Common Law and, for that purpose, proving the actual damages which have been sustained.

24. Damages for non-completion (see also above)

This clause of the Contract is, by its very nature, likely to lead to controversy and will become from time to time the subject for Adjudication.

By the nature of things, the issue is likely to arise towards the end of the contract period so that any dispute regarding the appropriateness of the imposition of Liquidated and Ascertained damages by the Employer can encompass matters which have occurred throughout the duration of the contract. Variations, delays, arguments over extensions of time, genuine misunderstandings and deliberate confusion can all combine to provide a fertile field for disputes.

The Contract calls for the Architect to issue a certificate to the effect that if the Contractor fails to complete the works by the completion date then the Architect issues a certificate to that effect. In the case of *Jarvis Brent Ltd* v. *Rowlinson Construction Ltd* [1990] CILL620 it was decided that when, in that case, the owner's Quantity Surveyor wrote a letter and deductions were made of Liquidated Damages from the cheques paid to honour Interim Certificates and in this case it was held that this constituted 'requirements in writing within the meaning of Clause 24.1'.

In arguments on this subject the factual and contractual matrices are likely to be complex and will require a great deal of time and effort to untangle. Any allegations which are put forward in the form of a claim are likely to require considerable research before the responding Party can answer any charges which are made and it is difficult to see how Adjudication will provide a level playing field for such disputes to be resolved as the short timescale may give the referring Party the advantage of an ambush. It will be very important that the Architect, as a key player in the scene, maintains full and easily accessible records. The records, need to be retrieved quickly and reliably. If they are not, then the Adjudicator will have to reach a decision before the records are unearthed and it is more likely that it will go against the Employer and the Employer may seek redress against the Architect/Engineer.

The possibility of one side mounting an ambush on this subject is an intrinsic problem with the statutory time limits for Adjudication, and could make it a very unsatisfactory subject for resolution in this way. It would be very important that any Adjudicator dealing with these matters is experienced and knowledgeable in the conditions and situations arising in the type of work involved in any particular contract.

25. Extension of time

Clause 25 sets out in detail the requirement for a notice by the Contractor of any delay in progress and the fixing of a new completion date. It also provides a process to review the new completion date. There is an inherent problem with Adjudication in that Adjudication can be invoked at any time so that an Architect's extension of the Contract period under Clause 25 can be reviewed by the Adjudicator. The provisions in the Act do not provide for any review of an Adjudicator's decision so that there is a potential difficulty that if the Adjudicator comes to a decision on the first Architect's extension of a Contract period, this is, on the face of it, not a matter which can be re-opened by the Architect. It is however, possible for the Architect to review his first decision and it may be that when he undertakes such a review might come to the same conclusion as the Adjudicator, or he may not. We thus have the possibility that there will be the Architect's extension of the Contract period, which will be different to the Adjudicator's extension of the Contract period and the Architect may review his first decision which again may be different to the previous decisions and it would seem that the Adjudicator may be able to come in and review the Architect's second decision. The possibility of four different decisions would make an interesting background for an eventual Arbitration!

The judgment in *Balfour Beatty* v. *Chestermount Properties QBD* [1993] 62 BLR1 gives guidance on the position of extensions of time where variations have been issued after the completion date has elapsed, but where the contractor is in a period culpable delay.

Clause 25.4.6 is likely to be a part of Clause which may frequently be drawn to the attention of an Adjudicator since the argument is often advanced by Contractors that necessary instructions are delayed by Architects and when they seek appropriate extensions of time the Architect is reluctant to grant what they might consider to be due since by doing so, the Architect will lay himself open to criticism or possibly claims for compensation from the Employer. It is also true, of course, that Architects themselves are delayed by decisions which are not forthcoming from the Employer when they are reasonably necessary. The Adjudicator should have no particular difficulty in dealing with the issue as and when it arises, so long as all the relevant information is available to him.

26. Loss and expense caused by matters materially affecting regular progress of the Works

The matters contained within this section of the Contract spring from many other matters contained elsewhere in the contract and have to be considered in tandem with the various clauses referred to. Some sections of the Clause deals specifically with nominated subcontractors. Agreements between Contractors and subcontractors will have the same recourse to Adjudication procedures as any other construction contract and the effect of this may well be to accelerate consideration of items in the main contract triggered by Adjudicator's decisions on disputes between Contractor and Subcontractor.

27. Determination by Employer and 28. Determination by Contractor

Determination tends to be a complex subject in dispute resolution since it will often involve an assessment of the cumulative effect of a series of events asserted to have taken place which are argued to consolidate a particular legal position. The clauses in the contract lay down a somewhat complicated procedure and procedural irregularities may again be asserted as preserving or jeopardising a particular Party's position.

A fair assessment of these complicated matters will almost certainly involve the fine judgement of complex, detailed matters and the opportunity for a Respondent in such a case will probably be prejudiced by the strict time limits imposed by the statute on the Adjudicator. In the experience of the authors, determination as a subject matter of dispute is unsuited to Adjudication conducted under the terms of the 1996 Act.

Repudiations (see CILL March 1997).

29. Works by Employer or persons employed or engaged by Employer

No particular comments.

30. Certificates and payments

This covers the arrangements for interim certificates and valuations and the ascertainment of amounts due in interim certificates. The arrangements for off-site materials or goods, retention rules and the final adjustment of the Contract Sum and the issue of the Final Certificate are set out in very considerable detail. In due course the Contract Documents themselves are likely to be revised fully to take account the arrangements for payments contained in the Housing Grants, etc. Act.

In *Page* v. *Llandaff and Dinas Powis District Council* [1901] see Hudson's Building Contracts 4th edition, it was held that improper interference by the employer in the surveyor's valuation prevented the final certificate from being accepted as binding.

In *Lubbenham* v. *South Pembrokeshire District Council* [1986] 33 BLR 39 the Architects wrongly deducted money from an interim certificate. The judge took the view that the Architects, though in error, were 'doing their incompetent best' and decided that the certificate was not invalidated and that it should be paid as computed and any error should later be rectified or referred to Arbitration.

Disputes arising under Clause 30 may involve arguments dealing with various parts of the contract and if the matter is to go to Adjudication then an Adjudicator most suited to deal with the matters will need to be matched to the discipline most likely to throw light on the particular aspects of the particular dispute.

31. Finance (No. 2) Act 1975 – statutory tax deduction scheme

No comments.

32. and 33.
These are numbers not used in the Contract.

34. Antiquities, fossils, antiques and objects of interest

Conservation is a subject of increasing interest to the general public and is of prime interest to conservationists. Items which turn up on site as a result of demolition in city centres of historic origin or other centres can have extensive repercussions on construction programmes, particularly if the finds come as a complete surprise to those concerned. Churchyards and burial grounds going back to Roman times may excite the interests of the Local Planning Authority. Prior research into the history of the site may assist in formulating a policy to deal with such matters. The *House Builder* magazine for August 1997 contains an account of a typical situation.

JCT Agreement for minor building works incorporating amendments MW1–MW10, 1996

Introduction

This Contract is noted in Practice Note M2, issued August 1981 revised September 1988 and March 1994 as being generally suitable for contracts up to the value of £70,000 (1992 prices). The general pattern of the contract is similar to that of JCT 80 but dispenses with several detailed provisions to achieve a more compact format which appears to make it more attractive to many users. The Minor Works Contract does not contemplate the use of Bills of Quantities specifically, but a priced specification and a Schedule of Rates are referred to. There are no detailed arrangements incorporated for the nomination of Subcontract Works and no provisions for the consequences of naming subcontractors. Many of the general comments within the section on JCT 80 apply here again.

Articles 1–4

Articles 1–4 deal with the terms of the contract, the Architect/ Contract Administrator and an Arbitration Agreement.

1. Intentions of the Parties

Clause 1 sets out the intentions of the Parties with the Contractor's obligations and the Architect/Contract Administrator's duties.

2. Commencement and completion

The general approach found in JCT 80 is repeated in this document.

Clause 2 deals with commencement and completion dates, arrangements for any extension of the Contract period, damages for non-completion, practical completion and defects liability. Disputes concerning the interpretation of these arrangements frequently arise and would be suitable for Adjudication.

3. Control of Works, Assignments, subcontracting, etc.

Control of the Works, including Assignment and subcontracting are covered in Clause 3. It should be noted that Practice Note M2, comments on the Employer's control of the selection of subcontractors for specialist work and naming of same. There are no provisions in the form which deal with the consequences of such naming nor is there any standard form of subcontract which would be applicable to such selected subcontractors. Disputes concerning the reasonableness or unreasonableness of withholding consent to a subcontract could be referred to an Adjudicator. The authors' view is that the only action open to the Adjudicator, in those circumstances, would be either to rule that the withholding of consent was reasonable in the circumstances of the particular case, or, to award damages if the Adjudicator considered it was unreasonable in the circumstances, but the computation of any damages applicable might be a complex matter. We do not consider that the Adjudicator would have power to issue instructions to permit subcontracting as that must remain the duty of the Architect/Contract Administrator and the administration of the contract is likely to become disorderly if the Adjudicator seeks to supplant the Architect/Contract Administrator by taking over his role rather than merely coming to a decision on matters referred to him from a dispute or difference under the contract.

The provision that 'at all reasonable times' the Contractor should keep on the works a competent person in charge (3.3), might lead to a dispute as to what were 'all reasonable times', and this point could come to an Adjudicator. It is a point which should be capable of a fairly quick decision, but, as always, the onus for proving the case would be with the referring Party.

The same comment applies to the provision (3.4) that the Architect/Contract Administrator may (but not unreasonably or vexatiously) issue instructions regarding the exclusion from the Works of any person employed therein.

The Architect/Contract Administrator's Instructions and Variations (3.5 and 3.6) are similar, but not identical with the arrangements in JCT 80. The provision for variations carry an obligation to value any direct loss and expense incurred by the Contractor due to the regular progress of the works being affected by compliance with any variation instruction or, the price of the variation may be agreed prior to carrying out a variation instruction. The latter option has much to recommend it. Disputes arising under the provisions are clearly possibilities for Adjudication.

Clause 3.7 deals with Provisional Sums. Somewhat surprisingly disputes appear to arise on occasions over these matters and it is likely that they would be suitable for Adjudication.

4. Payment

Clause 4.0 deals with Payment Provisions, correction if inconsistencies in/or between Contract Drawings, Specification and Schedules and makes it clear that nothing in those documents shall override the interpretation of the Conditions. Progress payments and retention arrangements are set out in 4.2. Disputes over these points arise from time to time and are suitable matters for Adjudications.

The Penultimate Certificate, to be issued within 14 days of Practical Completion is dealt with in 4.3. Clause 4.4 details arrangements for the issue of the Final Certificate, the supply of documentation required for the computation of the amount to be certified and the payments associated with the Final Certificate. This process may trigger disputes which could be referred to Adjudication.

Clause 4.5 deals with Contribution, Levy and Tax Changes dealt with in Part A of the Supplementary Memorandum. Disputes and Adjudication could arise in this area.

Clause 4.6, Fixed Price arrangements are spelt out, the only exception to that rule being the provision of matters in Clause 4.5. The substantial part of the clause would not, in itself, appear to leave much room for dispute. The main potential for any disputes arising is likely to come about by ill-considered amendments to the original document and these could, in turn, give references to Adjudication.

5.   Statutory Obligations

Clause 5.0 deals with Statutory Obligations. Sub-clause 5.1 is headed Statutory Obligations, Notices, Fees and Charges and requires the Contractor to comply with Statutory matters, Rules, Orders, Regulations or Bye Laws applicable to the Works. The Contractor has an obligation to immediately give written Notices specifying any 'divergence' between Statutory requirements and the requirements of Contract Documents if he finds them. Subject to that obligation, the Contractor is not liable to the Employer under the Contract if the Works do not comply with Statutory requirements, if the work has been carried out to the instructions of the Architect/contract Administrator. This could, at times, become a disputatious area referable to Adjudication.

Sub-clause 5.2 deals with Value Added Tax. The Clause makes it clear that the sum or sums due to the Contractor will be exclusive of VAT and requires the Employer to pay what is properly chargeable by the Commissioners of Customs and Excise. The matters are detailed in the Supplementary Memorandum. Any disputes in this area would appear to be outside the jurisdiction of an Adjudicator under the 1996 Housing Grants Construction and Regeneration Act.

Sub-clause 5.3 Statutory Tax Deduction Scheme is covered by sub-clause 5.3. This also refers to the Supplementary Memorandum Part C. The provisions are explained in JCT Practice Note 8(1980). Any references of disputes to Adjudication from this sub clause and the Supplementary Memorandum may be limited by the Income and Corporation Tax Act 1988 or by the Income Tax (subcontractors in the construction industry) Regulations 1985 S.1. No. 1960 or any re-enactment or amendment or remaking thereof.

The sub-clause 5.5 deals with the prevention of corruption. Under this clause the Employer is entitled to cancel the contract and recover any loss resulting from the cancellation of the contract. If the Contractor has offered or given or agreed to give any gift or consideration to a person, or if the Contractor offended against the Prevention of Corruption Acts 1889–1916 or, if the Employer is a Local Authority, has given any fee or reward, the receipt of which would contravene Sub-section (2) of Section 117 of the Local Government Act 1972 or any re-enactment thereof.

Any dispute arising from this section may be open to Adjudication in theory, but in practice will almost certainly be so complex legally, that the Adjudicator would need to be a Lawyer with specialist knowledge of those aspects of law involved. The time limits, even if extended within the limits of the Act, are probably quite unrealistic to allow this matter to be dealt with properly in Adjudication except in the most simple type of dispute.

6. Injury, damage and insurance

Clause 6 deals with injury, damage and insurance. The consequences of default in these areas are potentially so serious that it is in the mutual interest of both Employer and Contractor to ensure that the necessary insurance cover is effected. Contractors of any standing are likely to have serial policies in force and the most effective way of ensuring that compliance is covered is for the Employer's Insurance Broker to meet the Contractor's Insurance Broker and sort the matters out to their mutual satisfaction, having regard to the particular clauses in the Contract.

Clause 6.1 is headed 'Injury to or Death of Persons'. 'The Contractor has an obligation and is liable for and shall indemnify the Employer against any expense, liability, loss, claim or proceeding whatsoever arising under any statute or at common law in respect of personal injury to or death of any person whomsoever arising out of the works, except to the extent that the same is due to any Act or neglect of the Employer or to any person for whom the Employer is responsible.' The Contractor is obliged to take out and maintain the insurance spelt out and cause any Subcontractor to take out and maintain similar insurance cover.

These requirements are clear obligations and do not require any instructions by the Architect/Contract Administrator. Failure to comply with the obligations could have extremely serious consequences. The duties are clear cut and unambiguous. Disputes and Adjudication are theoretically possible but the risks of any default are so serious that it is difficult to consider that this would arise, particularly bearing in mind that under sub-clause 6.4 the Employer may require the Contractor, and require any Subcontractor to produce evidence that he might reasonably require in relation to Clauses 6.1, 6.2 and where applicable 6.3A. Any disputes referred to an Adjudicator regarding these matters would require an Adjudicator with very specialist detailed insurance and associated legal expertise, except for the simplest cases.

Clause 6.2 deals with injury or damaged property and clauses 6.3A or 6.3B (and any existing structures) by fire, etc. Clause 6.3A applies where the Contractor is responsible and 6.3B where the Employer is responsible for fire insurance and this option is normally used where any existing structures are involved and where split responsibility for contiguous or close proximity buildings are best avoided by extending the same insurance policy to cover both existing buildings (and perhaps contents) and new work. The provisions empower the Employer to require evidence of insurance. Clause 6.4 applies to the above matters. The same comments on Adjudication under 6.1 apply to 6.2 and 6.3.

Clause 6.4 deals with evidence of insurance to be produced to the Employer. See above under 6.1, 6.2 and 6.3A or 6.3B above.

Adjudication regarding disputes under these provisions may be a theoretical possibility, but in fact, the issues are likely to be extremely complex and would require very specialised knowledge and legal expertise.

7. Determination

Clauses under 7 deal with determination. The requirements for necessary Notices are set out under 7.1, the circumstances under which the Employer may determine the Contract as set out under 7.2 and the circumstances under which the Contractor can determine the Contract as set out under 7.3. It is made clear under 7.4 that the provisions of Clauses 7.3.17.3.3 are without prejudice to any other rights and remedies which the Contractor may possess.

Determination may become a very disputatious area since the nature of the matters it deals with are in themselves often controversial and disputatious. These clearly may, in turn, become matters referred to an Adjudicator. Experience shows that they tend to be complex so far as factual matters are concerned, that expert opinion, if it is involved, may be controversial and that the legal or contractual arguments involved are likely to be complex as the whole situation tends to develop out of a sequential series of events. The cumulative effect of the sequence of events involved may call for fine judgement on the part of any Adjudicator and in practical terms, the main difficulty may be in the truncated time scales imposed by the terms of the Housing Grants, Construction and Regeneration Act. The time scales negate a level playing field for the Parties since the first Party to refer the matter has the advantage of carrying out its research in preparation for the case at its own pace, thus staging an ambush on the responding Party who has to work within the time limits of Adjudication. This context makes the whole subject most unsatisfactory for referral to Adjudication under the terms of the Act.

8. Supplementary memorandum

No comment.

9. Settlement of disputes – arbitration
No comment.

JCT standard form of contract with Contractor's design 1981 with supplementary provisions issued February 1988 for Adjudication

Introduction
This contract includes arrangements for Adjudication which obviously pre-date the provisions of the Act and the Adjudication arrangements as then envisaged are set out in clauses S1–S7.6 inclusive. If an Adjudication is conducted under the terms of the CONTRACT ADJUDICATION, the Adjudicator will need to cover arrangements for indemnity from the Parties in the terms of his appointment.

Statutory Adjudication, under the Scheme, should include indemnity arrangements in any case. Some of the implications under the new Act are set out on page 2 where both Contract Adjudication and Statutory Adjudication may apply.

The Articles deal with:

- the Contractor's obligations
- the Contract Sum
- the Employer's Agent
- the Employer's requirements and Contractor's proposals
- the settlement of disputes by Arbitration.

Conditions

1. Interpretation and definition

Definitions are dealt with in sub-clauses 1.1–1.3 and may need to be the first point of call for an Adjudicator where any question of interpretation and definitions arises.

2. Contractor's obligations

As this is what is popularly known as a 'turnkey' contract, the Contractor is responsible for the design of the works including specifications for any kinds and standards of materials of goods and workmanship so far as is not described or stated in the Employer's requirements or Contractor's proposals.

It is made clear that nothing contained in the Employer's requirements or the Contractor's proposals or the contract sum analysis shall override or modify the application or interpretation of that which is contained in the articles of agreement, the Conditions and where applicable the supplementary provisions or the Appendices. Any divergence between the Employer's Requirements and the definition of the site boundary has to be corrected by an instruction issued by the Employer which is deemed to be a change to which the provisions of clauses 12.4–12.6 apply. It also calls for both the Employer and the contractor, where they find any such divergence as referred to in Clause 2.3.1 to give immediate written notice to the other.

Where there are any discrepancies within the Employer's requirements, the Contractor's proposal shall prevail without any adjustment of the Contract sum. Where the Contractor's proposals do not deal with any discrepancy within the Employer's require-ments the Contractor is called upon to inform the Employer in writing of his proposed amendment to deal with the discrepancy and the Employer either agrees with that proposal or decides how this discrepancy shall be dealt with and any agreement or decision has to be notified by the Contractor and such notification is treated as a change in the Employer's requirements. If there is a discrepancy within the Contractor's proposals, the Contractor is asked to inform the Employer in writing of his proposed amendments to remove the discrepancy and the Employer decides between the discrepant items or otherwise may accept the Contractor's proposed amendment. The Contractor is obliged to comply with the decision or accept and supply the Employer without cost to the Employer.

Contractor's design warranty

Clause 2.5.1 places on the Contractor the same general design liability that the Employer would have where an Architect or other appropriate professional designer had supplied the design.

Where a dwelling or dwellings are involved, the Contractor also carries liability under the Defective Premises Act 1972.

Where the provisions of the Defective Premises Act 1972 are not involved, provided that such limitation does not apply to any damages which the Contractor could be required to pay or allow as liquidated or ascertained damages in the event of failure to complete the construction of the works by the completion date.

Clause 2.5.4 makes it clear that any design which the Contractor has prepared or shall prepare or issue for the works, shall include a reference to any design which the Contractor has caused or shall cause to be prepared or issued by others.

There are many disputes which could arise under matters covered by Clause 2. Disputes which arise are almost inevitably likely to be resolved by Adjudication in the first instance since there is no traditional Contract Administrator to deal with possible differences of view.

3. Contract sum – additions or deductions – adjustment – interim payments

This could be a disputatious area and differences which arise could be referred to Adjudication.

4. Employer's instructions

This contract differs from most JCT Contracts in that in the absence of a traditional Contract Administrator the Employer issues instructions direct. Disputes arising under this clause could be referred to Adjudication.

5. Custody and supply of documents

In this case the Contractor is to supply to the Employer copies of drawing specifications, detailed levels and dimensions, etc. which the Contractor prepares or uses for the purposes of the works. Disputes arising under this clause could be referred to Adjudication.

6. Statutory obligations, Notices, fees and charges

The usual requirements carried in other JCT Contracts are included here. Again Adjudication could be required if there are disputes under this clause.

7. Site boundaries

The Employer is required to define the boundaries of the site. This is obviously the only practicable arrangement in the circumstances of the contract. Disputes which might arise under this clause could be referred to Adjudication and it would probably be to the benefit of the Parties if any matters arise that they are dealt with as a matter of urgency.

8. Materials, goods and workmanship to conform to description – testing and inspection

This Clause is generally in a similar form to that of Clause 8 – Work Materials and Goods in JCT 80 except that it has to cater for a situation where there is no specific description or specification in the same terms that would be available with JCT 80 and there is a provision that the Contractor shall not substitute anything which is described within the Employer's requirements without the Employer's consent, though such consent cannot be unreasonably delayed or withheld and that consent does not relieve the Contractor from his other obligations.

A similar arrangement deals with workmanship and if there are no standards, particularly covered then the workmanship has to be of a standard appropriate for the works. There are provisions that the Contractor shall provide upon request of the Employer, vouchers to prove that materials and goods comply with the requirements of Clause 8.1.1. The Employer may issue instructions requiring the Contractor to open up for inspection and there are provisions for payment for that unless the inspection or test shows, that the materials, goods or work are not in accordance with the Contract. There follow arrangements that any work materials or good not in accordance with the contract may be removed on instructions or after the consultation with the Contractor there may be instructions requiring a change but there are not extensions of time or additions to the contract sum. A Code of Practice is appended to the Conditions to cover matters arising under instructions under Clause 8.3 to open up for inspection or to test. There are also arrangements for the provisional samples to the Employer.

9. Copyright, royalties and patent rights
These provisions follow the provisions of Clause 9 in JCT 80 and comments regarding Adjudication would apply again here.

10. Person in charge
No particular comment.

11. Access for Employer's Agent, etc. to the Works
No particular comment.

12. Changes in the Employer's requirements and provisional sums
This deals with the definition of the change to the Employer's requirements, the imposition by the Employer of any obligations or restrictions in regard to matters set out in Clause 12.1.2.1 on 12.1.2.4 and the execution of completion of the works in a specific order. Instructions in regard to Provisional Sums and the valuation of changes in the work and the Valuation Rules generally are also incorporated in Clauses 12.3–12.5. Matters in dispute under this clause could be referred to Adjudication.

13. Contract Sum

This may not be adjusted or altered in any way whatsoever otherwise than in accordance with the express provisions of the conditions. Disputes arising under this clause would be suitable for Adjudication.

14. Value Added Tax – Supplemental provisions

No particular comments.

15. Unfixed materials and goods

Generally follows Clause 16 of JCT 80 except that it does not cover materials and goods which are off site.

Disputes arising here could be adjudicated.

16. Practical completion and defects liability period

This generally follows Clause 18 in JCT 80 and the comments which apply there would apply here again.

17. Partial possession by Employer

If disputes arose under this clause they would be suitable for Adjudication.

18. Assignment and Subcontracts

This generally follows the equivalent arrangements in Clause 19 of JCT 80 and comments regarding Adjudication which apply here again.

19. Fair wages

No particular comment.

20. Injury to persons and property and indemnity to Employer
The provisions are generally similar to those in JCT 80 and the same comments would apply again regarding Adjudication.

21. Insurance against injury to persons or property
The previous comments on this type of insurance under JCT 80 would apply again and the comments about Adjudication are repeated.

22. Insurance of the Works
Comments as above.

23. Date of possession, completion and postponement
This generally follows Clause 23 of JCT 80 and the comments made there would apply here again.

24. Damages for non-completion
In general terms this is similar to Clause 24 in JCT 80, except that it is a case of the issue of a notice rather than a certificate which the Architect would issue under JCT 80. The general comments under JCT 80 in Clause 24 would apply here again.

25. Extension of time
Provisions generally follow the arrangements in Clause 25 of JCT 80. Comments regarding Adjudication under JCT 80 would apply here again.

26. Loss and expense caused by matters affecting regular progress of the Works
Again, these generally follow Clause 26 of JCT 80 and the comments there would follow again.

27. Determination by Employer and 28. Determination by Contractor

These provide provisions generally similar to those covered in JCT 80 and the comments there would apply again.

29. Execution of work not forming part of the Contract

Execution of work not forming part of the contract. Generally speaking follows Clause 30 – payments are similar in kind to Clause 30 in JCT 80 which covers certificates and payments but generally follows the arrangements of Clause 31 in JCT 80. Comments under JCT 80 under JCT 80 under the similar section apply here regarding Adjudication.

30. Payments

The arrangements for payments follow the general pattern adopted in other JCT contracts and the comments under JCT 80 regarding Adjudication apply here again.

31. Finance (No. 2) Act 1975 statutory tax deduction scheme

No particular comments.

32. Outbreak of hostilities

This deals with the outbreak of hostilities and Clause 33 deals with the question of war damage. No particular comments.

33. War damage, 34. Antiques and 35. Fluctuations

No particular comments except that if there are disputes in this area they could be dealt with by Adjudication.

36. Contribution, levy and tax fluctuations

No particular comments.

37. Labour and materials, cost and tax fluctuations
The arrangements are set out in considerable detail and in the case of disputes the matter could be referred to Adjudication.

38. Use of Price Adjustment Formula
Comments as for 39 above.

39. Settlement of disputes – Arbitration
No particular comments.

JCT Intermediate Form of Contract 1984 incorporating Amendments Nos 1–7 Inclusive and 9

The Intermediate Form of Contract 1984 (IFC 84) follows, in general, the format of JCT Contracts but is significantly different to JCT 80 in that the elaborate procedures for subcontracting are simplified by introducing named persons as subcontractors. The other general point about IFC 84 is that it tends to be written in more user friendly language than JCT 80 and is intended for use with contracts intermediate between those for which JCT 80 are suitable and the Minor Works form, where the proposed building works are of simple content involving normally recognised trades and skills of the industry, without any building service installations of a complex nature or other specialised work of a similar nature and where adequately specified or billed documentation is available prior to the invitation of tenders.

Articles 1–5 deal respectively with the Contractor's obligations, the contract sum, the Architect/the Contract Administrator, the Quantity Surveyor and the settlement of disputes by Arbitration.

Condition 1: the intentions of the Parties

The Contractor's obligations are dealt with in a manner similar to that in JCT 80. The quantity and quality of work are to be defined either by Specifications, Schedules of Work or Contract Bills. The priority of Contract documents makes it clear that nothing contained in the Specification/Schedules of Work/Contract Bills shall over-ride or modify the application or interpretation which is contained in the Articles, Conditions, Supplemental Conditions or Appendix.

Instructions as to inconsistencies, errors and omissions are catered for in 1.4 and 1.5 indicates the Bills of Quantities should have been prepared in accordance with SMM7.

The Contract documents are directed to remain in the custody of the Employer but to be available at all reasonable times for inspection by the Contractor and there is an obligation that the Architect/Contract Administrator to provide the Contractor, without charge, with one certified copy of the contract documents.

Further drawings and details are to be provided in accordance with 1.7 and in general terms the same arrangements as included in JCT 80 at 5 are included here. There are limits to the use of documents for the purposes of the contract.

Certificates issued by the Architect or Contract Administrator are issued to the Employer with a duplicate supplied simultaneously to the Contractor.

Sub-clauses 1.0 and 1.11 deal with unfixed materials of goods and the passing of property and the arrangements for off site materials and goods and the passing of property.

Various matters covered by this clause are suitable for Adjudication.

Condition 2: possession and completion

Arrangements for the site to be given into the possession of the Contractor for the purposes of the works are set out in 2.1 and there is an obligation on the Contractor to begin and proceed regularly and diligently with the works to complete the same on or before the Date of Completion. There are provisions for the Employer to, with the consent in writing of the Contractor, occupy and use part of the site for the purposes of the storage of goods or otherwise than before the issue of the Certificate of Practical Completion. Arrangements are included for notification to Insurers in such circumstances.

Clause 2.2 provides for deferment of possession from the date stated in Appendix for a period which should not exceed six weeks.

Disputes arising under this clause might be suitable for Adjudication.

Extension of time

The arrangements for extension of time are generally in accordance with those provisions in Clause 23 of JCT 80. Arrangements for further delay or extension of time are dealt with in Clause 2.5 and arrangements for Certificate of Non-completion in 2.6.

Liquidated Damages for Non-completion are spelt out under Clause 2.7 together with repayment of liquidated damages under 2.8.

Comments regarding Adjudication are as set out under clause 23 of JCT 80.

Practical completion

Practical completion is covered in 2.9 together with arrangements for the issue of Certificates to that effect. The comments under Clause 17 of JCT 80 apply here.

Defects liability

The arrangements for Defects liability generally follows the same lines as Clause 17 in JCT 80. Many issues could arise under this clause which could be suitable for Adjudication.

Condition 3: control of the Works

The arrangements and limitations of assignment, and subcontracting, are dealt with under Clauses 3.1, 3.2, 3.2.1 and 3.2.2.

Named persons as Subcontractors

As stated previously the arrangements for naming subcontractors enables simplified procedures in comparison with those provided in

JCT 80 and these are set out in detail in Clauses 3.3.1–3.3.9 inclusive.

Contractor's person in charge

This generally follows the arrangements of JCT 80 in Clause 10.

Architects/Contract Administrator's instructions

These are dealt with under Clause 3.5.1. Matters are generally expressed in somewhat similar terms as those used in Clause 4 of JCT 80 and the same observations apply. Variations are covered in Clause 3.6 and follow the provisions generally of JCT 80 in Clause 13. The same observations as those made under JCT 80 at Clause 13 apply here. Instruction to expend provisional sums are dealt with in 3.8. Levels and setting out are dealt with in 3.9 and are analogous to those in Clause 7 of JCT 80.

Clerk of Works is dealt with in Clause 3.10 and follows generally the provision in JCT 80 of Clause 12.

Work not forming part of the contract which is to be carried out by the Employer or persons employed or engaged by the Employer is dealt with in Clause 3.11 and is similar in effect to those in Clause 29 of JCT 80.

Instructions as to inspection – tests are dealt with in 3.12 and instructions following failure of work in 3.13.1 and 3.13.2 with instructions for removal of work, etc. covered in 3.14.1 and 3.14.2 with instructions as to postponement dealt with in 3.15.

Any disputes arising under these matters would be suitable for Adjudication.

Condition 4: payment

Clause 4 deals with payment, the contract sum is defined in 4.1. The arrangements for interim payment in 4.2 and an interim payment on Practical Completion in 4.3.

Clause 4.4 makes it clear that where the Employer is not a Local Authority the Employer's interest in the percentage of the total value, not included in amounts in interim payments to be certified under Clauses 4.2 and 4.3 shall be regarded as fiduciary as Trustee and that the Contractors beneficial interest therein remains and that the Employer only has recourse thereto for any amount to which he is entitled under the provisions of the contract, to deduct.

Clause 4.5 deals with the computation of the adjusted Contract Sum. The arrangements for the issue of the Final Certificate in 4.6 and the effect of the Final Certificate is spelt out in 4.7.

The effect of Certificates other than Final Certificate is set out in 4.8 and arrangements for fluctuations in 4.9 and for fluctuations with named persons in 4.10. Disturbance of the regular progress of the works is deal with in 4.11 and the matters referred to in 4.11 are set out in detail in 4.12.

Disputes arising regarding payment would probably be suitable for Adjudication and, indeed, this was an area originally intended to be covered in the Latham recommendations.

Condition 5: statutory obligations, etc.

Statutory obligations are set out under Clause 5 together with arrangements for emergency compliance with same, Value Added Tax: Supplemental Condition A and the Statutory Tax Deduction Scheme: Supplemental Condition B. There are no particular comments on these sections.

Condition 6: injury, damage and insurance

The sub-clauses under this section generally follow the arrangements in JCT 80 and the Minor Works Contract and the comments there apply again in this case.

Condition 7: determination

- Determination by Employer
- Determination by Contractor.

These clauses generally follow the pattern established under Clause 27 and 28 of JCT 80 and the comments which apply there apply again in this case.

Condition 8: interpretation, etc.

Section 8 deals with references to clauses, etc., articles etc, to be treated as a whole, and definitions. They also cover the terms, the Architect/the Contract Administrator and the references to priced specification or priced Schedules of Work. These clauses may need to be the first port of call for an Adjudicator where disputes arise which involve interpretation of the contract and the definition of various parts of the same.

Condition 9: Settlement of disputes – Arbitration

No particular comments.

10

'Other contracts'

The ACA Form of Building Agreement, Second Edition 1984

This form is intended to be used for a wide range of contracts. It contains provisions for Adjudication which, obviously, pre-date the Act. Alternative arrangements for dispute resolution include either Adjudication, or Arbitration or Litigation.

In this Contract the Adjudicator is intended to be appointed at the pre-contract stage. If he was called on he was required to give his decision within five working days. If there was any disagreement by either of the Parties with the decision the matter could be referred to Arbitration at the stage when the works were taken over. The areas which the Adjudicator could deal with included any dispute or difference concerning:

- any adjustment or alteration of the Contract Sum
- Contractor's extensions of time
- Contractor's compliance with contract documents in the execution of the works
- either Party's entitlement to terminate the Contractor's employment.

Reasonableness of any Contractor's objection to instructions regarding named subletting and instructions to permit work or installations not forming part of the contract by others.

In this context the Adjudicator acts as an *Expert* and not as an Arbitrator, and if the Adjudicator does not produce his decision within the time limit, the dispute is to be referred to a person to be agreed between the Parties or nominated by the President or Vice President of the Chartered Institute of Arbitrators.

The arrangement for the Adjudicator in the ACA Form of contract is now anomalous with regard to the statutory position and this could lead to serious confusion until the contract is updated in line with the Act.

JCT 1987 Management Contract: Works Contract 1 and Works Contract 2

The Management Contract is intended for large contracts in which there will be:

- a professional team
- a Management Contractor employed by the Employer
- a Works Contractor employed by the Management Contractor.

The Management Contract contains two phases: first, the Pre-construction Period; second, the Construction Period. The Management Contractor has certain duties to advise and co-operate with the professional team during both the Pre-construction Period and during the Construction Period and receives a fee for both stages. Both the Management Contractor and the Works Contractor may have responsibilities for certain design aspects, as well as the professional team.

There is room for disputes to arise at all those points in which they may arise in other JCT contracts and in addition to aspects of design input from either or both the Management Contractor and the Works Contractor. This means that Adjudication can pass up or down the contractual chain and laterally into the professional team.

As elsewhere, Adjudication may be suitable to deal with simple disputes but it is unlikely to be suitable for complex cases and in this contract many situations are likely to be complex by the very nature of the arrangements contained therein.

11

Consultant's contracts

Introduction

Details of the arrangements for consultants' contracts should be clarified at the earliest possible stage. Architects or Engineers will need to be clear if they are offering simply the services of an Architect or Engineer, or whether they are offering a composite package of consultants' services. If it is a package of services, then the question arises as to whether the organisation providing the services will be a multidisciplinary one, and will provide the whole package, or if some of the components will be subcontracted and bought in from other organisations. If the answer to this question is 'yes', then it is important to remember that 'pay-when-paid' arrangements are outlawed by the Construction Act 1996 and arrangements for subcontractor's fee payment will have to be honoured by the lead Organisation, even though the Employer has not yet paid the lead Consultant. The Association of Consultant Architects' Publication *Project Team Guide Lines*, which was updated in 1988 discusses many of the matters arising when a Project Team are sorting out fees and working relationships.

If there is a dispute between Employer and Consultant and the dispute goes to Adjudication, the Adjudicator should make a decision on the basis of the contract arrangements. If the Consultant is himself preparing the Contract, then it needs to cover all the necessary points. If the Employer is drafting the Contract it is necessary to check every point and seek clarification if there is doubt, ambiguity or insufficient information on any item. In either case it would be wise to clear all the items of the Contract with Professional Indemnity Insurer.

The first stage will probably be to advise generally and comprehensively on what services and charges are likely to be and agree as many details as possible with the Employer. The services which the Consultant is to provide should be defined as precisely as possible and it should be made clear what other Consultants, Clerk of Works, Site staff (if any), will be required. The first discussion should be clarified in a detailed document which follows any meeting to discuss the arrangements. The consultant should always draft the detailed arrangements understanding that the employer may wish, at a later stage to have additional services, which have not been considered in the inception stage, or may wish to dispense with some part; and it is useful to have the associated changes spelt out in the early correspondence so that when any request for additional services or reduced services arises, immediate reference can be made to the related charges. If disbursements and expenses are to be reimbursed, this should be made clear. There should be no ambiguity or room to interpret the contract as implying that the consultant will do anything that turns up which the Employer would like the Consultant to deal with for an all inclusive fee: That may be the problem with a simple exchange of letters. While it may be desirable to adopt a 'can do' attitude, it is important to see that payment is made for the services rendered. If each sectional charge cannot stand alone the point needs to be clarified. As arrangements for fee payments have become more complex and specifically tailored to particular job circumstances and increasingly detailed, special, statutory services are increasingly required and more sophisticated conditions of engagement have been necessary. It may be convenient to use standard institutional publications or a specially generated document giving details for the agreement, but simply providing a copy of a standard document without details and specific references may not clarify the actual detailed terms of the contract between Employer and Consultant, and both Parties may form different views as to what their particular contract contains.

The ACA published in 1996 a document entitled *The Appointment of a Consultant Architect*. This includes a brief reference to Adjudication where, in the event of a dispute, Adjudication under the Act occurs. At the time of writing, the RIBA 'Form of Appointment CE/98' appeared to be on course for publication in the spring of 1998.

If a consultant is uneasy at the prospect of Adjudication, provision should be made for immediate Arbitration following an Adjudication, and/or arrangements for conciliation which may be a more 'user friendly' alternative for both Parties.

The following strategic items may need to be considered and covered:

- fees and expenses for a package of services either on a percentage basis or time charges; if a particular percentage is quoted and relates to a band of capital cost, the overall cost level should be specified with a note that the percentage will vary with the overall cost level
- particular and isolated additional charges for specialist services or costs associated with collateral warranties
- details of any special arrangements including termination of services
- time details for payments and arrangements for fees paid late (time limit and interest)
- confirmation of lines of communication between Employer and Consultant; otherwise, where two or more people in the same organisation are concerned, there is room subsequently to deny that any other than the current person was authorised to give instructions
- notes of any items of Employer's specific input and a note as to the timing of these arrangements if it is critical for the project as a whole
- approximate time periods and indications where uncertainty may exist, as for example with planning applications, should be indicated
- Adjudication and/or Arbitration arrangements should be set out.

It is suggested that it would generally be advantageous in a dispute in a Consultant's contract for the Adjudicator to be of the same discipline as the Consultant. Adjudication Rules should be set out in the appointment document. It is important to make sure that any rules adopted are acceptable to the Professional Indemnity Insurer or an Adjudicator's decision which goes against the Consultant may result in liability for payment by the consultant and the Professional Indemnity Insurer may deny liability. At the time of writing it has been extremely difficult or impossible to get clarification as to exactly what Professional Indemnity Insurers will cover. Points which have emerged are that: (i) Adjudication arrangements in which the Adjudicator's decision is FINAL and BINDING are not acceptable and (ii) schemes which allow the Adjudicator to make a decision on a basis of commercial fairness as opposed to legal liability are not acceptable.

- Charges for additional services provided by the Consultant if or when Adjudication occurs on the Employer/Contractor Contracts should be spelt out as time charges.
- If the Architect or Engineer is the lead Consultant, the terms of agreement, or at least any details of duties or services which other Consultants are to perform, need to be understood. If any arrangements are vague or inadequate so far as other Consultant's duties are concerned, clarification should be sought from the Employer at the earliest possible stage.
- It should be made clear that any shortcomings in the services provided by other Consultants are solely the responsibility of the other Consultant and not the lead Consultant.

The following areas of activity are likely to be encountered by the Architect or Engineer acting as a lead Consultant in a particular construction project:

- Initial feasibility
- Preliminary study
- Sketch design
- Developed design

- Working drawings, specification and Bills of Quantities
- Tender procedure
- Contract finalisation
- Site work leading to completion
- Other services.

These are set out in more detail in the checklist at the end of the chapter.

Definition of performance and limit of liability

There are differences in the definition of performance normally applied to professional organisations and Building Contractors which should be recognised in contracts for professionals. A professional is normally expected to undertake *reasonable skill and care* while a Building Contractor, when providing a 'turnkey' or 'package deal' is expected to provide a building which is *fit for its purpose*.

The difference is significant. A professional is unwise to agree to provide the latter service, not only because it undertakes a potentially much wider liability, but also because that service will probably be uninsurable so far as his Professional Indemnity Insurance policy is concerned. The 'turnkey' contract will probably also contain a considerably larger margin of profit to compensate for any wider liability.

Any limitations of liability (such as limited to the extent of the value of the fees) should be spelt out in the contract. These arrangements may have particular importance if Adjudication occurs, as the Adjudicator's jurisdiction will be, under the terms of the Act, limited to disputes arising under the contract.

Categories of disputes

Disputes over professional services tend to fall into one of two categories; either fees or allegations of professional negligence, or both. If either of these aspects are referred to Adjudication, the Adjudicator needs to see that whoever is making a claim establishes that claim within the terms of a written contract by legal and contractual argument or reference and provides the factual evidence to back it up. In the past many Consultant's contracts have been on an informal basis or the only definition may have been in a short letter. It should also be remembered that where there is ambiguity in these matters, the Courts will tend to interpret them *contra preferentum*, that is to say, against the Party who prepared the document. The Adjudicator will be on firm ground in following that precedent.

Traditionally, many professionals have conducted their affairs with their clients on a less commercial basis than that which is adopted by construction contractors. One possible effect of Adjudication will probably be to enforce more precise contractual arrangements and in doing so induce a more formal and less flexible relationship and that, in turn, is likely to generate more disputes. In some cases, where a dispute might have hung around and festered, Adjudication may bring the issues to a head more quickly and remove the canker, or reveal, at an early stage, serious problems. (The sooner the better.)

Where professional negligence is alleged, an Adjudicator and the Parties may find many difficulties, primarily due to lack of time. The process is unfortunately, open to abuse by ambush by one side where the allegations involving a complex build-up of information or evidence over a long time period, which can be done surreptitiously, and then sprung on the other side who need to respond very quickly to enable the Adjudicator to speak within the time limit of the process. The types of issues involved may cover complex factual situations, divided expert opinion and elaborate legal arguments and these have little in common with the original impetus for Adjudication, which was to safeguard reasonable cash flow in an industry where cash flow was the life blood.

In cases of this sort, the Adjudicator may feel justified in seeking agreement from the referring Party for additional time (the Act allows a further 14 days and this may still be insufficient) and it may be quite unrealistic to deal with allegations within the limited time frame. It will probably be found that legislation needs to be amended to deal with this very intractable type of problem. If this is found to be the case, write to your MP and tell him or her. Many people have previously made the point, but the DETR have refused to accept it in the past.

In any case, Expert opinion will probably be essential, particularly if the Adjudicator is not qualified in the discipline involved. If expert opinion, facts and law are held in a fine balance and presented imperfectly within truncated time-scales, it will need a very skilled Adjudicator to produce a reliable decision, and the matter will almost certainly be appealed by the losing Party at the earliest opportunity. If the Adjudicator is acting under the Scheme, the consultant should require the Adjudicator to give reasons for his decision. It is probably important to ask for reasons in any case, but unless under the Scheme, there is a possibility that reasons may not be mandatory on request.

The CIC Model Adjudication procedure is a concise procedure, which is clearly written and is probably best suited to Adjudication between relatively sophisticated Parties, as would generally be the case with Consultant's Contracts.

By comparison with other procedures the following points should be noted:

- Paragraph 17(v) entitled the Adjudicator to meet the Parties separately. The procedure does not require the Adjudicator to inform the other Party of the discussions at a private meeting, but this would obviously be necessary in the interests of fairness and impartiality as required by paragraphs 1 and 2.
- Paragraph 21 states clearly that 'The Adjudicator shall determine the rights and obligations of the Parties in accordance with the law of the Contract'.
- The Adjudicator may resign at any time on giving notice in writing to the Parties in accordance with paragraph 23. No reasons need to be given for his resignation, but the Parties are not going to be happy when they have to start again with a different adjudicator.

- Paragraph 24 enables the Adjudicator to withhold delivery of his decision until his fees and expenses have been paid.
- If the decision is late, it will still be effective if it is reached before the dispute is referred to a replacement Adjudicator.
- It may be necessary to add requirements for reasons in the reference to CIC Adjudication procedure in contracts.

One effect of Adjudication in professional contracts is that allegations of professional negligence may first be decided by Adjudicators and professionals will need to ensure that their Professional Indemnity Policy will pay out on claims established in this way. Unless they do, Professional Indemnity Insurance cover could be worthless, since a professional could become bankrupt if called upon to meet the claim without insurance backup operation in force in the first place.

The importance of dispute avoidance

The most positive approach in regard to disputes so far as Consultant Contracts are concerned and indeed for the whole process of construction is to adopt more thorough techniques of Project Management to avoid many of the difficulties which have arisen in the past.

There are indications that some large and influential clients are beginning to understand the positive advantages of developing long-term relationships with professional teams and contractors with proven track-records. The result may be, that if these trends continue, cowboy operators will be left with unenlightened employers where misunderstandings and disputes proliferate, while enlightened employers and reliable contractors develop smoother, more efficient, and more profitable contracts. In other words, the Act may become a watershed in separating the more truly professional organisations from the rest.

The Architect's Registration Board

The Housing Grants Construction and Regeneration Act 1996 not only includes the proposals for Adjudication but also contains, in Part III, arrangements for the Architect's Registration Board to which allegations may be made that a registered Architect is guilty of serious professional incompetence. These matters are likely to be the subject of disagreement and a dispute could arise under a Construction Contract regarding allegations of serious professional incompetence, so that this could also be referable to Adjudication. It is thus possible that the same matters may be referred to different tribunals at different times or indeed at the same time.

At the time of writing, the Architect's Registration Board do not appear fully to understand the way in which dispute resolution procedures operate and what is practicable with regard to their Code.

It is not quite clear why Architects should be singled out for a further layer of action than those which are available to the other professions in the Construction Industry. It could well be that those who are in process of training for professional practice in construction might wonder what advantage there is in training to be qualified and registered as an Architect and thereby laying oneself open to a further layer of disciplinary action. Taking into consideration with the more commercially oriented horizons of the Engineering professions which are more likely to enable opportunities to be available for practice abroad and in particular in the expanding economies of other geographical areas, would lead to the conclusion that an Engineering qualification is preferable to an architectural qualification and indeed, currently qualified and registered Architects might well be considering whether they adopt a different discipline or title under which to practice.

Checklist for activities in consultant/employer contracts

0.00 **General.** Only accept liability for 'reasonable skill and care', *not*, 'Fit for Purpose'.
1.00 **Initial feasibility**
1.01 Initial appointment and briefing by Client.

1.02 Particular construction methods and services.

1.03 Health and Safety aspects.

1.04 Procurement.

1.05 Initial approach to planning and Building Regulation approval.

1.06 Timetable.

2.00 **Preliminary study**

2.01 Prepare preliminary scheme and budget.

2.02 Client approval of preliminary scheme and budget.

2.03 Preparation of outline planning application.

3.00 **Sketch design**

3.01 Evolve scheme to full sketch design.

3.02 Develop estimated cost plan.

3.03 Develop proposals with all Consultants and input from services suppliers.

3.04 Make informal approach to planning and Building Control Authorities.

3.05 Develop full application for Planning Authority.

3.06 Client approval of developed sketch scheme.

3.07 Submit full planning application.

4.00 **Develop design**

4.01 Develop details and check costs.

4.02 Progress arrangements with all Consultants, Health and Safety, etc. for full detailing and designing.

4.03 Clear proposals with Building Control Authorities.

4.04 Decide Contract/Tender arrangements with Client.

4.05 Client approval of developed design.

5.00 **Working drawings, Specification and Bills of Quantities**

5.01 Complete working drawings.

5.02 Prepare Specification/Schedules, etc. for Bills of Quantities.

5.03 Harmonise and integrate the Consultant's proposals.

5.04 Check estimates.

5.05 Submit drawings for Building Regulation approval and give any necessary Notices, etc.

5.06 Clear proposals with any other Authorities (e.g. Finance provider) concerned in project.

5.07 Obtain Certificates from Consultants that all necessary preparations have been completed.

5.08 Clarify insurance arrangements with Employer and advise consultation with his Insurance Broker.

6.00 **Tender procedures**

6.01 Client approval for Tender or negotiated contract(s).

6.02 Invite Tenders and appraise and report on same.

6.03 Negotiate any relevant item or contract.

6.04 Make any necessary revisions to documentation.

7.00 **Tender finalisation**

7.01 Client approval and subsequent appointment of Contractor(s).

7.02 Finalise Contract.

7.03 Issue documents and information required by Contract, Health and Safety and Consultants.

7.04 Insurance and bond arrangements to be cleared by Employer.

8.00 **Site work leading to Completion**

8.01 Administer Building Contract.

8.02 Monitor progress of Contractors and Consultants with meetings and records, etc. and periodic reviews.

8.03 Inspect work in progress, investigate, make any tests or investigations. Co-ordinate progress with all Consultants and Health and Safety representative.

8.04 Issue detailed drawings, Schedules, etc., as necessary.

8.05 Make valuations and certificates as appropriate.

8.06 Issue maintenance documentation, prepare as-built records.

8.07 Notify Client of completion and insurance arrangements, etc.

9.00 **Other services**

9.01 Project Management.

9.02 Site selection.

9.03 Survey.

9.04 Model making/presentation aids.

9.05 Geotechnical/soil surveys/groundwater-flooding.

9.06 Building appraisal.

9.07 Dilapidation report(s).

9.08 Selection of consultants.

9.09 Fire damage.

9.10 Fire protection.

9.11 Upgrading existing buildings.

9.12 Investigation of building failures.

9.13 Structural surveys.

9.14 CDM.

9.15 Energy Conservation.

9.16 Sound insulation or acoustic treatment.

9.17 Valuation.

9.18 Furnishing requirements.

9.19 Specialist Engineering or design skills: mechanical handling.

9.20 Conservation: Historic, Ecological, Industrial, Ecclesiastical, Soil or coastal erosion, water.

9.21 Environmental matters generally.

9.22 Landscape.

9.23 Special planning negotiations.

9.24 Ground contamination and clearance.

9.25 IT applications.

9.26 Dispute Resolution. (Litigation, Arbitration and/or Adjudication.)

9.27 Expert Witness work.

9.28 Maintenance manuals.

9.29 Landlord requirements.

9.30 Grant applications.

9.31 Special valuations.

9.32 Extra requirements for insolvency of any other Party.

12

Legal notes

Any review of the law relating to Adjudication as envisaged in the new Act must be of necessity extremely limited. It follows that much of the interest in this facet of Adjudication must be speculative. This is not only because the Act is a new feature of the building industry, but because there are inherent features of the provisions of the Act which, as discussed in the earlier chapters, leave uncertainties in interpretation and difficulties in the day to day management of the quasi-judicial functions of the Adjudicator.

Such case law as exists in the narrower practice of Adjudication under the earlier consensual provisions of the JCT subcontracts and the like is unlikely to be of much relevance to the statutory requirements under the new legislation. The Act, while providing some rigid requirements, leaves much of the implementation of the provisions to the terms of standard form contracts or to the government's Scheme. While the Scheme will apply only to those contracts which do not comply with Section 108 provisions, its influence will probably bear heavily on legal interpretation of matters arising from the practice of Adjudication.

Notwithstanding these reservations certain general principles may be discerned at this stage. The following matters appear to the authors to be prudent to consider.

The appointment
The Act is silent on questions of appointment. Of course, like appointments of arbitrators, the appointment may be consensual.

The Act prescribes such a short time-scale for the appointment to become effective (the aim being to allow the dispute to be settled quickly) that, unless the appointment is made before the building contract is entered into, consensus may rarely be feasible. Even then the Parties will not be aware whether the Adjudicator would have appropriate qualifications and would be available when required. Nevertheless the Scheme makes elaborate provisions whereby reference may be made to 'an Adjudicator nominating body' which is defined as a body which holds itself out publicly as a body which will select an Adjudicator when requested to do so. Apart from the fact the Adjudicator nominating body should not be a natural person nor a Party to the dispute, there seems to be remarkably little qualification or control of such bodies; although the debate in committee suggests that DETR may publish a list of approved bodies later.

It would be prudent for an appointing body to have a panel of Adjudicators each of whom is properly qualified and ready and willing to take up the appointment in less than seven days. The corollary is that the appointing body should equally have administrative support to give effect to its appointing function without delay.

On receipt of an application for an appointment the appointing body may need to discover some details, for example:

- Is the contract controlled by the Act?
- Is there a formulated dispute or difference?
- Is the dispute current?
- What professional qualifications should the Adjudicator have?
- Is the potential appointee available?
- Does that person have any connections with either of the Parties or the subject matter of the dispute? (The Scheme requires that the person selected as an Adjudicator *shall declare* any interest, financial or otherwise, in any matter relating to the dispute.)
- Are the contract provisions applicable or does the Scheme apply?

Some institutes already have panels in place but not all will have the time and/or the resources to check these points. While the appointing body may not have full authority to make all such investigations before making the appointment, it may be that its reputation could be tarnished if proper checks are not made. Many institutes may consider the use of carefully worded application forms and standard letters of use to obtain the desired information. Time limits are likely to prevent the responding Party from making submissions to the appointing body on the suitability of the appointee (see below). There may further be occasions when the operative terms of the contract need to be checked before the Adjudicator becomes active. These points would have to be ascertained and checked thoroughly, but quickly, by the appointing body. If it does not check these points the onus must be on the appointee to do so without delay and before expense is incurred. It is important that the potential Adjudicator should be aware that the appointing body may not have made all inquiries and that therefore problems (particularly of jurisdiction or bias) could arise. In most cases it would be sensible not to delay but in others the Adjudicator should consider his position very carefully.

Section 108 provides that a Party to a construction contract has the right to refer a dispute, which includes any 'difference', arising *under* the contract for Adjudication. The inclusion of a difference in the definition in Section 108 may avoid some of the uncertainties which have hitherto dogged the arbitral process where in the alleged absence of a dispute the arbitrator would have been reluctant to act.

Mustill and Boyd suggest that the word 'difference' has a wider scope than 'dispute' although they declare that they know of no case where the distinction has been decisive on an issue of jurisdiction. Most disputes stem from claims although some disputes come into existence before a formal contractual claim has been made.

The Act restricts disputes or differences leading to the statutory Adjudication to those arising 'under' the contract. Such disputes may have a narrower scope than those arising 'out of' a contract. While terms such as 'in connection with' a contract or those 'in relation to' a contract may appear to give a degree of latitude, early case law relating to arbitration suggests otherwise. Other terms include 'in respect of' or 'with regard to', both of which have in the past allowed arbitrators to look beyond the immediate provisions of the contract.

It is submitted that Adjudication may have a more confined role than arbitration and that, until Adjudication case law becomes established, any disputes arising out of collateral matters would be outside the Adjudicator's jurisdiction. As to any argument that there may not be a dispute, compare recent case law (for example, *Halki Shipping* v. *Sopex Oils* [1997] 1 WLR 1268, affirmed by the Court of Appeal, *The Times*, 19 January 1998) albeit a case on the provisions for a stay in the 1996 Arbitration Act.

The qualifications of the Adjudicator may often be self-obvious. In matters of quality under a building contract he would normally be an Engineer or an Architect, matching the duties of the certifier under the contract. Equally, in contracts for professional services, it would not be wise to appoint a professional outside the expertise of the consultant Party to the dispute unless there are exceptional circumstances. However there may be occasions when a dispute is so confined to valuation that another professional would be better suited.

The provisions of the Act set such a tight timescale for the resolution of the dispute that the prospective Adjudicator must be able to devote time immediately to the Adjudication process. It is inevitable that the Adjudicator will want to be intricately involved in the procedure from the start and must stay available throughout the period in which the Parties are engaged. The statutory provisions appear not to contemplate any adjournment unless both Parties clearly express a wish to delay the process for any reason. However the Scheme envisages a prolongation of time where the appointment process fails or where the Adjudicator resigns; in either case the nomination procedure starts afresh.

The Act expressly imposes a duty on the Adjudicator to act impartially, as does the Scheme. It is, as the authors see it, essential in any event that a quasi-judicial function should be exercised within the rules of natural justice - those basic principles of fair procedure which demand freedom from interest or bias and the right to a fair hearing for those who are immediately affected by the Adjudicator's decision. Thus it may be necessary for any appointing body to ensure that the appointee has no overt or latent connection with the Parties or with the contract from which the dispute has arisen (see above and paragraph 4 of the Scheme) and it would be wrong for an Adjudicator to proceed if there is any doubt as to his ability to act impartially.

A further point is that since the Act states that a Party may give notice *at any time* of his intention to refer a dispute to arbitration, there may be rare occasions when the reference may be time-barred under the Limitation Acts. Equally the provision enables a referring Party to take time to build up a case against the responding Party to the latter's disadvantage where the time scales are circumscribed (see below).

Section 107 requires that the contract is in writing, and examines the several ways in which an agreement in writing is construed. It is unnecessary to analyse these interpretations here other than to warn appointing bodies and future Adjudicators that this is an aspect which must be ascertained before embarking on an Adjudication lest the question of the Adjudicator's jurisdiction is raised, whether promptly or otherwise.

Is it possible for two Adjudications to run simultaneously between the same Parties? It may be that each Party may serve notice to appoint on the same dispute but to different appointing bodies. Equally, the Parties may appoint separate Adjudicators for different issues. In general terms the law frowns on concurrent dispute resolution unless there is a clear distinction between the matters in issue. While there is nothing in the Act or the Scheme to prevent simultaneous Adjudication, enforcement of incompatible decisions may create difficulties.

There have been suggestions that the contract Architect or Engineer may act as the Adjudicator. While it is right that if the Parties are truly and fully in agreement to that course at the time a dispute arises there can be no objection, but in most cases the Architect or Engineer would be ruling on his own actions or decisions and the law would require him to act fairly and with a mind that is not closed to argument.

Powers and duties of the Adjudicator

Inevitably, as with any form of judicial or quasi-judicial decision making, the Adjudicator must respect and give effect to the agreements made by the Parties. Although controlled by statute, Adjudication is a consensual process; it is based on the contract. Thus any specific terms of the contract cannot be ignored. In particular it is essential that the Adjudicator should respect any provisions for finality in the contract. An example which springs to mind is a provision that a final certificate (in for example the JCT Standard Form) is final and binding unless challenged within the period set out in the contract (see *Crown Estate Commissioners* v. *Mowlem* 70 BLR 1). Some commentators have mooted the proposition that paragraph 20(a) of the Scheme may encourage the authors of *ad hoc* contracts to confer finality on any certificates (including those for interim payments) in order to avoid the Adjudication provisions. However such measures would be fraught with difficulties. In any case if the Parties want to go straight to litigation or arbitration they may do so; the Act only provides a right (not an obligation) to adjudicate.

There is no provision in the Act for a challenge to the Adjudicator's jurisdiction. No doubt this is deliberate because such a challenge would be an obvious target for a reluctant responding Party and would delay what is meant to be a speedy process. The Scheme specifically states at paragraph 10 that an objection to the appointment of a particular Adjudicator shall not invalidate his appointment. Thus in ordinary circumstances the Adjudicator facing a challenge to his jurisdiction should continue. It is, though, important that there should be a mechanism to remove an unsuitable Adjudicator who fails some of the tests set out in the Scheme. While the Parties may agree to revoke the appointment (paragraph 11), it appears that the most swift and effective remedy where only one Party objects, but where the appointment is clearly inappropriate or blatantly improper, would be recourse to an injunction to prevent him from acting.

The Act places emphasis on an expeditious resolution of the disputes which come to Adjudication. Accordingly it is not surprising to find that there is an indication that the Adjudicator may act inquisitorially; Section 108(2)(f) states that the contract shall enable the Adjudicator to take the initiative in ascertaining the facts and the law. While this may be a useful tool, perhaps the prudent Adjudicator should take care in using this power. The provision to take the initiative is repeated in paragraph 13 of the Scheme but has to be compared with the stipulation in paragraph 12(a) that the decision should be reached in accordance with the applicable law in relation to the contract.

There are inherent hazards to 'entering the ring' or appearing not to comply with the duty placed by the statute on the Adjudicator to act impartially. The power requires a sensitive and delicate approach to avoid giving the appearance of siding with one Party. The power is largely alien to the English legal system (although compare Section 34(2)(g) of the 1996 Arbitration Act) and it may be that the Act envisages more of an investigative role such as tracking down documents or seeing one Party in the absence of the other (see paragraph 13(c) of the Scheme) rather than cross-examining those who may appear before him in any oral hearings. In a recent case (*Dyason* v. *Secretary of State for the Environment*, (1998) unrep) the Court of Appeal gave a reminder that in inquisitorial proceedings the need to proceed efficiently should not be at the expense of fairness to the Parties. A fair and thorough investigation can be expected by a Party who has a right to be heard whichever procedure is followed. Where the Adjudicator takes evidence he may, of course, administer the oath if he deems it appropriate. If the Adjudicator does see one Party in private the other Party must be kept informed in order to comply with the rules of natural justice. The Act is silent on an Adjudicator's power to use his own expert knowledge but it appears that, given the short time scales, he is bound to make use of his experience even though he may be wise not to indicate the extent to which he has done so in publishing his reasons.

It is obvious from the provisions made in the Act that the Adjudicator should take a leading role in controlling the procedure. It is not unlikely that one of the Parties will be recalcitrant and uncooperative. There is no time to wait for the submissions of a Party in response to an application on a procedural point. One might expect some reference to the issue of a subpoena to bring forward a witness or document, but the Act and the Scheme are silent on the matter, mainly, presumably, in the interests of speed. It may be that the Adjudicator should continue without such information and draw his own conclusions.

The underlying thrust of the Scheme (for example paragraph 10) seems to be that the Adjudicator should proceed, once appointed, irrespective of the force of any objection to his jurisdiction. However, it is thought he should take a balanced view and refuse to act in those cases where it is patently obvious that he could not act impartially or where it is clear that he does not have proper expertise. Furthermore, where such problems arise expressly only because of the terms of the Scheme, common law considerations suggest that the Adjudicator should bear these matters in mind in any event.

For these reasons, while the Adjudicator must ensure that no time should be lost, jurisdictional and procedural considerations may lead to the conclusion that a preliminary meeting would be desirable. Such a meeting would enable the Adjudicator to see and check the contract and to understand what it is the referring Party seeks. Examination of the scope of the notice will, in most cases, determine what procedures are most suitable.

Of course, the Adjudicator has power to extend time with the consent of both Parties. Otherwise, any extension may be made only within strict limits. He may extend the overall period with the consent of the Party by whom the dispute was referred. Clearly this provision is to prevent the responding Party from delaying resolution of the dispute. The effect of the failure to reach a decision appears from paragraph 19(2) of the Scheme to allow either Party to serve a fresh notice and to request another Adjudicator to act.

If the failure to reach that point within the statutory period or the extended time rests with one of the Parties, it appears that the intention is that the Adjudicator should give his decision on the information (however deficient) which he has received. There is no indication, though, of any penalty which the Adjudicator faces for his failure to act within the time allowed by the Act. Indeed, Section 108(4) requires the contract to provide that the Adjudicator is not liable for anything done *or omitted* in the discharge of his functions. Even where the Adjudicator's appointment is revoked by the Parties, he is entitled to the payment of reasonable fees unless due to his fault or misconduct (paragraph 11(1) where the Scheme applies).

It could be that the lack of a decision from the Adjudicator, while defeating the object of the strategy envisaged in the Act, could be remedied by a reference to arbitration. Indeed the first draft proposals for the Government's Scheme provided for revocation of the Adjudicator's authority by application to the Court to remove an Adjudicator. The grounds for doing so would have included the Adjudicator's refusal or failure to use the necessary despatch in conducting the proceedings or making a decision.

Paragraph 20(a) of the Scheme grants powers to the Adjudicator to open up, revise and review any decision or certificate given by the person named in the contract. These powers had particular significance until recently when the House of Lords decided that *NRHA v. Crouch* (1984) 26 BLR 1 had been wrongly decided. The position now is that unless the building contract expressly grants such powers to the Adjudicator, only Adjudicators appointed under the Scheme may open up and review certificates. The court's powers to do so are not limited.

The Scheme makes extensive provision for payment of the Adjudicator. He may set his own fee and is to be entitled to the payment of such reasonable amount as he may determine. The Parties are to be jointly and severally liable for any sum which remains outstanding following the making of any determination which he makes on how the payment shall be apportioned.

The Scheme is silent on any lien which the Adjudicator may have in respect of his fees. It is submitted that although the Adjudicator is required to reach a decision within 28 days after referral, there is no reason why he should not give notice of his decision within the required period but not release his decision until paid. An arbitrator's lien was only given statutory force in the 1996 Act but it had been the practice in common law to retain a lien before then.

Set-off

It would not be sensible in this chapter to examine all aspects of law which may arise but there appears to be a strong possibility that many Adjudicator's decisions might invoke a cross claim from the responding Party where monies paid or certified are in dispute. Thus the Adjudicator should be clear as to his powers to reduce any monies otherwise due in recognition of such a cross claim even though this may be less important in Adjudication than in arbitration in view of the continuous review of interim certificates which the nature and process of Adjudication may offer.

In a series of cases in the 1970s the Courts held that where two Parties had similar relationships in more than one contract a defendant was not permitted to set-off monies due under one contract against those due under another unless the contracts were so closely linked that it would be fair and equitable to do so. Where there is only one contract it may be permissible to weigh one claim against another but this is an area of law which has some pitfalls for the unwary.

The first question to be addressed is whether the cross claim is an intrinsic consideration in the issue to be decided or whether it is simply a separate claim upon which the responding Party seeks a ruling at the same time. If it is the former then it is clearly right to weigh both arguments in reaching a decision. However there are other implications and it is not always possible to draw a line between those matters which can be taken into account and those which cannot.

In building disputes it will be apparent that where, for example, defective work has to be made good, the resulting delay usually leads to monetary ramifications, as indeed will any cause of delay. Most Adjudicators will be aware of contract provisions in, say, DOM/1 or NSC/C subcontracts where set-off is limited by the specific terms, usually notice in writing. Where such provisions apply but the limitations are not met it *may* be possible to raise the law of abatement, but again that defence is also bounded by strict limitations. In brief, for a Party to rely on the common law right to abate the price which is paid for goods supplied or work done, he must be able to show that the breach of contract relied upon has directly affected the *actual value* of the goods or work. (These principles are explained by the Court of Appeal in *Mellowes Archital Ltd v. Bell Products Ltd* (1997) CILL 1320.)

As a rough guide, when faced by a claim to set-off sums otherwise due to the referring Party, the Adjudicator should first examine the contract provisions for set-off; if any condition precedent has not been complied with, the nature of the claim should be reviewed to see whether extraneous cross claims are made, or whether such cross claims are fundamental to the main claim. In any event there must be 'a close relationship between the dealings and transactions which gave rise to the respective claims' (*Hanak* v. *Green* 1 BLR 1; and see also *Hargreaves* v. *Action 2000* 62 BLR 72). Secondly, it is submitted the Adjudicator may need to consider whether the matters on which the responding Party relies have directly affected the value of the work itself. It is interesting to note that in *Overland Shoes* v. *Schenkers* (*The Times*, 26 February 1998) a 'no set-off' clause satisfied the requirement of reasonableness in the Unfair Contract Terms Act 1977.

The cross claims may be called counter claims, cross claims or set-offs, but their effect may depend on their validity, as often what is termed a counter claim may be, in effect, merely a defence to the claim dressed up to give it more impact.

Legal advice for the Adjudicator

Most Adjudicators will have comparatively little legal training. Whereas in arbitration or other similar proceedings the arbitrator will have the law explained to him by the advocates for the Parties, in Adjudication the likelihood of oral hearings at which lawyers address the decision maker is small, despite provisions in the Scheme for lawyers to represent Parties. At the same time the

Adjudicator is obliged by the Scheme to carry out his duties in accordance with any terms of the contract and, as noted above, *in accordance with the applicable law in relation to the contract*: see paragraph 12(a).

As noted above, Section 108(2)(f) makes provision for the Adjudicator to take the initiative in ascertaining not only the facts but also the law. If the amount in dispute warrants sufficient expenditure, a legal advisor could thus be appointed with the consent of both Parties, and this is confirmed in paragraph 13(f) of the Scheme. Equally, the Adjudicator may seek advice from a solicitor or a barrister. However, it is submitted that he has a duty to the Parties to ascertain first the likely fee. In the experience of the authors, not all solicitors have extensive knowledge of the intricacies of construction law unless they specialise in that subject. Most professions in the building industry have Direct Professional Access to specialist barristers for the purposes of advice.

Many large public reference libraries have a law section. Alternatively many universities allow access for reference purposes. The main works on construction law are *Keating On Building Contracts* and *Hudson's Building and Engineering Contracts*.

If individual modern cases are sought these can mainly be found in *Building Law Reports* (BLR) or *Construction Law Reports* (ConLR). As the name suggests these are a series of volumes several of which are published each year and each containing a number of recent cases together with a commentary on each of them.

Many other and older cases are in the *Law Reports* published by the Incorporated Council of Law Reporting. Since 1891 these are confined to the following series:

- Appeal Cases, abbreviated as AC (restricted to House of Lords or Privy Council decisions);
- Chancery Division, Ch;
- Queen's (or King's) Bench Division, QB or KB; and
- Probate Division, P (since 1972 known as Family, Fam).

These are then referred to by the year of the case, the abbreviation above and the page number on which the report of each case starts. Thus, for example, *Calderbank v. Calderbank* will be referred to under the reference [1976] Fam 93.

The Council also publishes a weekly series known as Weekly Law Reports, WLR, and these are usually bound into an annual volume or volumes. Other privately owned series include: the All England Law Reports, All ER; Lloyds Law Reports (in which many arbitration cases are published), Ll L Rep. Reference is made to all of these in the same way.

Leading cases

Until statutory Adjudication develops, case-law will be limited to general principles and to disputes under other contract arrangements. There are a few indications, though, of the approach made by the Courts to this form of dispute resolution; where Adjudication has been examined by the Courts in the past it has usually arisen under standard form subcontracts. The following notes of cases, to which, where possible, the reports in BLR are given for ease of reference, may give some guidance:

Cameron v. John Mowlem (1990) 52 BLR 24

A decision of an Adjudicator under clause 24 of DOM/1 was binding only until the determination by the arbitrator on a disputed claim to a set-off. It was not an award within the meaning of S 26 of the Arbitration Act 1950 and could not be enforced under that section.

Drake & Scull v. McLaughlin & Harvey (1992) 60 BLR 102

Another DOM/1 case. In contrast to the above case, it was held that the only possible reason for refusing to comply with an Adjudicator's award would be if the Adjudicator had exceeded his jurisdiction by ordering a deposit which was greater than the amount due from the contractor to the subcontractor in respect of which the contractor had exercised the right of set-off. Since the obligation to comply with the Adjudicator's decision was a contractual matter, a mandatory injunction would be granted.

Cape Durasteel v. Rosser and Russell (1995) 46 Con LR

A subcontract made provisions in two parts for the settlement of disputes. The first sub-clause provided for Adjudication, but the second took account of a dispute which covered matters which the main contractor 'has or is contemplating referring to arbitration or Adjudication under the Principal Contract ...'. In deciding whether the case should be stayed to arbitration the judge examined the meaning of 'Adjudication' and concluded that 'Adjudication' taken by itself meant a process by which a dispute is resolved in a judicial manner but as yet it had no special meaning in the construction industry. In this case there was no purpose in ascribing to the Parties an intention that all their disputes should be submitted to such a procedure but without the possibility of review or reversal; the judge was unable to accept that 'Adjudication' is a procedure which cannot be arbitration or that it has an established meaning in construction contracts which precludes it being an arbitration.

Chatbrown Ltd v. Alfred McAlpine (1986) 35 BLR 44

In considering claims for a set-off against monies due to a subcontractor for loss and expense, it was held that it was not sufficient to argue that a liability which could lead to loss and expense in the *future*, it was necessary that loss and/or expense should have actually occurred prior to a notice to that effect. Thus, while a contractor may be able to claim additional expenses by reason of disruption at an early stage, delay is likely to present greater problems and claims are normally for loss and expense assessed at the end of the main contract period. The case also demonstrates that the Courts will determine arguable points of law on an application for summary judgment so long as to do so would not involve an investigation of contested facts; and in that case the presence of an arbitration clause makes no difference.

Archital Luxfer v. Dunning (1987) 47 BLR 1

Another of a number of cases on a contractor's claim to set-off monies otherwise due to a subcontractor. On an application for summary judgment in respect of set-off, the Court of Appeal held that where an arbitrator is appointed, mixed questions of law and fact were pre-eminently a matter for the arbitrator.

As to modern cases concerning damages

Ruxley Electronics v. Forsyth (1993) 66 BLR 23

Where work does not accord with the contract, the measure of damages is the loss truly suffered by the promisee. It may not always be the cost of replacement and it would be unreasonable to treat as a loss the cost of carrying out work which would never in fact be done. Reasonableness plays a central part in determining the basis of recovery.

Murphy v. Brentwood (1991) 50 BLR 1

Although a case concerning housing authorities where claims for economic loss arise, the case established that the requirements for the existence of a duty of care are that the loss should be foreseeable; there should be a special relationship of proximity; there should be reliance by the plaintiff on the defendant; and the existence of the duty should be just and reasonable. A residual liability of public or private defendants may be left where positive actions or representations amount to a voluntary assumption of responsibility. One effect is to focus attention on the Defective Premises Act 1972. There may, though, be a liability in tort where catastrophic damage has occurred in parts of the whole building consequent upon defects in another or limited part of the building: for example, defective electrical work which causes fire in the building as a whole.

Time limits

The Act requires the contract to 'provide a timetable *with the object of* securing the appointment of the Adjudicator and referral of the dispute to him within 7 days of [the] notice'. However, the notice may be given at any time. Taken together these provisions may give rather more scope for setting up the Adjudication process than appears at first sight.

Thereafter the normal process would require the Adjudicator to reach his decision within 28 days of the referral to him. That period may be extended only by the agreement of the Parties, in which case they have freedom to extend time to suit their purposes; or, presumably failing agreement, the Party who refers the dispute may grant the Adjudicator an extension of time limited to 14 days.

There is no doubt that this imposes a heavy burden on the Adjudicator to complete his decision within the time allowed. Nevertheless by section 108(4) the Adjudicator is not liable for anything omitted in the discharge of his functions as Adjudicator. There is thus no redress for a Party deprived of a decision which may, in turn, delay progress of the contract works.

Setting the last point aside, it appears that the Adjudicator must carefully select procedures which will allow each Party's case to be adequately presented without generating excessive documentation. Even though he has power under Section 104(2)(f) to take the initiative in ascertaining the facts and the law, he should take care not to shut out vital information which a Party wishes to draw to his attention, either by way of original submissions or reply to new points raised by his opponent. On the other hand, paragraph 15 in the Scheme allows the Adjudicator to proceed *ex parte* or to draw inferences from the failure of a Party to comply with a request, direction or timetable.

Reasons

The Act makes no provision for the Adjudicator's decision to be accompanied by reasons, but paragraph 22 of the Scheme requires the Adjudicator to give reasons if requested to do so by one of the

Parties; and in committee the Minister stated that 'it would be contrary to the principles of natural justice to come up with a decision without giving the reasons'. If no application is made it may be wise not to give reasons, but the Adjudicator should consider carefully whether the circumstances warrant a reasoned decision. In many instances reasons will not be appropriate, particularly where the decision is essentially an interim valuation. Nevertheless the Adjudicator should not be blind to circumstances where reasons are desirable.

In recent years the Courts have expressed a predilection for reasons to be given in many fields. It is sometimes suggested that there may be an implied right for a Party to be given reasons as part of the general obligation to let a person know the case he has to answer where there is a right of appeal. The right to appeal under the Act is clear (S 108(3)).

Equally it may be necessary as part of the decision making process to acquaint the Parties with the current state of the decision-maker's thinking. In some circumstances the Courts may infer from the absence of reasons that there are no good reasons for a decision. (See *Padfield* v. *Minister of Agriculture* [1968] AC 997.) Finally while ordinary courtesy may require the giving of reasons, the time within which the decision should be given suggests that any reasons should be concise (and precise).

What reasons should be given?

Another way of expressing this question is: what grounds of challenge may arise? In the GCHQ case *Council of Civil Service Unions* v. *Minister for the Civil Service* [1985] AC 374, Lord Diplock identified the grounds of challenge into illegality, irrationality and procedural impropriety.

Illegality

In the context of decision making, illegality is a way of saying that the decision maker has got the law wrong. Thus there is a need for an Adjudicator to check the law in respect of the matters before him. Even where a statute confers a wide discretion the Courts will consider that the discretion has not been properly exercised.

Irrationality
The Courts require that all powers and duties must be exercised reasonably. That is not to say that the Courts will substitute their own view of what is reasonable. The only interference on this ground where a decision 'is so outrageous in its defiance of logic or of accepted moral standards that no sensible person who had applied his mind to the question to be decided could have arrived at it' (see the GCHQ case above).

Procedural impropriety
Principally, the decision maker must abide with the rules of natural justice. There must be no discernible bias either before or during the decision-making process. The decision must be confined to the matters before him and the process must accord with any statutory and contractual provisions.

As with any written decision it must be expressed so as to be unambiguous, certain, enforceable and it should address all matters put before the Adjudicator. In respect of this last point it does no harm to demonstrate in the reasons for the decision that all those matters have been addressed.

Enforcement and remedies
The Adjudicator will not, normally, be concerned with the machinery for enforcement of his decision. That will be for the Parties to pursue. Nevertheless, since many Architects and Engineers will encounter Adjudication in their capacity as consultants for Parties to the contract, the following notes may be of interest.

Whereas the Arbitration Acts set out a series of remedies, the Act which provides for Adjudication is largely silent. While the statute sets out a wide discretion for Adjudication, section 108(3) indicates provision for final determination by legal proceedings, by arbitration or by agreement. This seems to indicate that the decision is to be regarded as a temporary finding only. How then can the Courts be expected to consider an application to enforce an Adjudicator's decision at an early stage of a building contract? There are indications of the Court's support for the Adjudication process in that senior judges have taken part in consultations leading to the statute and in discussions concerning the Scheme.

Perhaps the most intriguing aspect of potential applications to the Court from Adjudication will be to see what status the Adjudicator's decision will have. It is not unlikely that a good number of, if not most, Adjudications will arise in consequence of interim certificates. In many cases the decision will be equivalent to or replace the Architect or Engineer's certificate. The provisional or transient nature of such certificates have usually been treated with caution by the Courts, particularly on applications for summary judgement (Order 14). This approach arises because: first, some contracts have previously reserved to arbitration the powers to open up, review and revise any certificates and thus the Courts have been slow to intervene; secondly, the Courts have recognised that it would require time to investigate the material leading to the certificate before it would be known whether it was really open to challenge and before it would be possible to particularise the matters which required to be determined (to paraphrase the judgement of Kerr LJ in *C M Pillings* v. *Kent Investments Ltd* (1985) 30 BLR 80 at 94).

Against that background it is more than possible that an application for summary judgement to enforce an Adjudicator's decision may be met by an application to stay to arbitration. The Arbitration Act 1996 has strengthened provisions for ensuring that arbitration clauses are given effect. The first major judicial decision under the 1996 Arbitration Act on an application to stay a case to arbitration (*Halki Shipping* v. *Sopex Oils* see above at paragraph 2.7) robustly supports the new provisions; while in *Channel Tunnel* v. *Balfour Beatty* (1993) 61 BLR 1 the House of Lords upheld an application for a stay to the Parties' chosen contractual machinery for dispute resolution even though there was no arbitration clause as such.

The new clause 41A of the JCT Contract states that the Adjudicator may take the initiative in ascertaining the facts and the law as he considers necessary which may include opening up, reviewing and revising any certificate, etc. Similar provisions are included in the ICE contract.

Interest has been focused on whether the Courts would want to discourage protracted legal proceedings during the currency of the contract works or whether the judiciary would aim for certainty during that period. Would the Courts be encouraged to defer to the arbitrator's jurisdiction the task of reviewing a certificate? Two primary routes have been suggested. One is to seek arbitration on a single issue, e.g. 'Is the Adjudicator's decision enforceable?'. However, the JCT Adjudication provisions seek enforcement through litigation while the ICE has amended its contract by the inclusion of clause 66(9)(a) which now reads: 'All disputes arising under or in connection with the Contract or the carrying out of the Works other than failure to give effect to a decision of an Adjudicator shall be finally determined by reference to arbitration.'

One other route to enforcement of an Adjudicator's decision may be injunctive relief (see *Drake & Scull* v. *McLaughlin* above). If so, the guiding principles to be applied require, among other things, consideration of the balance of convenience. Again, such an action may, of course, be met with an application to stay to arbitration.

There is a curious provision in the Scheme whereby the Adjudicator may, if he thinks fit, order any of the Parties to comply with a peremptory order, compliance with which is subject to Section 42 of the Arbitration Act 1996. It has been suggested that the Adjudicator's decision on the dispute should be issued as a peremptory order to ensure enforcement. However, it is submitted that it is no part of an Adjudicator's duties to ensure enforcement when the statute is explicit in providing final determination by legal proceedings or arbitration. In any event, Section 42 appears to be directed to interlocutory matters where there has been default by one of the Parties. It has been suggested that Section 66 would have been a better vehicle but it appears that the government made a deliberate decision not to allow for finality in respect of a process of quick rough justice.

Many of these problems have been resolved as this book was going to press. In the first major case to consider enforcement of an adjudicator's decision (*Macob Civil Engineering Ltd v Morrison Construction Ltd*) Dyson J. has provided helpful guidance on these matters. The plaintiff sought to enforce an adjudicator's decision. The defendant contended that the decision was invalid because of procedural error in breach of the rules of natural justice, and issued a summons seeking to stay the plaintiff's proceedings under section 9 of the Arbitration Act 1996, since the contract contained an arbitration clause. On the natural justice point, he formed the view that the challenge was hopeless, and that such a construction would drive a coach and horses through the legislation. Declining to stay to arbitration, he distinguished between a dispute to the merits of a decision and a dispute as to the validity of the decision, as in that case, but added that there was nothing in *Halki* which prevented the Court from deciding that the defendant was precluded by its election from seeking a stay to arbitration under section 9.

In the particular circumstances of the case, Dyson J. found that the Court could enforce the Adjudicator's decision under section 42, although he said that ordinarily an agreement would exclude that power. He also considered other routes to enforcement, including summary judgement or mandatory injunction. He concluded that it would rarely be appropriate to grant injunctive relief to enforce an obligation to pay, although different considerations would apply when an adjudicator ordered the performance of some other obligation.

Thus, section 42 apart, Dyson J. concluded that the usual remedy for failure to pay in accordance with an adjudicator's decision would be to issue proceedings claiming the sum due, followed by an application for summary judgement.

Adjudicator's liability
There is, of course, a requirement in the statute for the contract to provide immunity for the Adjudicator in the discharge of his functions as an Adjudicator. As is well known such a provision

cannot prevent action against the Adjudicator from anyone who is not a signatory to the contract but who may be affected by the Adjudicator's decision. Since most construction industry projects within the scope of the Act are executed with any number of subcontractors, not to mention a variety of consultants, the scope for complaint from those not Parties to the Adjudication could be significant.

Thus the Adjudicator is in a different situation from that of an arbitrator who now has express immunity under the Arbitration Act 1996. There is therefore no doubt that anyone expecting to practise as an Adjudicator would be imprudent not to obtain professional indemnity insurance cover if it is available.

However, while the statute requires contractual immunity, the Scheme simply states 'the Adjudicator shall not be liable ...'. As a statutory instrument, the Scheme is effectively delegated legislation. Thus the Adjudicator may be better protected when acting in compliance with the Scheme than he would be when the contract has Adjudication provisions which comply with Section 108. The prudent Adjudicator may insist on a contract for his own appointment with provisions for his immunity beyond those incorporated into the Act and/or the Scheme.

Payment provisions

Adjudicators should be aware that the Act makes provision for payment by instalments, stage payments or other periodic payments for any work under such contracts that exceed, or are likely to exceed, 45 days. These, like other parts of the Act, apply also to the contracts between consultants and their clients.

The Parties are free to agree the amounts of the payments and the intervals at which, or the circumstances in which, they become due. If no provision is made in the contract, Part II of the Scheme will apply. These initial provisions are found in Section 109 of the Act.

Essentially the Scheme sets the 'relevant period' between payments at 28 days. Any interim payment becomes due either seven days after the end of the relevant period or the making of a claim by the payee, whichever is the later. Similarly, the final periodic payment becomes due 30 days after completion of the work or, again, on a claim by the payee. The final date for any payment is 17 days after it becomes due.

Section 110 and the Scheme require a notice to be served by a Party who is obliged to make a payment within five days of that payment becoming due. The notice should set out the amount made or due to be made, and the basis on which that amount was calculated. The implication seems to be that neither a cheque nor a certificate is sufficient in itself unless there is some explanation of the sum paid.

The other side of the coin is that if the paying Party intends to withhold payment he has to give notice to that effect not later than seven days before the final date for payment of any interim or other payment. The Scheme makes no provision for the contents of the notice but Section 110(2) sets out three matters which might prevent a sum from falling due. These are: non-performance of the contractual obligations; set-off; or abatement. As to set-off and abatement, see the points referred to above in this chapter.

The remedy for failure to pay, apart from Adjudication itself, lies in the right to suspend work. Section 112 provides that the right to suspend depends on three factors:

- a sum of money falling due under the contract
- there being no effective notice of withholding payment, and
- a seven-day notice of the intention to suspend.

Nevertheless, the right to suspend work has to be viewed in the light of the fact that a judge or arbitrator may disregard the Adjudicator's decision, and the right of a contractor to direct loss and expense may be lost.

Finally, the Scheme prohibits 'pay-when-paid' provisions in contracts. Paragraph 9 states that any such arrangements will be ineffective.

Conclusions

The Act is one of few statutory interventions into the principle of freedom of contract in English law. While, for example, The Unfair Contracts Terms Act 1977 and other such statutes are directed mainly at the effects of contractual provisions, there are few Acts which require a contract to include dispute resolution procedures. No-one is obliged to incorporate an arbitration clause into a contract; indeed this Act only introduces the requirement by a fall-back provision (the Scheme). Nevertheless, while the intention of regular payments in building contracts is to keep the contractor in funds to finish the work, that may be frustrated by non-payment or the Architect or Engineer certifies too little. The Act aims to overcome these difficulties.

Much remains to be clarified about the operation of the Act, and the extent to which practices in the building industry will have to change. JCT and ICE contracts now make pragmatic provisions for the appointment and conduct of Adjudications without recourse to the Scheme. Only *ad hoc* or less significant contracts will invoke the provisions of the Scheme. The major concern, though, is the uncertainty of enforcement of Adjudicators' decisions and the effect of those decisions on the subsequent performance of the building contracts in which there has been an Adjudication.

The Act provides no requirement for Adjudication to be a condition precedent to arbitration or litigation. Nor is there any machinery to prevent rolled-up (or global) claims being brought to Adjudication at an advanced stage of a contract. As noted above there is no time bar to claims in Adjudication. These may be the target of amendments to the present Act and Scheme after a suitable period of use has exposed any shortcomings.

Cases referred to

Antino v. *Epping Forest* (1991) 53 BLR 56; (1991) 155 JP 663;
  (1991) JPN 426; *The Times* 11 March 1991, DC
Archital Luxfer v. Dunning (1987) 47 BLR 1; [1987] 1 FTLR 372;
  (1989) 5 Constr LJ 47, CA
Balfour Beatty v. *Chestermount Properties* (1993) 62 BLR 1
Calderbank v. *Calderbank* [1976] Fam 93; [1975] 3 All ER 333,CA
  Cameron v. *John Mowlem* (1990) 52 BLR 24, CA
Cape Durasteel v. *Rosser & Russell* (1995) 46 ConLR
Channel Tunnel v. *Balfour Beatty* (1993) 61 BLR 1; [1993] AC 334;
  [1993] 2 WLR 262; [1993] 1 All ER 664; [1993] 1 Ll L Rep 291
  and others
Chatbrown Ltd v. *Alfred McAlpine* (1987) 35 BLR 44; (1987) 3
  Constr LJ 104; (1988) 11 Con LR 1, CA
Council of Civil Service Unions v. *Minister for the Civil Service* [1985]
  AC 374
  Crown Estate Commissioners v. *Mowlem* (1994) 70 BLR 1
Drake & Scull v. *McLaughlin & Harvey* (1992) 60 BLR 102
Dyason v. *Secretary of State for the Environment* (1998) unrep, CA
Halki Shipping v. *Sopex Oils* (1998) *The Times*, 19 January 1998 CA
  affirming [1997] 1 WLR 1268; (1997) CILL 1278
Hanak v. *Green* (1958) 1 BLR 1; [1958] 2 QB 9; [1958] 2 WLR
  755; [1958] 2 All ER 141, CA
Hargreaves v. *Action 2000* (1993) 62 BLR 72; [1993] BCLC 1111
Jarvis Brent Ltd v. *Rowlinson Construction Ltd* (1990) CILL 620; 6
  Constr LJ 192

Lubbenham v. South Pembrokeshire (1986) 933 BLR 39; (1986) 6 Con LR 85; 2 Constr LJ 111, CA

Mellowes Archital Ltd v. *Bell Projects Ltd* (1997) CILL 1320

Murphy v. *Brentwood* (1991) 50 BLR 1; [1991] 1 AC 398; [1990] 3 WLR 414; [1990] 2 All ER 908

Northern Regional Health Authority v. *Crouch Construction Ltd* (1984) 26 BLR 1; [1984] QB 644; [1984] 2 WLR 676; [1984] 2 All ER 175, CA

Overland Shoes Ltd v. *Schenker Ltd* (1998) *The Times* 26 February 1998

Padfield v. *Minister of Agriculture* [1968] AC 997

Page v. *Llandaff & Dinas Powys DC* (1901) Hudson 4th edition, Vol 2 p 316

CM *Pillings* v. *Kent Investments Ltd* (1985) 30 BLR 80

Rotherham MBC v. *Frank Haslam Milan & Co and M J Gleeson (Northern) Ltd* (1996) 78 BLR 1

Ruxley Electronics v. *Forsythe* (1993) 66 BLR 23; [1994] 1 WLR 650, CA

Bibliography

Bevin A. *Alternative Dispute Resolution.* Sweet & Maxwell (1992).

Campbell P. (ed.). *Construction Disputes.* Whittles Publishing (1997).

Cheshire G.C., Fifoot C.H.S. and Furmston M.P. *Law of Contract,* 12th edn. Butterworths (1991).

Cottam G.D.G. *Adjudication under the Scheme for Construction Contracts, including payment provisions.* Thomas Telford, London (1998).

Cottam G.D.G. and Hawker G.H. *Dispute procedures under ICE contracts – a practical guide.* Thomas Telford, London (to be published 1999).

Dancaster C. and Riches J. *Construction Adjudication.* LLP (1999).

Fay E. *Official Referee's Business,* 2nd edn. Sweet & Maxwell (1988).

General Council of The Bar and The Law Society. *Civil Justice on Trial – The Case for Change. Report of the Independent Working Party* (1993).

Kendall J. *Dispute Resolution: Expert Determination.* Longman (1992).

Lupton S. *Architect's Guide to Arbitration.* RIBA Publications (1997).

Mackie K. *ADR Route Map.* Centre for Dispute Resolution (1991).

Mustill M.J. and Boyd S.C. *Commercial Arbitration,* 2nd edn. Butterworths (1989).

NJCC. *Alternative Dispute Resolution.* Guidance Note No. 7 (1993).

Reynold M.P. and King P.S.D. *The Expert Witness and his Evidence,* 2nd edn. Blackwell Scientific (1992).

Timpson J. *The Architect in Dispute Resolution.* RIBA Publications (1994).

Totterdill B.W. *ICE Adjudication Procedure (1997): a user's guide and commentary.* Thomas Telford, London (1998).

Uff J. *Construction Contract Reform: A plea for Sanity.* Construction Law Press (1997).

Uff J. *Construction Law*, 5th edn. Sweet & Maxwell (1991).

Woolf Lord. *Access to Justice. Final Report by Right Hon. the Lord Woolf.* HMSO (1996).

Appendix 1

Part II: Housing Grants, Construction and Regeneration Act 1996

The text of Part II of the Housing Grants, Construction and Regeneration Act 1996 is reproduced below.

Part II Construction contracts

Introductory provisions

104 Construction contracts

(1) In this Part a "construction contract" means an agreement with a person for any of the following—

    (*a*) the carrying out of construction operations;

    (*b*) arranging for the carrying out of construction operations by others, whether under subcontract to him or otherwise;

    (*c*) providing his own labour, or the labour of others, for the carrying out of construction operations.

(2) References in this Part to a construction contract include an agreement—

    (*a*) to do architectural, design or surveying work, or

    (*b*) to provide advice on building, engineering, interior or exterior decoration or on the laying-out of landscape,

in relation to construction operations.

(3) References in this Part to a construction contract do not include a contract of employment (within the meaning of the Employment Rights Act 1996).

(4) The Secretary of State may by order add to, amend or repeal any of the provisions of subsection (1), (2) or (3) as to the agreements which are construction contracts for the purposes of this Part or are to be taken or not to be taken as included in references to such contracts.

No such order shall be made unless a draft of it has been laid before and approved by a resolution of each of (*sic*) House of Parliament.

(5) Where an agreement relates to construction operations and other matters, this Part applies to it only so far as it relates to construction operations.

An agreement relates to construction operations so far as it makes provision of any kind within subsection (1) or (2).

(6) This Part applies only to construction contracts which—

(*a*) are entered into after the commencement of this Part, and

(*b*) relate to the carrying out of construction operations in England, Wales or Scotland.

(7) This Part applies whether or not the law of England and Wales or Scotland is otherwise the applicable law in relation to the contract.

105 Meaning of "construction operations"

(1) In this Part "construction operations" means, subject as follows, operations of any of the following descriptions—

(*a*) construction, alteration, repair, maintenance, extension, demolition or dismantling of buildings, or structures forming or to form, part of the land (whether permanent or not);

(*b*) construction, alteration, repair, maintenance, extension, demolition or dismantling of any works forming, or to form, part of the land, including (without prejudice to the foregoing) walls, roadworks, power-lines, telecommunication apparatus, aircraft runways, docks and harbours, railways, inland waterways, pipe-lines, reservoirs, water-mains, wells, sewers, industrial plant and installations for purposes of land drainage, coast protection or defence;

(c) installation in any building or structure of fittings forming part of the land, including (without prejudice to the foregoing) systems of heating, lighting, air-conditioning, ventilation, power supply, drainage, sanitation, water supply or fire protection, or security or communications systems;

(d) external or internal cleaning of buildings and structures, so far as carried out in the course of their construction, alteration, repair, extension or restoration;

(e) operations which form an integral part of, or are preparatory to, or are for rendering complete, such operations as are previously described in this subsection, including site clearance, earth-moving, excavation, tunnelling and boring, laying of foundations, erection, maintenance or dismantling of scaffolding, site restoration, landscaping and the provision of roadways and other access works;

(f) painting or decorating the internal or external surfaces of any building or structure.

(2) The following operations are not construction operations within the meaning of this Part—

(a) drilling for, or extraction of, oil or natural gas;

(b) extraction (whether by underground or surface working) of minerals; tunnelling or boring, or construction of underground works, for this purpose;

(c) assembly, installation or demolition of plant or machinery, or erection or demolition of steelwork for the purposes of supporting or providing access to plant or machinery, on a site where the primary activity is—

(i) nuclear processing, power generation, or water or effluent treatment, or (*ii*) the production, transmission, processing or bulk storage (other than warehousing) of chemicals, pharmaceuticals, oil, gas, steel or food and drink;

(*d*) manufacture or delivery to site of—

(*i*) building or engineering components or equipment,

(*ii*) materials, plant or machinery, or

(*iii*) components for systems of heating, lighting, air-conditioning, ventilation, power supply, drainage, sanitation, water supply or fire protection, or for security or communications systems,

except under a contract which also provides for their installation;

(*e*) the making, installation and repair of artistic works, being sculptures, murals and other works which are wholly artistic in nature.

(3) The Secretary of State may by order add to, amend or repeal any of the provisions of subsection (1) or (2) as to the operations and work to be treated as construction operations for the purposes of this Part.

(4) No such order shall be made unless a draft of it has been laid before and approved by a resolution of each House of Parliament.

106 Provisions not applicable to contract with residential occupier

(1) This Part does not apply—

(*a*) to a construction contract with a residential occupier (see below), or

(*b*) to any other description of construction contract excluded from the operation of this Part by order of the Secretary of State.

(2) A construction contract with a residential occupier means a construction contract which principally relates to operations on a dwelling which one of the parties to the contract occupies, or intends to occupy, as his residence.

In this subsection "dwelling" means a dwelling-house or a flat; and for this purpose—

"dwelling-house" does not include a building containing a flat; and

"flat" means separate and self-contained premises constructed or adapted for use for residential purposes and forming part of a building from some other part of which the premises are divided horizontally.

(3) The Secretary of State may by order amend subsection (2).

(4) No order under this section shall be made unless a draft of it has been laid before and approved by a resolution of each House of Parliament.

107 Provisions applicable only to agreements in writing

(1) The provisions of this Part apply only where the construction contract is in writing, and any other agreement between the parties as to any matter is effective for the purposes of this Part only if in writing.

The expressions "agreement", "agree" and "agreed" shall be construed accordingly.

(2) There is an agreement in writing—

(*a*) if the agreement is made in writing (whether or not it is signed by the parties),

(*b*) if the agreement is made by exchange of communications in writing, or

(*c*) if the agreement is evidenced in writing.

(3) Where parties agree otherwise than in writing by reference to terms which are in writing, they make an agreement in writing.

(4) An agreement is evidenced in writing if an agreement made otherwise than in writing is recorded by one of the parties, or by a third party, with the authority of the parties to the agreement.

(5) An exchange of written submissions in adjudication proceedings, or in arbitral or legal proceedings in which

the existence of an agreement otherwise than in writing is alleged by one party against another party and not denied by the other party in his response constitutes as between those parties an agreement in writing to the effect alleged.

(6) References in this Part to anything being written or in writing include its being recorded by any means.

Adjudication

108 Right to refer disputes to adjudication

(1) A party to a construction contract has the right to refer a dispute arising under the contract for adjudication under a procedure complying with this section.

For this purpose "dispute" includes any difference.

(2) The contract shall—

(*a*) enable a party to give notice at any time of his intention to refer a dispute to adjudication;

(*b*) provide a timetable with the object of securing the appointment of the adjudicator and referral of the dispute to him within seven days of such notice;

(*c*) require the adjudicator to reach a decision within 28 days of referral or such longer period as is agreed by the parties after the dispute has been referred;

(*d*) allow the adjudicator to extend the period of 28 days by up to 14 days, with the consent of the party by whom the dispute was referred;

(*e*) impose a duty on the adjudicator to act impartially; and

(*f*) enable the adjudicator to take the initiative in ascertaining the facts and the law.

(3) The contract shall provide that the decision of the adjudicator is binding until the dispute is finally determined by legal proceedings, by arbitration (if the contract provides for arbitration or the parties otherwise agree to arbitration) or by agreement.

The parties may agree to accept the decision of the adjudicator as finally determining the dispute.

(4) The contract shall also provide that the adjudicator is not liable for anything done or omitted in the discharge or purported discharge of his functions as adjudicator unless the act or omission is in bad faith, and that any employee or agent of the adjudicator is similarly protected from liability.

(5) If the contract does not comply with the requirements of subsections (1) to (4), the adjudication provisions of the Scheme for Construction Contracts apply.

(6) For England and Wales, the Scheme may apply the provisions of the Arbitration Act 1996 with such adaptations and modifications as appear to the Minister making the Scheme to be appropriate.

For Scotland, the Scheme may include provision conferring powers on courts in relation to adjudication and provision relating to the enforcement of the adjudicator's decision.

Payment

109 Entitlement to stage payments

(1) A party to a construction contract is entitled to payment by instalments, stage payments or other periodic payments for any work under the contract unless—

(a) it is specified in the contract that the duration of the work is to be less than 45 days, or

(b) it is agreed between the parties that the duration of the work is estimated to be less than 45 days.

(2) The parties are free to agree the amounts of the payments and the intervals at which, or circumstances in which, they become due.

(3) In the absence of such agreement, the relevant provisions of the Scheme for Construction Contracts apply.

(4) References in the following sections to a payment under the contract include a payment by virtue of this section.

110 Dates for payment

(1) Every construction contract shall—

    (*a*) provide an adequate mechanism for determining what payments become due under the contract, and when, and

    (*b*) provide for a final date for payment in relation to any sum which becomes due.

    The parties are free to agree how long the period is to be between the date on which a sum becomes due and the final date for payment.

(2) Every construction contract shall provide for the giving of notice by a party not later than five days after the date on which a payment becomes due from him under the contract, or would have become due if—

    (*a*) the other party had carried out his obligations under the contract, and

    (*b*) no set-off or abatement was permitted by reference to any sum claimed to be due under one or more other contracts,

    specifying the amount (if any) of the payment made or proposed to be made, and the basis on which that amount was calculated.

(3) If or to the extent that a contract does not contain such provision as is mentioned in subsection (1) or (2), the relevant provisions of the Scheme for Construction Contracts apply.

111 Notice of intention to withhold payment

(1) A party to a construction contract may not withhold payment after the final date for payment of a sum due under the contract unless he has given an effective notice of intention to withhold payment.

    The notice mentioned in section 110(2) may suffice as a notice of intention to withhold payment if it complies with the requirements of this section.

(2) To be effective such a notice must specify—

    (*a*) the amount proposed to be withheld and the ground for withholding payment, or

    (*b*) if there is more than one ground, each ground and the amount attributable to it,

    and must be given not later than the prescribed period before the final date for payment.

(3) The parties are free to agree what that prescribed period is to be.

    In the absence of such agreement, the period shall be that provided by the Scheme for Construction Contracts.

(4) Where an effective notice of intention to withhold payment is given, but on the matter being referred to adjudication it is decided that the whole or part of the amount should be paid, the decision shall be construed as requiring payment not later than—

    (*a*) seven days from the date of the decision, or

    (*b*) the date which apart from the notice would have been the final date for payment,

whichever is the later.

112 Right to suspend performance for non-payment

(1) Where a sum due under a construction contract is not paid in full by the final date for payment and no effective notice to withhold payment has been given, the person to whom the sum is due has the right (without prejudice to any other right or remedy) to suspend performance of his obligations under the contract to the party by whom payment ought to have been made ("the party in default").

(2) The right may not be exercised without first giving to the party in default at least seven days' notice of intention to suspend performance, stating the ground or grounds on which it is intended to suspend performance.

(3) The right to suspend performance ceases when the party in default makes payment in full of the amount due.

(4) Any period during which performance is suspended in pursuance of the right conferred by this section shall be disregarded in computing for the purposes of any contractual time limit the time taken, by the party exercising the right or by a third party, to complete any work directly or indirectly affected by the exercise of the right.

Where the contractual time limit is set by reference to a date rather than a period, the date shall be adjusted accordingly.

113 Prohibition of conditional payment provisions

(1) A provision making payment under a construction contract conditional on the payer receiving payment from a third person is ineffective, unless that third person, or any other person payment by whom is under the contract (directly or indirectly) a condition of payment by that third person, is insolvent.

(2) For the purposes of this section a company becomes insolvent—

(*a*) on the making of an administration order against it under Part II of the Insolvency Act 1986,

(*b*) on the appointment of an administrative receiver or a receiver or manager of its property under Chapter I of Part III of that Act, or the appointment of a receiver under Chapter II of that Part,

(*c*) on the passing of a resolution for voluntary winding-up without a declaration of solvency under section 89 of that Act, or

(*d*) on the making of a winding-up order under Part IV or V of that Act.

(3) For the purposes of this section a partnership becomes insolvent—

(*a*) on the making of a winding-up order against it under any provision of the Insolvency Act 1986 as applied by an order under section 420 of that Act, or

(b) when sequestration is awarded on the estate of the partnership under section 12 of the Bankruptcy (Scotland) Act 1985 or the partnership grants a trust deed for its creditors.

(4) For the purposes of this section an individual becomes insolvent—

    (a) on the making of a bankruptcy order against him under Part IX of the Insolvency Act 1986, or

    (b) on the sequestration of his estate under the Bankruptcy (Scotland) Act 1985 or when he grants a trust deed for his creditors.

(5) A company, partnership or individual shall also be treated as insolvent on the occurrence of any event corresponding to those specified in subsection (2), (3) or (4) under the law of Northern Ireland or of a country outside the United Kingdom.

(6) Where a provision is rendered ineffective by subsection (1), the parties are free to agree other terms for payment.

In the absence of such agreement, the relevant provisions of the Scheme for Construction Contracts apply.

Supplementary provisions
114 The Scheme for Construction Contracts

(1) The Minister shall by regulations make a scheme ("the Scheme for Construction Contracts") containing provision about the matters referred to in the preceding provisions of this Part.

(2) Before making any regulations under this section the Minister shall consult such persons as he thinks fit.

(3) In this section "the Minister" means—

    (a) for England and Wales, the Secretary of State, and

    (b) for Scotland, the Lord Advocate.

(4) Where any provisions of the Scheme for Construction Contracts apply by virtue of this Part in default of

contractual provision agreed by the parties, they have effect as implied terms of the contract concerned.

(5) Regulations under this section shall not be made unless a draft of them has been approved by resolution of each House of Parliament.

115 Service of notices, &c

(1) The parties are free to agree on the manner of service of any notice or other document required or authorised to be served in pursuance of the construction contract or for any of the purposes of this Part.

(2) If or to the extent that there is no such agreement the following provisions apply.

(3) A notice or other document may be served on a person by any effective means.

(4) If a notice or other document is addressed, pre-paid and delivered by post—

(a) to the addressee's last known principal residence or, if he is or has been carrying on a trade, profession or business, his last known principal business address, or

(b) where the addressee is a body corporate, to the body's registered or principal office,

it shall be treated as effectively served.

(5) This section does not apply to the service of documents for the purposes of legal proceedings, for which provision is made by rules of court.

(6) References in this Part to a notice or other document include any form of communication in writing and references to service shall be construed accordingly.

116 Reckoning periods of time

(1) For the purposes of this Part periods of time shall be reckoned as follows.

(2) Where an act is required to be done within a specified period after or from a specified date, the period begins immediately after that date.

(3) Where the period would include Christmas Day, Good Friday or a day which under the Banking and Financial Dealings Act 1971 is a bank holiday in England and Wales or, as the case may be, in Scotland, that day shall be excluded.

117 Crown application

(1) This Part applies to a construction contract entered into by or on behalf of the Crown otherwise than by or on behalf of Her Majesty in her private capacity.

(2) This Part applies to a construction contract entered into on behalf of the Duchy of Cornwall notwithstanding any Crown interest.

(3) Where a construction contract is entered into by or on behalf of Her Majesty in right of the Duchy of Lancaster, Her Majesty shall be represented, for the purposes of any adjudication or other proceedings arising out of the contract by virtue of this Part, by the Chancellor of the Duchy or such person as he may appoint.

(4) Where a construction contract is entered into on behalf of the Duchy of Cornwall, the Duke of Cornwall or the possessor for the time being of the Duchy shall be represented, for the purposes of any adjudication or other proceedings arising out of the contract by virtue of this Part, by such person as he may appoint.

Source: *The Housing Grants, Construction and Regeneration Act 1996.* HMSO, London, 1996.

Appendix 2

The Scheme for Construction Contracts (England and Wales) Regulations 1998

The text of the above is reproduced below.

Citation, commencement, extent and interpretation

1. (1) These Regulations may be cited as The Scheme for Construction Contracts (England and Wales) Regulations 1998 and shall come into force at the end of the period of 8 weeks beginning with the day on which it is made (the "commencement date").

    (2) These Regulations shall extend only to England and Wales.

    (3) In these Regulations, "the Act" means the Housing Grants, Construction and Regeneration Act 1996.

The Scheme for Construction Contracts

2. Where a construction contract does not comply with the requirements of section 108(1) to (4) of the Act, the adjudication provisions in Part 1 of the Schedule to these Regulations shall apply.

3. Where—

    (a) the parties to a construction contract are unable to reach agreement for the purposes mentioned respectively in sections 109, 111 and 113 of the Act, or

    (b) a construction contract does not make provision as required by section 110 of the Act, the relevant provisions in Part II of the Schedule to these Regulations shall apply.

4. The provisions in the Schedule to these Regulations shall be the Scheme for Construction Contracts for the purposes of section 114 of the Act.

Part I. Adjudication
Notice of Intention to seek Adjudication

1. (1) Any party to a construction contract (the "referring party") may give written notice (the "notice of adjudication") of his intention to refer any dispute arising under the contract to adjudication.

   (2) The notice of adjudication shall be given to every other party to the contract.

   (3) The notice of adjudication shall set out briefly—
      (a) the nature and a brief description of the dispute and of the parties involved.
      (b) details of where and when the dispute has arisen,
      (c) the nature of the redress which is sought, and
      (d) the names and addresses of the parties to the contract (including, where appropriate, the addresses which the parties have specified for the giving of notices).

2. (1) Following the giving of a notice of adjudication and subject to any agreement between the parties to the dispute as to who shall act as adjudicator—
      (a) the referring party shall request the person (if any) specified in the contract to act as adjudicator, or
      (b) if no person is named in the contract or the person named has already indicated that he is unwilling or unable to act, and the contract provides for a specified nominating body to select a person, the referring party shall request the nominating body named in the contract to select a person to act as adjudicator, or
      (c) where neither paragraph (a) nor (b) above applies, or where the person referred to in (a) has already indicated

that he is unwilling or unable to act and (*b*) does not apply, the referring party shall request an adjudicator nominating body to select a person to act as adjudicator.

(2) A person requested to act as adjudicator in accordance with the provisions of paragraph (1) shall indicate whether or not he is willing to act within two days of receiving the request.

(3) In this paragraph, and in paragraphs 5 and 6 below, an "adjudicator nominating body" shall mean a body (not being a natural person and not being a party to the dispute) which holds itself out publicly as a body which will select an adjudicator when requested to do so by a referring party

3. The request referred to in paragraphs 2, 5 and 6 shall be accompanied by a copy of the notice of adjudication.

4. Any person requested or selected to act as adjudicator in accordance with paragraphs 2, 5 or 6 shall be a natural person acting in his personal capacity. A person requested or selected to act as an adjudicator shall not be an employee of any of the parties to the dispute and shall declare any interest, financial or otherwise, in any matter relating to the dispute.

5. (1) The nominating body referred to in paragraphs 2(1)(*b*) and 6(1)(*b*) or the adjudicator nominating body referred to in paragraphs 2(1)(*c*), 5(2)(*b*) and 6(1)(*c*) must communicate the selection of an adjudicator to the referring party within five days of receiving a request to do so.

(2) Where the nominating body or the adjudicator nominating body fails to comply with paragraph (1) the referring party may—

   (*a*) agree with the other parties to the dispute to request a specified person to act as adjudicator, or

   (*b*) request any other adjudicator nominating body to select a person to act as adjudicator.

(3) The person requested to act as adjudicator in accordance with the provisions of paragraphs (1) or (2) shall indicate

whether or not he is willing to act within two days of receiving the request.

6. (1) Where another adjudicator who is named in the contract indicates to the parties that he is unable or unwilling to act or where he fails to respond in accordance with paragraph 2(2), the referring party may—

   (a) request another person (if any) specified in the contract to act as adjudicator or

   (b) request the nominating body (if any) referred to in the contract to select a person to act as adjudicator, or

   (c) request any other adjudicator nominating body to select a person to act as adjudicator.

   (2) The person requested to act in accordance with the provisions of paragraph (1) shall indicate whether or not he is willing to act within two days of receiving the request.

7. (1) Where an adjudicator has been selected in accordance with paragraphs 2, 5 or 6, the referring party shall, not later than seven days from the date of the notice of adjudication, refer the dispute in writing (the "referral notice") to the adjudicator.

   (2) A referral notice shall be accompanied by copies of, or relevant extracts from, the construction contract and such other documents as the referring party intends to rely upon.

   (3) The referring party shall, at the same time as he sends to the adjudicator the documents referred to in paragraphs (1) and (2), send copies of those documents to every other party to the dispute.

8. (1) The adjudicator may, with the consent of all the parties to those disputes, adjudicate at the same time on one or more disputes under the same contract.

   (2) The adjudicator may, with the consent of all the parties to those disputes, adjudicate at the same time on related disputes under different contracts, whether or not one or more of those parties is a party to those disputes.

(3) All the parties in paragraphs (1) and (2) respectively, may agree to extend the period within which the adjudicator may reach a decision in relation to all or any of these disputes.

(4) Where an adjudicator ceases to act because a dispute is to be adjudicated on by another person in terms of this paragraph, that adjudicator's fees and expenses shall be determined in accordance with paragraph 25.

9. (1) An adjudicator may resign at any time on giving notice in writing to the parties to the dispute.

(2) An adjudicator must resign where the dispute is the same or substantially the same as one which has previously been referred to adjudication, and a decision has been taken in that adjudication.

(3) Where an adjudicator ceases to act under paragraph 9(1)—

(a) the referring party may serve a fresh notice under paragraph 1 and shall request an adjudicator to act in accordance within paragraphs 2 to 7; and

(b) if requested by the new adjudicator and insofar as it is reasonably practicable, the parties shall supply him with copies of all documents which they had made available to the previous adjudicator.

(4) Where an adjudicator resigns in the circumstances referred to in paragraph (2), or where a dispute varies significantly from the dispute referred to him in the referral notice and for that reason he is not competent to decide it, the adjudicator shall be entitled to the payment of such reasonable amount as he may determine by way of fees and expenses reasonably incurred by him. The parties shall be jointly and severally liable for any sum which remains outstanding following the making of any determination on how the payment shall be apportioned.

10. Where any party to the dispute objects to the appointment of a particular person as adjudicator, that objection shall not

invalidate the adjudicator's appointment nor any decision he may reach in accordance with paragraph 20.

11. (1) The parties to a dispute may at any time agree to revoke the appointment of the adjudicator. The adjudicator shall be entitled to the payment of such reasonable amount as he may determine by way of fees and expenses incurred by him. The parties shall be jointly and severally liable for any sum which remains outstanding following the making of any determination on how the payment shall be apportioned.

(2) Where the revocation of the appointment of the adjudicator is due to the default or misconduct of the adjudicator, the parties shall not be liable to pay the adjudicator's fees and expenses.

Powers of the adjudicator

12. The adjudicator shall—

(a) act impartially in carrying out his duties and shall do so in accordance with any relevant terms of the contract and shall reach his decision in accordance with the applicable law in relation to the contract; and

(b) avoid incurring unnecessary expense.

13. The adjudicator may take the initiative in ascertaining the facts and the law necessary to determine the dispute, and shall decide on the procedure to be followed in the adjudication. In particular he may—

(a) request any party to the contract to supply him with such documents as he may reasonably require including, if he so directs, any written statement from any party to the contract supporting or supplementing the referral notice and any other documents given under paragraphs 7(2),

(b) decide the language or languages to be used in the adjudication and whether a translation of any document is to be provided and if so by whom,

(c) meet and question any of the parties to the contract and their representatives, (*d*) subject to obtaining any necessary consent from a third party or parties, make such site visits and inspections as he considers appropriate, whether accompanied by the parties or not,

(*e*) subject to obtaining any necessary consent from a third party or parties, carry out any tests or experiments,

(*f*) obtain and consider such representations and submissions as he requires, and, provided he has notified the parties of his intention, appoint experts, assessors or legal advisers,

(*g*) give directions as to the timetable for the adjudication, any deadlines, or limits as to the length of written documents or oral representations to be complied with, and

(*h*) issue other directions relating to the conduct of the adjudication.

14. The parties shall comply with any request or direction of the adjudicator in relation to the adjudication.

15. If, without showing sufficient cause, a party fails to comply with any request, direction or timetable of the adjudicator made in accordance with his powers, fails to produce any document or written statement requested by the adjudicator or in any other way fails to comply with a requirement under these provisions relating to the adjudication, the adjudicator may—

(*a*) continue the adjudication in the absence of that party or of the document or written statement requested,

(*b*) draw such inferences from that failure to comply as circumstances may, in the adjudicator's opinion, be justified, and

(*c*) make a decision on the basis of the information before him attaching such weight as he thinks fit to any evidence submitted to him outside any period he may have requested or directed.

16. (1) Subject to any agreement between the parties to the contrary and to the terms of paragraph (2) below, any party to the dispute may be assisted by, or represented by such

advisers or representatives (whether legally qualified or not) as he considers appropriate.

(2) Where the adjudicator is considering oral evidence or representations, a party to the dispute may not be represented by more than one person, unless the adjudicator gives directions to the contrary.

17. The adjudicator shall consider any relevant information submitted to him by any of the parties to the dispute and shall make available to them any information to be taken into account in reaching his decision.

18. The adjudicator and any party to the dispute shall not disclose to any other person any information or document provided to him in connection with the adjudication which the party supplying it has indicated is to be treated as confidential, except to the extent that it is necessary for the purposes of, or in connection with, the adjudication.

19. (1) The adjudicator shall reach his decision not later than—

   (*a*) twenty eight days after the date of the referral notice mentioned in paragraph 7(1), or

   (*b*) forty two days after the date of the referral notice if the referring party so consents, or

   (*c*) such period exceeding twenty eight days after the referral notice as the parties to the dispute may, after the giving of that notice, agree.

(2) Where the adjudicator fails, for any reason, to reach his decision in accordance with paragraph (1)

   (*a*) any of the parties to the dispute may serve a fresh notice under paragraph 1 and shall request an adjudicator to act in accordance with paragraphs 2 to 7; and

   (*b*) if requested by the new adjudicator and insofar as it is reasonably practicable, the parties shall supply him with copies of all documents which they had made available to the previous adjudicator.

(3) As soon as possible after he has reached a decision, the adjudicator shall deliver a copy of that decision to each of the parties to the contract.

Adjudicator's decision

20. The adjudicator shall decide the matters in dispute. He may take into account any other matters which the parties to the dispute agree should be within the scope of the adjudication or which are matters under the contract which he considers are necessarily connected with the dispute. In particular, he may—

    (a) open up, revise and review any decision taken or any certificate given by any person referred to in the contract unless the contract states that the decision or certificate is final and conclusive,

    (b) decide that any of the parties to the dispute is liable to make a payment under the contract (whether in sterling or some other currency) and, subject to section 111(4) of the Act, when that payment is due and the final date for payment,

    (c) having regard to any term of the contract relating to the payment of interest decide the circumstances in which, and the rates at which, and the periods for which simple or compound rates of interest shall be paid.

21. In the absence of any directions by the adjudicator relating to the time for performance of his decision, the parties shall be required to comply with any decision of the adjudicator immediately on delivery of the decision to the parties in accordance with this paragraph.

22. If requested by one of the parties to the dispute, the adjudicator shall provide reasons for his decision.

Effects of the decision

23. (1) In his decision, the adjudicator may, if he thinks fit, order any of the parties to comply peremptorily with his decision or any part of it.

(2) The decision of the adjudicator shall be binding on the parties, and they shall comply with it until the dispute is finally determined by legal proceedings, by arbitration (if the contract provides for arbitration or the parties otherwise agree to arbitration), or by agreement between the parties.

24. Section 42 of the Arbitration Act 1996 shall apply to this Scheme subject to the following modifications—
    (a) in subsection (2) for the word "tribunal" wherever it appears there shall be substituted the word "adjudicator",
    (b) in subparagraph (b) of subsection (2) for the words "arbitral proceedings" there shall be substituted the word "adjudication",
    (c) subparagraph (c) of subsection (2) shall be deleted, and
    (d) subsection (3) shall be deleted.

25. The adjudicator shall be entitled to the payment of such reasonable amount as he may determine by way of fees and expenses reasonably incurred by him. The parties shall be jointly and severally liable to pay any sum which remains outstanding following the making of any determination on how the payment shall be apportioned.

26. The adjudicator shall not be liable for anything done or omitted in the discharge or purported discharge of his functions as adjudicator unless the act or omission is in bad faith, and any employee or agent of the adjudicator shall be similarly protected from liability.

Part II. Payment

Entitlement to and amount of stage payments

1. Where the parties to a relevant construction contract fail to agree—
    (a) the amount of any instalment or stage or periodic payment for any work under the contract, or
    (b) the intervals at which, or circumstances in which, such payments become due under that contract, or

    (c) both of the matters mentioned in sub-paragraphs (a) and (b) above, the relevant provisions of paragraphs 2 to 4 below shall apply.

2. (1) The amount of any payment by way of instalments or stage or periodic payments in respect of a relevant period shall be the difference between the amount determined in accordance with sub-paragraph (2) and the amount determined in accordance with sub-paragraph (3).

    (2) The aggregate of the following amounts—

        (a) an amount equal to the value of any work performed in accordance with the relevant construction contract during the period from the commencement of the contract to the end of the relevant period (excluding any amount calculated in accordance with sub-paragraph (b)),

        (b) where the contract provides for payment for materials, an amount equal to the value of any materials manufactured on site or brought onto site for the purposes of the works during the period from the commencement of the contract to the end of the relevant period, and

        (c) any other amount or sum which the contract specifies shall be payable during or in respect of the period from the commencement of the contract to the end of the relevant period.

    (3) The aggregate of any sums which have been paid or are due for payment by way of instalments, stage or periodic payments during the period from the commencement of the contract to the end of the relevant period.

    (4) An amount calculated in accordance with this paragraph shall not exceed the difference between—

        (a) the contract price, and

        (b) the aggregate of the instalments or stage or periodic payments which have become due.

Dates for payment

3. Where the parties to a construction contract fail to provide an adequate mechanism for determining either what payments become due under the contract, or when they become due for payment, or both, the relevant provisions of paragraphs 4 to 7 shall apply.

4. Any payment of a kind mentioned in paragraph 2 above shall become due on whichever of the following dates occurs later—

    (*a*) the expiry of 7 days following the relevant period mentioned in paragraph 2(1) above, or

    (*b*) the making of a claim by the payee.

5. The final payment payable under a relevant construction contract, namely the payment of an amount equal to the difference (if any) between—

    (*a*) the contract price, and

    (*b*) the aggregate of any instalment or stage or periodic payments which have become due under the contract,

    shall become due on the expiry of—

    (*a*) 30 days following completion of the work, or

    (*b*) the making of a claim by the payee,

    whichever is the later.

6. Payment of the contract price under a construction contract (not being a relevant construction contract) shall become due on—

    (*a*) the expiry of 30 days following the completion of the work, or

    (*b*) the making of a claim by the payee

    whichever is the later.

7. Any other payment under a construction contract shall become due—

    (*a*) on the expiry of 7 days following the completion of the work to which the payment relates, or

    (*b*) the making of a claim by the payee,

    whichever is the later.

Final date for payment

8. (1) Where the parties to a construction contract fail to provide a final date for payment in relation to any sum which becomes due under a construction contract, the provisions of this paragraph shall apply.

(2) The final date for the making of any payment of a kind mentioned in paragraphs 2, 5, 6 or 7, shall be 17 days from the date that payment becomes due.

Notice specifying amount of payment

9. A party to a construction contract shall, not later than 5 days after the date on which any payment—

(*a*) becomes due from him, or

(*b*) would have become due, if—

    (*i*) the other party had carried out his obligations under the contract, and

    (*ii*) no set-off or abatement was permitted by reference to any sum claimed to be due under one or more other contracts,

give notice to the other party to the contract specifying the amount (if any) of the payment he has made or proposes to make, specifying to what the payment relates and the basis on which that amount is calculated.

Notice of intention to withhold payment

10. Any notice of intention to withhold payment mentioned in section 111 of the Act shall be given not later than the prescribed period, which is to say not later than 7 days before the final date for payment determined either in accordance with the construction contract, or where no such provision is made in the contract, in accordance with paragraph 8 above.

Prohibition of conditional payment provisions

11. Where a provision making payment under a construction contract conditional on the payer receiving payment from a third person is ineffective as mentioned in section 113 of the Act, and the parties have not agreed other terms for payment, the relevant provisions of –

(*a*) paragraphs 2, 4, 5, 7, 8, 9 and 10 shall apply in the case of a relevant construction contract, and

(*b*) paragraphs 6, 7, 8, 9 and 10 shall apply in the case of any other construction contract.

Interpretation

12. In this Part of the Scheme for Construction Contracts—

"claim by the payee" means a written notice given by the party carrying out work under a construction contract to the other party specifying the amount of any payment or payments which he considers to be due and the basis on which it is, or they are calculated;

"contract price" means the entire sum payable under the construction contract in respect of the work;

"relevant construction contract" means any construction contract other than one which specifies that the duration of the work is to be less than 45 days, or in respect of which the parties agree that the duration of the work is estimated to be less than 45 days;

"relevant period" means a period which is specified in, or is calculated by reference to the construction contract or where no such period is so specified or is so calculable, a period of 28 days:

"value of work" means an amount determined in accordance with the construction contract under which the work is performed or where the contract contains no such provision, the cost of any work performed in accordance with that contract together with an amount equal to any overhead or profit included in the contract price;

"work" means any of the work or services mentioned in section 104 of the Act.

Explanatory note
(This note is not part of the Order)
Part II of the Housing Grants, Construction and Regeneration Act 1996 makes provision in relation to construction contracts. Section 114 empowers the Secretary of State to make the Scheme for Construction Contracts. Where a construction contract does not comply with the requirements of sections 108 to 111 (adjudication of disputes and payment provisions), and section 113 (prohibition of conditional payment provisions), the relevant provisions of the Scheme for Construction Contracts have effect.

The Scheme which is contained in the Schedule to these Regulations is in two parts. Part I provides for the selection and appointment of an adjudicator, gives powers to the adjudicator to gather and consider information, and makes provisions in respect of his decisions. Part II makes provision with respect to payments under a construction contract where either the contract fails to make provision or the parties fail to agree—

(*a*) the method for calculating the amount of any instalment, stage or periodic payment,

(*b*) the due date and the final date for payments to be made, and

(*c*) prescribes the period within which a notice of intention to withhold payment must be given.

Appendix 3

The Scheme for Construction Contracts (Scotland) Regulations 1998

The text of the above is reproduced below.

Citation, commencement and extent

1. (1) These Regulations may be cited as the Scheme for Construction Contracts (Scotland) Regulations 1998 and shall come into force at the end of the period of 8 weeks beginning with the day on which they are made.
   (2) These Regulations extend to Scotland only.

Interpretation

2. In these Regulations, "the Act" means the Housing Grants, Construction and Regeneration Act 1996.

The Scheme for Construction Contracts (Scotland)

3. Where a construction contract does not comply with the requirements of subsections (1) to (4) of section 108 of the Act, the adjudication provisions in Part I of the Schedule to these Regulations shall apply.
4. Where—
   (a) the parties to a construction contract are unable to reach agreement for the purposes mentioned respectively in sections 109, 111 and 113 of the Act; or

(b) a construction contract does not make provision as required by section 110 of the Act,

the relevant provisions in Part II of the Schedule to these Regulations shall apply.

5. The provisions in the Schedule to these Regulations shall be the Scheme for Construction Contracts (Scotland) for the purposes of section 114 of the Act.

Part I. Adjudication

Notice of intention to seek adjudication

1. (1) Any party to a construction contract ("the referring party") may give written notice ("the notice of adjudication") of his intention to refer any dispute arising under the contract to adjudication.

   (2) The notice of adjudication shall be given to every other party to the contract.

   (3) The notice of adjudication shall set out briefly—
      (a) the nature and a brief description of the dispute and of the parties involved;
      (b) details of where and when the dispute has arisen;
      (c) the nature of the redress which is sought; and
      (d) the names and addresses of the parties to the contract (including, where appropriate, the addresses which the parties have specified for the giving of notices).

2. (1) Following the giving of a notice of adjudication and subject to any agreement between the parties to the dispute as to who shall act as adjudicator—
      (a) the referring party shall request the person (if any) specified in the contract to act as adjudicator;
      (b) if no person is named in the contract or the person named has already indicated that he is unwilling or unable to act, and the contract provides for a specified nominating body to select a person, the referring party shall request the nominating body named in the contract to select a person to act as adjudicator; or

      (c) where neither head (*a*) nor (*b*) above applies, or where the person referred to in (*a*) has already indicated that he is unwilling or unable to act and (*b*) does not apply, the referring party shall request an adjudicator nominating body to select a person to act as adjudicator.

    (2) A person requested to act as adjudicator in accordance with the provisions of sub-paragraph (1) shall indicate whether or not he is willing to act within two days of receiving the request.

    (3) In this paragraph, and in paragraphs 5 and 6 below, "an adjudicator nominating body" shall mean a body (not being a natural person and not being a party to the dispute) which holds itself out publicly as a body which will select an adjudicator when requested to do so by a referring party.

3. The request referred to in paragraphs 2, 5 and 6 shall be accompanied by a copy of the notice of adjudication.

4. Any person requested or selected to act as adjudicator in accordance with paragraphs 2, 5 or 6 shall be a natural person acting in his personal capacity. A person requested or selected to act as an adjudicator shall not be an employee of any of the parties to the dispute and shall declare any interest, financial or otherwise, in any matter relating to the dispute.

5. (1) The nominating body referred to in paragraphs 2(1)(*b*) and 6(1)(*b*) or the adjudicator nominating body referred to in paragraphs 2(1)(*c*), 5(2)(*b*) and 6(1)(*c*) must communicate the selection of an adjudicator to the referring party within five days of receiving a request to do so.

    (2) Where the nominating body or the adjudicator nominating body fails to comply with sub-paragraph (1), the referring party may—

      (*a*) agree with the other party to the dispute to request a specified person to act as adjudicator; or

      (*b*) request any other adjudicator nominating body to select a person to act as adjudicator.

(3) The person requested to act as adjudicator in accordance with the provisions of sub-paragraph (1) or (2) shall indicate whether or not he is willing to act within two days of receiving the request.

6. (1) Where an adjudicator who is named in the contract indicates to the parties that he is unable or unwilling to act, or where he fails to respond in accordance with paragraph 2(2), the referring party may—

   (*a*) request another person (if any) specified in the contract to act as adjudicator;

   (*b*) request the nominating body (if any) referred to in the contract to select a person to act as adjudicator; or

   (*c*) request any other adjudicator nominating body to select a person to act as adjudicator.

   (2) The person requested to act in accordance with the provisions of sub-paragraph (1) shall indicate whether or not he is willing to act within two days of receiving the request.

7. (1) Where an adjudicator has been selected in accordance with paragraphs 2, 5 or 6, the referring party shall, not later than seven days from the date of the notice of adjudication, refer the dispute in writing ("the referral notice") to the adjudicator.

   (2) A referral notice shall be accompanied by copies of, or relevant extracts from, the construction contract and such other documents as the referring party intends to rely upon.

   (3) The referring party shall, at the same time as he sends to the adjudicator the documents referred to in sub-paragraphs (1) and (2), send copies of those documents to every other party to the dispute.

8. (1) The adjudicator may, with the consent of all the parties to those disputes, adjudicate at the same time on more than one dispute under the same contract.

   (2) The adjudicator may, with the consent of all the parties to those disputes, adjudicate at the same time on related disputes under different contracts, whether or not one or more of those parties is a party to those disputes.

(3) All the parties in sub-paragraphs (1) and (2) respectively may agree to extend the period within which the adjudicator may reach a decision in relation to all or any of these disputes.

(4) Where an adjudicator ceases to act because a dispute is to be adjudicated on by another person in terms of this paragraph, that adjudicator's fees and expenses shall be determined and payable in accordance with paragraph 25.

9. (1) An adjudicator may resign at any time on giving notice in writing to the parties to the dispute.

(2) An adjudicator must resign where the dispute is the same or substantially the same as one which has previously been referred to adjudication, and a decision has been taken in that adjudication.

(3) Where an adjudicator ceases to act under sub-paragraph (1)—

(*a*) the referring party may serve a fresh notice under paragraph 1 and shall request an adjudicator to act in accordance with paragraphs 2 to 7; and

(*b*) if requested by the new adjudicator and insofar as it is reasonably practicable, the parties shall supply him with copies of all documents which they had made available to the previous adjudicator.

(4) Where an adjudicator resigns in the circumstances mentioned in sub-paragraph (2), or where a dispute varies significantly from the dispute referred to him and for that reason he is not competent to decide it, that adjudicator's fees and expenses shall be determined and payable in accordance with paragraph 25.

10. Where any party to the dispute objects to the appointment of a particular person as adjudicator, that objection shall not invalidate the adjudicator's appointment nor any decision he may reach in accordance with paragraph 20.

11. (1) The parties to a dispute may at any time agree to revoke the appointment of the adjudicator and in such circumstances

the fees and expenses of that adjudicator shall, subject to sub-paragraph (2), be determined and payable in accordance with paragraph 25.

(2) Where the revocation of the appointment of the adjudicator is due to the default or misconduct of the adjudicator, the parties shall not be liable to pay the adjudicator's fees and expenses.

Powers of the adjudicator

12. The adjudicator shall—

   (a) act impartially in carrying out his duties and shall do so in accordance with any relevant terms of the contract and shall reach his decision in accordance with the applicable law in relation to the contract; and

   (b) avoid incurring unnecessary expense.

13. The adjudicator may take the initiative in ascertaining the facts and the law necessary to determine the dispute, and shall decide on the procedure to be followed in the adjudication. In particular, he may—

   (a) request any party to the contract to supply him with such documents as he may reasonably require including, if he so directs, any written statement from any party to the contract supporting or supplementing the referral notice and any other documents given under paragraph 7(2);

   (b) decide the language or languages to be used in the adjudication and whether a translation of any document is to be provided and, if so, by whom;

   (c) meet and question any of the parties to the contract and their representatives;

   (d) subject to obtaining any necessary consent from a third party or parties, make such site visits and inspections as he considers appropriate, whether accompanied by the parties or not;

   (e) subject to obtaining any necessary consent from a third party or parties, carry out any tests or experiments;

(f) obtain and consider such representations and submissions as he requires, and, provided he has notified the parties of his intention, appoint experts, assessors or legal advisers;

(g) give directions as to the timetable for the adjudication, any deadlines, or limits as to the length of written documents or oral representations to be complied with; and

(h) issue other directions relating to the conduct of the adjudication.

14. The parties shall comply with any request or direction of the adjudicator in relation to the adjudication.

15. If, without showing sufficient cause, a party fails to comply with any request, direction or timetable of the adjudicator made in accordance with his powers, fails to produce any document or written statement requested by the adjudicator, or in any other way fails to comply with a requirement under these provisions relating to the adjudication, the adjudicator may—

(a) continue the adjudication in the absence of that party or of the document or written statement requested;

(b) draw such inferences from that failure to comply as may, in the adjudicator's opinion, be justified in the circumstances; and

(c) make a decision on the basis of the information before him, attaching such weight as he thinks fit to any evidence submitted to him outside any period he may have requested or directed.

16. (1) Subject to any agreement between the parties to the contrary and to the terms of sub-paragraph (2), any party to the dispute may be assisted by, or represented by, such advisers or representatives (whether legally qualified or not) as he considers appropriate.

(2) Where the adjudicator is considering oral evidence or representations, a party to the dispute may not be represented by more than one person, unless the adjudicator gives directions to the contrary.

17. The adjudicator shall consider any relevant information submitted to him by any of the parties to the dispute and shall make available to them any information to be taken into account in reaching his decision.

18. The adjudicator and any party to the dispute shall not disclose to any other person any information or document provided to him in connection with the adjudication which the party supplying it has indicated is to be treated as confidential, except to the extent that it is necessary for the purposes of, or in connection with, the adjudication.

19. (1) The adjudicator shall reach his decision not later than—

    (a) twenty eight days after the date of the referral notice mentioned in paragraph 7(1);

    (b) forty two days after the date of the referral notice if the referring party so consents; or

    (c) such period exceeding twenty eight days after the referral notice as the parties to the dispute may, after the giving of that notice, agree.

  (2) Where the adjudicator fails, for any reason, to reach his decision in accordance with sub-paragraph (1)—

    (a) any of the parties to the dispute may serve a fresh notice under paragraph 1 and shall request an adjudicator to act in accordance with paragraphs 2 to 7; and

    (b) if requested by the new adjudicator and insofar as it is reasonably practicable, the parties shall supply him with copies of all documents which they had made available to the previous adjudicator.

    (c) As soon as possible after he has reached a decision, the adjudicator shall deliver a copy of that decision to each of the parties to the contract.

Adjudicator's decision

20. (1) The adjudicator shall decide the matters in dispute and may make a decision on different aspects of the dispute at different times.

(2) The adjudicator may take into account any other matters which the parties to the dispute agree should be within the scope of the adjudication or which are matters under the contract which he considers are necessarily connected with the dispute and, in particular, he may—

(*a*) open up, review and revise any decision taken or any certificate given by any person referred to in the contract, unless the contract states that the decision or certificate is final and conclusive;

(*b*) decide that any of the parties to the dispute is liable to make a payment under the contract (whether in sterling or some other currency) and, subject to section 111(4) of the Act, when that payment is due and the final date for payment;

(*c*) having regard to any term of the contract relating to the payment of interest, decide the circumstances in which, the rates at which, and the periods for which simple or compound rates of interest shall be paid.

21. In the absence of any directions by the adjudicator relating to the time for performance of his decision, the parties shall be required to comply with any decision of the adjudicator immediately on delivery of the decision to the parties in accordance with paragraph 19(3).

22. If requested by one of the parties to the dispute, the adjudicator shall provide reasons for his decision.

Effects of the decision

23. (1) In his decision, the adjudicator may, if he thinks fit, order any of the parties to comply peremptorily with his decision or any part of it.

(2) The decision of the adjudicator shall be binding on the parties, and they shall comply with it, until the dispute is finally determined by legal proceedings, by arbitration (if the contract provides for arbitration or the parties otherwise agree to arbitration), or by agreement between the parties.

24. Where a party or the adjudicator wishes to register the decision for execution in the Books of Council and Session, any other party shall, on being requested to do so, forthwith consent to such registration by subscribing the decision before a witness.

25. (1) The adjudicator shall be entitled to the payment of such reasonable amount as he may determine by way of fees and expenses incurred by him and the parties shall be jointly and severally liable to pay that amount to the adjudicator.

    (2) Without prejudice to the right of the adjudicator to effect recovery from any party in accordance with sub-paragraph (1), the adjudicator may by direction determine the apportionment between the parties of liability for his fees and expenses.

26. The adjudicator shall not be liable for anything done or omitted in the discharge or purported discharge of his functions as adjudicator unless the act or omission is in bad faith, and any employee or agent of the adjudicator shall be similarly protected from liability.

Part II. Payment
Entitlement to and amount of stage payments

1. Where the parties to a relevant construction contract fail to agree—

    (a) the amount of any instalment or stage or periodic payment for any work under the contract;

    (b) the intervals at which, or circumstances in which, such payments become due under that contract; or

    (c) both of the matters mentioned in sub-paragraphs (a) and (b),

the relevant provisions of paragraphs 2 to 4 shall apply.

2. (1) The amount of any payment by way of instalments or stage or periodic payments in respect of a relevant period shall be the difference between the amount determined in accordance with sub-paragraph (2) and the amount determined in accordance with sub-paragraph (3).

(2) The aggregate of the following amounts:—

(*a*) an amount equal to the value of any work performed in accordance with the relevant construction contract during the period from the commencement of the contract to the end of the relevant period (excluding any amount calculated in accordance with head (*b*));

(*b*) where the contract provides for payment for materials, an amount equal to the value of any materials manufactured on site or brought onto site for the purposes of the works during the period from the commencement of the contract to the end of the relevant period; and

(*c*) any other amount or sum which the contract specifies shall be payable during or in respect of the period from the commencement of the contract to the end of the relevant period.

(3) The aggregate of any sums which have been paid or are due for payment by way of instalments, stage or periodic payments during the period from the commencement of the contract to the end of the relevant period.

(4) An amount calculated in accordance with this paragraph shall not exceed the difference between—

(*a*) the contract price; and

(*b*) the aggregate of the instalments or stage or periodic payments which have become due.

Dates for payment

3. Where the parties to a construction contract fail to provide an adequate mechanism for determining either what payments become due under the contract, or when they become due for payment, or both, the relevant provisions of paragraphs 4 to 7 shall apply.

4. Any payment of a kind mentioned in paragraph 2 above shall become due on whichever of the following dates occurs later—

(*a*) the expiry of seven days following the relevant period mentioned in paragraph 2(1); or

(*b*) the making of a claim by the payee.

5. The final payment payable under a relevant construction contract, namely the payment of an amount equal to the difference (if any) between—

(*a*) the contract price; and

(*b*) the aggregate of any instalment or stage or periodic payments which have become due under the contract,

shall become due on—

(*i*) the expiry of thirty days following completion of the work; or

(*ii*) the making of a claim by the payee,

whichever is the later.

6. Payment of the contract price under a construction contract (not being a relevant construction contract) shall become due on—

(*a*) the expiry of thirty days following the completion of the work; or

(*b*) the making of a claim by the payee,

whichever is the later.

7. Any other payment under a construction contract shall become due on—

(*a*) the expiry of seven days following the completion of the work to which the payment relates; or

(*b*) the making of a claim by the payee,

whichever is the later.

Final date for payment

8. (1) Where the parties to a construction contract fail to provide a final date for payment in relation to any sum which becomes due under a construction contract, the provisions of this paragraph shall apply.

(2) The final date for the making of any payment of a kind mentioned in paragraphs 2, 5, 6 or 7 shall be 17 days from the date that payment becomes due.

Notice specifying amount of payment

9. A party to a construction contract shall, not later than 5 days after the date on which any payment—

(*a*) becomes due from him; or

(*b*) would have become due, if—

    (*i*) the other party had carried out his obligations under the contract; and

    (*ii*) no set-off or abatement was permitted by reference to any sum claimed to be due under one or more other contracts,

give notice to the other party to the contract specifying the amount (if any) of the payment he has made or proposes to make, specifying to what the payment relates and the basis on which that amount is calculated.

Notice of intention to withhold payment

10. Any notice of intention to withhold payment mentioned in section 111 of the Act shall be given not later than the prescribed period, which is to say not later than seven days before the final date for payment determined either in accordance with the construction contract or, where no such provision is made in the contract, in accordance with paragraph 8.

Prohibition of conditional payment provisions

11. Where a provision making payment under a construction contract conditional on the payer receiving payment from a third person is ineffective as mentioned in section 113 of the Act and the parties have not agreed other terms for payment, the relevant provisions of—

(*a*) paragraphs 2, 4, 5 and 7 to 10 shall apply in the case of a relevant construction contract; and

(*b*) paragraphs 6 to 10 shall apply in the case of any other construction contract.

Interpretation

12. In this Part—

"claim by the payee" means a written notice given by the party carrying out work under a construction contract to the other party specifying the amount of any payment or payments which he considers to be due, specifying to what the payment relates (or payments relate) and the basis on which it is, or they are, calculated;

"contract price" means the entire sum payable under the construction contract in respect of the work;

"relevant construction contract" means any construction contract other than one—

(*a*) which specifies that the duration of the work is to be less than 45 days; or

(*b*) in respect of which the parties agree that the duration of the work is estimated to be less than 45 days;

"relevant period" means a period which is specified in, or is calculated by reference to, the construction contract or, where no such period is so specified or is so calculable, a period of 28 days;

"value of work" means an amount determined in accordance with the construction contract under which the work is performed or, where the contract contains no such provision, the cost of any work performed in accordance with that contract together with an amount equal to any overhead or profit included in the contract price;

"work" means any of the work or services mentioned in section 104 of the Act.

Explanatory Note
(This note is not part of the Regulations)

Part II of the Housing Grants, Construction and Regeneration Act 1996 makes provision in relation to construction contracts. Section 114 empowers the Lord Advocate to make the Scheme for Construction Contracts (as regards Scotland). Where a construction contract does not comply with the requirements of sections 108 to 111 (adjudication of disputes and payment provisions), and section 113 (prohibition of conditional payment provisions), the relevant provisions of the Scheme for Construction Contracts have effect.

The Scheme which is contained in the Schedule to these Regulations is in two parts. Part I provides for the selection and appointment of an adjudicator, gives powers to the adjudicator to gather and consider information, and makes provisions in respect of his decisions. Part II makes provision with respect to payments under a construction contract where either the contract fails to make provision or the parties fail to agree—

(*a*) the method for calculating the amount of any instalment, stage or periodic payment;

(*b*) the due date and the final date for payments to be made; and

(*c*) the prescribed period within which a notice of intention to withhold payment must be given.

Appendix 4

The Construction Contracts (England and Wales) Exclusion Order 1998

The text of the above is reproduced below.

Citation, commencement and extent

1. (1) This Order may be cited as the Construction Contracts (England and Wales) Exclusion Order 1998 and shall come into force at the end of the period of 8 weeks beginning with the day on which it is made ("the commencement date").

(2) This Order shall extend to England and Wales only.

Interpretation

2. In this Order, "Part II" means Part II of the Housing Grants, Construction and Regeneration Act 1996.

Agreements under statute

3. A construction contract is excluded from the operation of Part II if it is—

(*a*) an agreement under section 38 (power of highway authorities to adopt by agreement) or section 278 (agreements as to execution of works) of the Highways Act 1980[1];

---

1   1980 c.66: section 38 was amended by and section 278 substituted by the New Roads and Street Works Act 1991 (c.22) sections 22 and 23.

(b) an agreement under section 106 (planning obligations), 106A (modification or discharge of planning obligations) or 299A (Crown planning obligations) of the Town and Country Planning Act 1990[2];

(c) an agreement under section 104 of the Water Industry Act 1991[3] (agreements to adopt sewer, drain or sewage disposal works); or

(d) an externally financed development agreement within the meaning of section 1 of the National Health Service (Private Finance) Act 1997[4] (powers of NHS Trusts to enter into agreements).

Private finance initiative

4. (1) A construction contract is excluded from the operation of Part II if it is a contract entered into under the private finance initiative, within the meaning given below.

(2) A contract is entered into under the private finance initiative if all the following conditions are fulfilled—

(a) it contains a statement that it is entered into under that initiative or, as the case may be, under a project applying similar principles;

(b) the consideration due under the contract is determined at least in part by reference to one or more of the following—

(i) the standards attained in the performance of a service, the provision of which is the principal purpose or one of the principal purposes for which the building or structure is constructed;

(ii) the extent, rate or intensity of use of all or any part of the building or structure in question; or

---

2 1990 c.8: section 106 was substituted and the other sections inserted by section 12 of the Planning and Compensation Act 1991 (c.34).

3 1991 c.56.

4 1997 c.56.

      (*iii*)   the right to operate any facility in connection with the building or structure in question; and

  (*c*) one of the parties to the contract is—

      (*i*)   a Minister of the Crown;

      (*ii*)   a department in respect of which appropriation accounts are required to be prepared under the Exchequer and Audit Departments Act 1866[5];

      (*iii*)   any other authority or body whose accounts are required to be examined and certified by or are open to the inspection of the Comptroller and Auditor General by virtue of an agreement entered into before the commencement date or by virtue of any enactment;

      (*iv*)   any authority or body listed in Schedule 4 to the National Audit Act 1983[6] (nationalised industries and other public authorities);

      (*v*)   a body whose accounts are subject to audit by auditors appointed by the Audit Commission;

      (*vi*)   the governing body or trustees of a voluntary school within the meaning of section 31 of the Education Act 1996[7] (county schools and voluntary schools), or

      (*vii*)   a company wholly owned by any of the bodies described in paragraphs (*i*) to (*v*).

---

5   1866 c.39.

6   1983 c.44: amended by the Telecommunication Act 1984; (c.12) Schedule 7, Part III, the Oil and Pipelines Act 1985 (c.12) Schedule 4, Part II; the Broadcasting Act 1990, (c.42) Schedule 20, paragraph 36, S.I. 1991/510, article 5(4) and the Coal Industry Act 1994, (c.21) Schedule 9, paragraph 29.

7   1996 c.56.

Finance agreements

5. (1) A construction contract is excluded from the operation of Part II if it is a finance agreement, within the meaning given below.

(2) A contract is a finance agreement if it is any one of the following—

(a) any contract of insurance;

(b) any contract under which the principal obligations include the formation or dissolution of a company, unincorporated association or partnership;

(c) any contract under which the principal obligations include the creation or transfer of securities or any right or interest in securities;

(d) any contract under which the principal obligations include the lending of money;

(e) any contract under which the principal obligations include an undertaking by a person to be responsible as surety for the debt or default of another person, including a fidelity bond, advance payment bond, retention bond or performance bond.

Development agreements

6. (1) A construction contract is excluded from the operation of Part II if it is a development agreement, within the meaning given below.

(2) A contract is a development agreement if it includes provision for the grant or disposal of a relevant interest in the land on which take place the principal construction operations to which the contract relates.

(3) In paragraph (2) above, a relevant interest in land means—

(a) a freehold; or

(b) a leasehold for a period which is to expire no earlier than 12 months after the completion of the construction operations under the contract.

Explanatory Note

(This note is not part of the Order)

Part II of the Housing Grants, Construction and Regeneration Act 1996 makes provision in relation to the terms of construction contracts. Section 106 confers power on the Secretary of State to exclude descriptions of contracts from the operation of Part II. This Order excludes contracts of four descriptions.

Article 3 excludes agreements made under specified statutory provisions dealing with highways works, planning obligations, sewage works and externally financed NHS Trust agreements. Article 4 excludes agreements entered into by specified public bodies under the private finance initiative (or a project applying similar principles). Article 5 excludes agreements which primarily relate to the financing of works. Article 6 excludes development agreements, which contain provision for the disposal of an interest in land.

Appendix 5

The Construction Contracts (Scotland) Exclusion Order 1998

Citation, commencement and extent

1. (1) This Order may be cited as the Construction Contracts (Scotland) Exclusion Order 1998 and shall come into force at the end of the period of 8 weeks beginning with the day on which it is made.

   (2) This Order shall extend to Scotland only.

Interpretation

2. In this Order, "Part II" means Part II of the Housing Grants, Construction and Regeneration Act 1996.

Agreements under statute

3. A construction contract is excluded from the operation of Part II if it is—

   (a) an agreement under section 48 (contributions towards expenditure on constructing or improving roads) of the Roads (Scotland) Act 1984[1];

   (b) an agreement under section 75 (agreements regulating development or use of land) or 246 (agreements relating to

---

1   1984 c.54.

Crown land) of the Town and Country Planning (Scotland) Act 1997[2];

(c) an agreement under section 8 (agreements as to provision of sewers, etc. for new premises) of the Sewerage (Scotland) Act 1968[3]; or

(d) an externally financed development agreement within the meaning of section 1 (powers of NHS Trusts to enter into agreements) of the National Health Service (Private Finance) Act 1997[4].

Private finance initiative

4. (1) A construction contract is excluded from the operation of Part II if it is a contract entered into under the private finance initiative, within the meaning given below.

(2) A contract is entered into under the private finance initiative if all the following conditions are fulfilled:

(a) it contains a statement that it is entered into under that initiative or, as the case may be, under a project applying similar principles;

(b) the consideration due under the contract is determined at least in part by reference to one or more of the following:

(i) the standards attained in the performance of a service, the provision of which is the principal purpose or one of the principal purposes for which the building or structure is constructed;

(ii) the extent, rate or intensity of use of all or any part of the building or structure in question; or

(iii) the right to operate any facility in connection with the building or structure in question; and

(c) one of the parties to the contract is—

---

2   1997 c.8.
3   1968 c.47.
4   1997 c.56.

(*i*)   a Minister of the Crown;

(*ii*) a department in respect of which appropriation accounts are required to be prepared under the Exchequer and Audit Departments Act 1866[5];

(*iii*) any other authority or body whose accounts are required to be examined and certified by or are open to the inspection of the Comptroller and Auditor General by virtue of an agreement entered into before the date on which this Order comes into force, or by virtue of any enactment;

(*iv*) any authority or body listed in Schedule 4 (nationalised industries and other public authorities) to the National Audit Act 1983[6];

(*v*)   a body whose accounts are subject to audit by auditors appointed by the Accounts Commission for Scotland;

(*vi*) a water and sewerage authority established under section 62 (new water and sewerage authorities) of the Local Government etc. (Scotland) Act 1994[7];

(*vii*) the board of management of a self-governing school within the meaning of section 1(3) (duty of Secretary of State to maintain self-governing schools) of the Self-Governing Schools, etc. (Scotland) Act 1989[8]; or

(*viii*) a company wholly owned by any of the bodies described in heads (*i*) to (*v*) above.

---

5   1866 c.39.

6   1983 c.44: amended by the Telecommunications Act 1984 (c.12), Schedule 7, Part III; the Oil and Pipelines Act 1985 (c.12), Schedule 4, Part II; the Broadcasting Act 1990 (c.42), Schedule 20, paragraph 36, S.I. 1991/510, article 5(4) and the Coal Industry Act 1994 (c.21), Schedule 9, paragraph 29.

7   1994 c.39.

8   1989 c.39.

Finance agreements

5. (1) A construction contract is excluded from the operation of Part II if it is a finance agreement, within the meaning given below.

   (2) A contract is a finance agreement if it is any one of the following:

   (*a*) any contract of insurance;

   (*b*) any contract under which the principal obligations include the formation or dissolution of a company, unincorporated association or partnership;

   (*c*) any contract under which the principal obligations include the creation or transfer of securities or any right or interest in securities;

   (*d*) any contract under which the principal obligations include the lending of money;

   (*e*) any contract under which the principal obligations include an undertaking by a person to be responsible as surety for the debt or default of another person, including a fidelity bond, advance payment bond, retention bond or performance bond.

Development agreements

6. (1) A construction contract is excluded from the operation of Part II if it is a development agreement, within the meaning given below.

   (2) A contract is a development agreement if it includes provision for the grant or disposal of a relevant interest in the land on which take place the principal construction operations to which the contract relates.

   (3) In paragraph (2) above, a relevant interest in land means—

   (*a*) ownership; or

   (*b*) a tenant's interest under a lease for a period which is to expire no earlier than 12 months after the completion of the construction operations under the contract.

Explanatory note
(This note is not part of the Order)

Part II of the Housing Grants, Construction and Regeneration Act 1996 makes provision in relation to the terms of construction contracts. Section 106 confers power on the Secretary of State to exclude descriptions of contracts from the operation of Part II. This Order excludes, as regards Scotland, contracts of four descriptions.

Article 3 excludes agreements made under specified statutory provisions dealing with works relating to roads, planning obligations, sewerage works and externally financed NHS Trust agreements. Article 4 excludes agreements entered into by specified public bodies under the private finance initiative (or a project applying similar principles). Article 5 excludes agreements which primarily relate to the financing of works. Article 6 excludes development agreements, which contain provision for the disposal of an interest in land.

Appendix 6

Amendments to the ICE Conditions of Contract 6th Edition to take into account The Housing Grants, Construction and Regeneration Act 1996 (Part II)

The Sponsoring Bodies of the Conditions of Contract and Forms of Tender, Agreement, Bond, and Contract Schedule for use in connection with Works of Civil Engineering Construction have approved amendments to cover the introduction of the Housing Grants, Construction and Regeneration Act 1996 ("the Act").

It is recommended that these amendments are incorporated into the ICE Conditions of Contract 6th Edition (January 1991), the Corrigenda (August 1993), Guidance Note (March 1995) and Amendments (Reference ICE/6th Edition/Tax/February 1998). The 6th Edition was reprinted in November 1995 and November 1997.

Notes for Guidance

Clause 60
Payment Provisions
The payment provisions have been amended to take account of the requirements of ss. 109–111 of the Act with respect to timing and the provision of information.

The traditional procedures for payment against interim and final certificates are retained. The date for the commencement of submission of monthly statements under Clause 60(1) is defined as within one month after the Works Commencement Date (s. 109(2)).

Clause 60(2) requires the Engineer to certify within 25 days of delivery of the Contractor's monthly statement, so that payment can take place within 28 days of such delivery. Payments become due upon certification and the "final date for payment" (s. 110(1)(b)) is within 28 days of delivery of the monthly statement. Similar provisions have been inserted in Clause 60(4) with regard to the final account.

Clause 60(9) provides that the Engineer's certificate shall also serve as the Employer's notification to the Contractor of the amount to be paid and its basis of calculation (s. 110(2)), the words of the Section now appearing in the Clause. In sending the certificate to the Contractor "on the Employer's behalf" the Engineer is acting as the Employer's agent for this purpose. The certificate must be issued at least three days before the "final date for payment" (s. 110(1)).

Clause 60(10) requires the Employer to notify the Contractor if payment is to differ from that certified not less than one day before the "final date for payment" (i.e. not later than the 27th day after delivery of the monthly statement (s. 111)). Failure to pay in full in the absence of such timely notice may entitle the Contractor to suspend performance for non-payment (s. 112).

Clause 66

The purpose of the revised Clause is to overcome where possible the causes of disputes and in those cases where disputes are likely still to arise to facilitate their clear definition and early resolution preferably by agreement. Where agreement is not reached the procedure set out in Clause 66 shall apply for the avoidance and settlement of disputes.

Reference on dissatisfaction

Clause 66(2) provides that if at any time the Employer or the Contractor is dissatisfied with any decision opinion instruction direction certificate or valuation of the Engineer or with any other matter in connection with or arising out of the Contract or the carrying out of the Works the matter has to be referred to and settled by the Engineer.

If either party is dissatisfied with the Engineer's decision or if a decision has not been given within the time allowed either party may serve a Notice of Dispute.

Settlement of disputes

The disputes procedure now includes options for conciliation or adjudication before there is a reference to arbitration. It is anticipated that most disputes or differences will be dealt with as soon as possible after they arise. With the potential for the prompt settlement of many minor disputes or differences that can arise on a Contract this should lead to considerable savings in time and cost.

After service of a Notice of Dispute the dispute can be considered under the provisions of the Institution of Civil Engineers' Conciliation Procedure 1994 or, after Notice of Adjudication has been given, may be referred to an adjudicator under the terms of the contract.

These two alternatives provide a route to a speedy settlement of most disputes.

If the recommendation of a conciliator or the decision of an adjudicator is not acceptable to either party, or if the parties at any time so decide, the dispute may be referred directly to arbitration by one party serving on the other party a written Notice to Refer. The reference shall be conducted in accordance with the procedure set out in the Appendix to the Form of Tender or any amendment or modification being in force at the time of the appointment of the arbitrator.

Adjudication

In accordance with the Act an adjudicator is empowered to deal with disputes arising under the Contract.

The statutory requirements set out in ss. 108(1) to 108(4) of the Act appear in Clause 66(6). The Contract incorporates by reference the ICE Adjudication Procedure (1997) (or any amendment or modification in force at the time of the Notice of Adjudication).

Following a Notice of Adjudication, 7 days are allowed for appointing the adjudicator and referring the dispute to him, whereupon he is given 28 days (or such other period as may be permitted) in which to reach his decision.

Once a decision has been reached and notified to the parties it becomes binding unless and until the dispute (not the decision) is referred to arbitration.

A failure to give effect to a decision is excluded from the arbitration agreement leaving the parties free to seek enforcement through the courts.

If a dispute on which a decision has been given is not referred to arbitration by issuing a Notice to Refer under Clause 66(9) within three months of the giving of the decision, that decision becomes final as well as binding and cannot thereafter be challenged.

Consequential Amendments

Save for the deletion of Clause 2(7) and some re-numbering of Clauses, the only small consequential amendment is that Clause 1(6) includes the substance of s. 107, in particular s. 107(6). The addition to Clause 44(1) meets the requirements of s. 112 of the Act. Also as a consequence of the Arbitration Act 1996 coming into force, Clause 67 has been suitably amended.

CCSJC opinions

The ICE Conditions of Contract Standing Joint Committee is constituted of members appointed by the sponsors of the ICE Conditions of Contract: The Institution of Civil Engineers, The Association of Consulting Engineers and The Civil Engineering Contractors Association[1], and its function is to keep the use of the ICE Forms of Contract under review. The Terms of Reference of the CCSJC exclude the provision of any legal interpretation.

Amendments to the ICE Conditions of Contract 6th Edition

Clause 1. Definitions and interpretation
Delete existing Clause 1(6) and insert new Clause 1(6) below:

Communications in writing
"(6) Communications which under the Contract are required to be "in writing" may be handwritten typewritten or printed and sent by hand post telex cable facsimile or other means resulting in a permanent record."

Clause 2. Engineer and Engineer's Representative
Delete existing Clause 2(7) and renumber existing Clause 2(8) to 2(7).

Clause 44. Commencement time and delays
Renumber existing Clause 44(1)(e) to 44(1)(f) and insert new 44(1)(e):
"(e) any delay impediment prevention or default by the Employer or"

Clause 60. Certificates and payment
Delete the existing first paragraph of Clause 60(1) and replace with new first paragraph below:
"(1) Unless otherwise agreed the Contractor shall submit to the Engineer at monthly intervals commencing within one month after the Works Commencement Date a statement (in such form if any as may be prescribed in the Specification) showing"
Delete existing Clause 60(2) and replace with new Clause 60(2) below:
"**Monthly payments**
(2) Within 25 days of the date of delivery of the Contractor's monthly statement to the Engineer or the Engineer's Repre-

sentative in accordance with sub-clause (1) of this clause the Engineer shall certify and within 28 days of the same date the Employer shall pay to the Contractor (after deducting any previous payments on account)

(*a*) the amount which in the opinion of the Engineer on the basis of the monthly statement is due to the Contractor on account of sub-clauses (1)(*a*) and (1)(*d*) of this Clause less a retention as provided in sub-clause (5) of this Clause and

(*b*) such amounts (if any) as the Engineer may consider proper (but in no case exceeding the percentage of the value stated in the Appendix to the Form of Tender) in respect of sub-clauses (1)(*b*) and (1)(*c*) of this Clause.

The payments become due on certification with the final date for payment being 28 days after the date of delivery of the Contractor's monthly statement.

The amounts certified in respect of Nominated Sub-contracts shall be shown separately in the certificate."

Delete the existing last paragraph of Clause 60(4) and replace with a new last paragraph below:

"Such amount shall subject to Clause 47 be paid to or by the Contractor as the case may require. The payment becomes due on certification. The final date for payment is 28 days later."

Delete the existing first paragraph of Clause 60(6)(*c*) and replace with a new first paragraph below:

"(*c*) At the end of the Defects Correction Period or if more than one the last of such periods the final date for payment of the remainder of the retention money to be paid to the Contractor is 14 days later notwithstanding that at that time there may be outstanding claims by the Contractor against the Employer."

Delete existing Clauses 60(9) and (10) and replace with new Clauses 60(9) and (10) below:

"Certificates and payment notices

(9) Every certificate issued by the Engineer pursuant to this Clause shall be sent to the Employer and on the Employer's behalf to the Contractor. By this certificate the Employer shall give

notice to the Contractor specifying the amount (if any) of the payment proposed to be made and the basis on which it was calculated.

Notice of intention to withhold payment

(10) Where a payment under Clause 60(2) or (4) is to differ from that certified or the Employer is to withhold payment after the final date for payment of a sum due under the Contract the Employer shall notify the Contractor in writing not less than one day before the final date for payment specifying the amount proposed to be withheld and the ground for withholding payment or if there is more than one ground each ground and the amount attributable to it."

Clause 66. Avoidance and settlement of disputes

Delete existing Clauses 66(1)–(9) and replace with new Clauses 66(1)–(12) below:

"Avoidance of disputes

(1) In order to overcome where possible the causes of disputes and in those cases where disputes are likely still to arise to facilitate their clear definition and early resolution (whether by agreement or otherwise) the following procedure shall apply for the avoidance and settlement of disputes.

Matters of dissatisfaction

(2) If at any time
   (a) the Contractor is dissatisfied with any act or instruction of the Engineer's Representative or any other person responsible to the Engineer or
   (b) the Employer or the Contractor is dissatisfied with any decision opinion instruction direction certificate or valuation of the Engineer or with any other matter arising under or in connection with the Contract or the carrying out of the Works

the matter of dissatisfaction shall be referred to the Engineer who shall notify his written decision to the Employer and the Contractor within one month of the reference to him.

Disputes

(3) The Employer and the Contractor agree that no matter shall constitute nor be said to give rise to a dispute unless and until in respect of that matter

    (*a*) the time for the giving of a decision by the Engineer on a matter of dissatisfaction under Clause 66(2) has expired or the decision given is unacceptable or has not been implemented and in consequence the Employer or the Contractor has served on the other and on the Engineer a notice in writing (hereinafter called the Notice of Dispute) or

    (*b*) an adjudicator has given a decision on a dispute under Clause 66(6) and the Employer or the Contractor is not giving effect to the decision, and in consequence the other has served on him and the Engineer a Notice of Dispute

and the dispute shall be that stated in the Notice of Dispute. For the purposes of all matters arising under or in connection with the Contract or the carrying out of the Works the word "dispute" shall be construed accordingly and shall include any difference.

(4) (*a*) Notwithstanding the existence of a dispute following the service of a Notice under Clause 66(3) and unless the Contract has already been determined or abandoned the Employer and the Contractor shall continue to perform their obligations.

    (*b*) The Employer and the Contractor shall give effect forthwith to every decision of

        (*i*) the Engineer on a matter of dissatisfaction given under Clause 66(2) and

        (*ii*) the adjudicator on a dispute given under Clause 66(6)

    unless and until that decision is revised by agreement of the Employer and Contractor or pursuant to Clause 66.

Conciliation

(5) (*a*) The Employer or the Contractor may at any time before service of a Notice to Refer to arbitration under Clause

66(9) by notice in writing seek the agreement of the other for the dispute to be considered under the Institution of Civil Engineers' Conciliation Procedure (1994) or any amendment or modification thereof being in force at the date of such notice.

(b) If the other party agrees to this procedure any recommendation of the conciliator shall be deemed to have been accepted as finally determining the dispute by agreement so that the matter is no longer in dispute unless a Notice of Adjudication under Clause 66(6) or a Notice to Refer to arbitration under Clause 66(9) has been served in respect of that dispute not later than 1 month after receipt of the recommendation by the dissenting party.

Adjudication

(6) (a) The Employer and the Contractor each has the right to refer a dispute as to a matter under the Contract for adjudication and either party may give notice in writing (hereinafter called the Notice of Adjudication) to the other at any time of his intention so to do. The adjudication shall be conducted under the Institution of Civil Engineers' Adjudication Procedure (1997) or any amendment or modification thereof being in force at the time of the said Notice.

(b) Unless the adjudicator has already been appointed he is to be appointed by a timetable with the object of securing his appointment and referral of the dispute to him within 7 days of such notice.

(c) The adjudicator shall reach a decision within 28 days of referral or such longer period as is agreed by the parties after the dispute has been referred.

(d) The adjudicator may extend the period of 28 days by up to 14 days with the consent of the party by whom the dispute was referred.

(e) The adjudicator shall act impartially.

(*f*)   The adjudicator may take the initiative in ascertaining the facts and the law.

(7)   The decision of the adjudicator shall be binding until the dispute is finally determined by legal proceedings or by arbitration (if the contract provides for arbitration or the parties otherwise agree to arbitration) or by agreement.

(8)   The adjudicator is not liable for anything done or omitted in the discharge or purported discharge of his functions as adjudicator unless the act or omission is in bad faith and any employee or agent of the adjudicator is similarly not liable.

Arbitration

(9)   (*a*)   All disputes arising under or in connection with the Contract or the carrying out of the Works other than failure to give effect to a decision of an adjudicator shall be finally determined by reference to arbitration. The party seeking arbitration shall serve on the other party a notice in writing (called the Notice to Refer) to refer the dispute to arbitration.

(*b*)   Where an adjudicator has given a decision under Clause 66(6) in respect of the particular dispute the Notice to Refer must be served within three months of the giving of the decision otherwise it shall be final as well as binding.

Appointment of arbitrator

(10)   (*a*)   The arbitrator shall be a person appointed by agreement of the parties.

President or Vice-President to act

(*b*)   If the parties fail to appoint an arbitrator within one month of either party serving on the other party a notice in writing (hereinafter called the Notice to Concur) to concur in the appointment of an arbitrator the dispute shall be referred to a person to be appointed on the application of either party by the President for the time being of the Institution of Civil Engineers.

(*c*)   If an arbitrator declines the appointment or after appointment is removed by order of a competent court or is incapable of acting or dies and the parties do not within one month of the vacancy arising fill the vacancy then either party may apply to the President for the time being of the Institution of Civil Engineers to appoint another arbitrator to fill the vacancy.

(d) In any case where the President for the time being of the Institution of Civil Engineers is not able to exercise the functions conferred on him by this Clause the said functions shall be exercised on his behalf by a Vice-President for the time being of the said Institution.

Arbitration – procedure and powers

(11) (a) Any reference to arbitration under this Clause shall be deemed to be a submission to arbitration within the meaning of the Arbitration Act 1996 or any statutory re-enactment or amendment thereof for the time being in force. The reference shall be conducted in accordance with the procedure set out in the Appendix to the Form of Tender or any amendment or modification thereof being in force at the time of the appointment of the arbitrator. Such arbitrator shall have full power to open up review and revise any decision opinion instruction direction certificate or valuation of the Engineer or an adjudicator.

(b) Neither party shall be limited in the arbitration to the evidence or arguments put to the Engineer or to any adjudicator pursuant to Clause 66(2) or 66(6) respectively.

(c) The award of the arbitrator shall be binding on all parties.

(d) Unless the parties otherwise agree in writing any reference to arbitration may proceed notwithstanding that the Works are not then complete or alleged to be complete.

Witnesses

(12) (a) No decision opinion instruction direction certificate or valuation given by the Engineer shall disqualify him from

being called as a witness and giving evidence before a conciliator adjudicator or arbitrator on any matter whatsoever relevant to the dispute.

(b)   All matters and information placed before a conciliator pursuant to a reference under sub-clause (5) of this Clause shall be deemed to be submitted to him without prejudice and the conciliator shall not be called as witness by the parties or anyone claiming through them in connection with any adjudication arbitration or other legal proceedings arising out of or connected with any matter so referred to him".

Clause 67. Application to Scotland and Northern Ireland

Clause 67(2)(b), line 1: delete "Arbitration Acts" and replace with "Arbitration Act 1996"

Clause 67(2)(c), line 2: delete "(1983)" and replace with "(1997)"; line 3, delete "and"

Clause 67(2)(d), line 4: delete "case". and replace with "case and" Insert new Clause 67(2)(e) below:

"(e) where the Employer or the Contractor wishes to register the decision of an adjudicator in the Books of Council and Session for preservation and execution the other party shall on being requested to do so forthwith consent to such registration by subscribing the said decision before a witness".

Clause 67(3): lines 3 and 4, delete all after "Northern Ireland" Delete existing Clause 67(4)

Appendix – Part 1. Form of Tender (Appendix)

Add:

21   The Arbitration Procedure to be used is (Clause 60(11)(a))

(a)   The Institution of Civil Engineers' Arbitration Procedure (1997)[g] or

(b)   The Construction Industry Model Arbitration Rules[g]

[g] Delete as appropriate

Appendix 7

The ICE Adjudication Procedure (1997)

Contents

Acknowledgements

The Adjudication Procedure (1997) has been produced by The Institution of Civil Engineers through its Conciliation and Adjudication Advisory Panel. It was drafted by Mr Brian Totterdill with the assistance of Mr Guy Cottam.

Members of the Conciliation and Adjudication Advisory Panel are

Mr B W Totterdill BSc(Hons)(Eng) CEng FICE FIStructE FIPENZ FCIArb MAE FFB (Chairman)

Mr D Carrick FInstCES FCIArb MAE MCIPS

Mr G D G Cottam BSc(Eng) CEng FICE FIEI FCIArb MAE

Mr I G Forrest EurIng CEng MICE Dip Arb FCIArb

Mr G F Hawker TD BSc(Eng) FEng FICE CEng FIEI FIStructE MSocIS(France) MConsE FCIArb EurIng Barrister

Mr D G Loosemore CEng MICE ACIArb FInstCES

Mr T W Weddell BSc CEng DIC FICE FIStructE ACIArb

ICE Secretariat

Mrs E A Stanton (Secretary)

Mr F N Vernon BSc(Eng) CEng MICE (Technical Adviser)

Although this Procedure (approved November 1997) has been prepared by The Institution of Civil Engineers principally for use with the ICE family of Conditions of Contract it may be suitable for use with other contracts.

The Institution of Civil Engineers'
ADJUDICATION PROCEDURE (1997)

1. General principles

1.1 The adjudication shall be conducted in accordance with the edition of the ICE Adjudication Procedure which is current at the date of issue of a notice in writing of intention to refer a dispute to adjudication (hereinafter called the Notice of Adjudication) and the Adjudicator shall be appointed under the Adjudicator's Agreement which forms a part of this Procedure. If a conflict arises between this Procedure and the Contract then this Procedure shall prevail.

1.2 The object of adjudication is to reach a fair, rapid and inexpensive determination of a dispute arising under the Contract and this Procedure shall be interpreted accordingly.

1.3 The Adjudicator shall be a named individual and shall act impartially.

1.4 In making a decision, the Adjudicator may take the initiative in ascertaining the facts and the law. The adjudication shall be neither an expert determination nor an arbitration but the Adjudicator may rely on his own expert knowledge and experience.

1.5 The Adjudicator's decision shall be binding until the dispute is finally determined by legal proceedings, by arbitration (if the Contract provides for arbitration or the Parties otherwise agree to arbitration), or by agreement.

1.6 The Parties shall implement the Adjudicator's decision without delay whether or not the dispute is to be referred to legal proceedings or arbitration. Payment shall be made in accordance with the payment provisions in the Contract, in the next stage payment which becomes due after the date of issue of the decision, unless otherwise directed by the Adjudicator or unless the decision is in relation to an effective notice under Section 111(4) of the Act.

2. The Notice of Adjudication

2.1 Any Party may give notice at any time of its intention to refer a dispute arising under the Contract to adjudication by giving a written Notice of Adjudication to the other Party. The Notice of Adjudication shall include:

(*a*) the details and date of the Contract between the Parties;

(*b*) the issues which the Adjudicator is being asked to decide;

(*c*) details of the nature and extent of the redress sought.

3. The appointment of the Adjudicator

3.1 Where an Adjudicator has either been named in the Contract or agreed by the Parties prior to the issue of the Notice of Adjudication, the Party issuing the Notice of Adjudication shall at the same time send to the Adjudicator a copy of the Notice of Adjudication and a request for confirmation, within four days of the date of issue of the Notice of Adjudication, that the Adjudicator is able and willing to act.

3.2 Where an Adjudicator has not been so named or agreed, the Party issuing the Notice of Adjudication may include with the Notice the names of one or more persons with their addresses who have agreed to act, any one of whom would be acceptable to the referring Party, for selection by the other Party. The other Party shall select and notify the referring Party and the selected Adjudicator within four days of the date of issue of the Notice of Adjudication.

3.3 If confirmation is not received under paragraph 3.1 or a selection is not made under paragraph 3.2 or the Adjudicator does not accept or is unable to act, then either Party may within a further three days request the person or body named in the Contract or if none is so named The Institution of Civil Engineers to appoint the Adjudicator. Such request shall be in writing on the appropriate form of application for the appointment of an adjudicator and accompanied by a copy of the Notice of Adjudication and the appropriate fee.

3.4 The Adjudicator shall be appointed on the terms and conditions set out in the attached Adjudicator's Agreement and Schedule and shall be entitled to be paid a reasonable fee together with his expenses. The Parties shall sign the agreement within seven days of being requested to do so.

3.5 If for any reason whatsoever the Adjudicator is unable to act, either Party may require the appointment of a replacement adjudicator in accordance with the procedure in paragraph 3.3.

4. Referral

4.1 The referring Party shall within two days of receipt of confirmation under 3.1, or notification of selection under 3.2, or appointment under 3.3 send to the Adjudicator, with a copy to the other Party, a full statement of his case which should include:

(*a*) a copy of the Notice of Adjudication;

(*b*) a copy of any adjudication provision in the Contract, and

(*c*) the information upon which he relies, including supporting documents.

4.2 The date of referral of the dispute to adjudication shall be the date upon which the Adjudicator receives the documents referred to in paragraph 4.1. The Adjudicator shall notify the Parties forthwith of that date.

5. Conduct of the adjudication

5.1 The Adjudicator shall reach his decision within 28 days of referral, or such longer period as is agreed by the Parties after the dispute has been referred. The period of 28 days may be extended by up to 14 days with the consent of the referring Party.

5.2 The Adjudicator shall determine the matters set out in the Notice of Adjudication, together with any other matters which the Parties and the Adjudicator agree should be within the scope of the adjudication.

5.3 The Adjudicator may open up, review and revise any decision (other than that of an adjudicator unless agreed by the Parties), opinion, instruction, direction, certificate or valuation made under or in connection with the Contract and which is relevant to the dispute. He may order the payment of a sum of money, or other redress but no decision of the Adjudicator shall affect the freedom of the Parties to vary the terms of the Contract or the Engineer or other authorised person to vary the Works in accordance with the Contract.

5.4 The other Party may submit his response to the statement under paragraph 4.1 within 14 days of referral. The period of response may be extended by agreement between the Parties and the Adjudicator.

5.5 The Adjudicator shall have complete discretion as to how to conduct the adjudication, and shall establish the procedure and timetable, subject to any limitation that there may be in the Contract or the Act. He shall not be required to observe any rule of evidence, procedure or otherwise, of any court. Without prejudice to the generality of these powers, he may:

(a) ask for further written information;

(b) meet and question the Parties and their representatives;

(c) visit the site;

(d) request the production of documents or the attendance of people whom he considers could assist;

(e) set times for (a)–(d) and similar activities;

(f) proceed with the adjudication and reach a decision even if a Party fails:

(i) to provide information;

(ii) to attend a meeting;

(iii) to take any other action requested by the Adjudicator;

(g) issue such further directions as he considers to be appropriate.

5.6 The Adjudicator may obtain legal or technical advice having first notified the Parties of his intention.

5.7 Any Party may at any time ask that additional Parties shall be joined in the Adjudication. Joinder of additional Parties shall be subject to the agreement of the Adjudicator and the existing and additional Parties. An additional Party shall have the same rights and obligations as the other Parties, unless otherwise agreed by the Adjudicator and the Parties.

6. The Decision

6.1 The Adjudicator shall reach his decision and so notify the Parties within the time limits in paragraph 5.1 and may reach a decision on different aspects of the dispute at different times. He shall not be required to give reasons.

6.2 The Adjudicator may in any decision direct the payment of such simple or compound interest at such rate and between such dates or events as he considers appropriate.

6.3 Should the Adjudicator fail to reach his decision and notify the Parties in the due time, either Party may give seven days notice of its intention to refer the dispute to a replacement adjudicator appointed in accordance with the procedures in paragraph 3.3.

6.4 If the Adjudicator fails to reach and notify his decision in due time but does so before the dispute has been referred to a replacement adjudicator under paragraph 6.3, his decision shall still be effective.

If the Parties are not so notified then the decision shall be of no effect and the Adjudicator shall not be entitled to any fees or expenses, but the Parties shall be responsible for the fees and expenses of any legal or technical adviser appointed under paragraph 5.6 subject to the Parties having received such advice.

6.5 The Parties shall bear their own costs and expenses incurred in the adjudication. The Parties shall be jointly and severally responsible for the Adjudicator's fees and expenses, including those of any legal or technical adviser appointed under paragraph 5.6, but in his decision the Adjudicator may direct a Party to pay all or part of his fees and expenses. If he makes no such direction the Parties shall pay them in equal shares.

6.6 At any time until seven days before the Adjudicator is due to reach his decision, he may give notice to the Parties that he will deliver it only on full payment of his fees and expenses. Any Party may then pay these costs in order to obtain the decision and recover the other Party's share of the costs in accordance with paragraph 6.5 as a debt due.

6.7 The Parties shall be entitled to the relief and remedies set out in the decision and to seek summary enforcement thereof, regardless of whether the dispute is to be referred to legal proceedings or arbitration. No issue decided by an adjudicator may subsequently be laid before another adjudicator unless so agreed by the Parties.

6.8 In the event that the dispute is referred to legal proceedings or arbitration, the Adjudicator's decision shall not inhibit the court or arbitrator from determining the Parties' rights or obligations anew.

6.9 The Adjudicator may on his own initiative, or at the request of either Party, correct a decision so as to remove any clerical mistake, error or ambiguity provided that the initiative is taken, or the request is made within 14 days of the notification of the decision to the Parties. The Adjudicator shall make his corrections within seven days of any request by a Party.

7. Miscellaneous provisions

7.1 Unless the Parties agree, the Adjudicator shall not be appointed arbitrator in any subsequent arbitration between the Parties under the Contract. No Party may call the Adjudicator as a witness in any legal proceedings or arbitration concerning the subject matter of the adjudication.

7.2 The Adjudicator shall not be liable for anything done or omitted in the discharge or purported discharge of his functions as Adjudicator unless the act or omission is in bad faith, and any employee or agent of the Adjudicator shall be similarly protected from liability. The Parties shall save harmless and indemnify the Adjudicator and any employee or agent of the Adjudicator against all claims by third parties and in respect of this shall be jointly and severally liable.

7.3 Neither The Institution of Civil Engineers nor its servants or agents shall be liable to any Party for any act, omission or misconduct in connection with any appointment made or any adjudication conducted under this Procedure.

7.4 All notices shall be sent by recorded delivery to the address stated in the Contract for service of notices, or if none, the principal place of business or registered office (in the case of a company). Any agreement required by this Procedure shall be evidenced in writing.

7.5 This Procedure shall be interpreted in accordance with the law of the Contract.

8. Definitions

8.1 (*a*) The "Act" means the Housing Grants, Construction and Regeneration Act 1996.

(*b*) The "Adjudicator" means the person named as such in the Contract or appointed in accordance with this Procedure.

(*c*) "Contract" means the contract or the agreement between the Parties which contains the provision for adjudication.

(*d*) "Party" means a Party to the Contract and references to either Party or the other Party or Parties shall include any additional Party or Parties joined in accordance with this Procedure.

9. Application to particular contracts

9.1 When this Procedure is used with The Institution of Civil Engineers' Agreement for Consultancy Work in Respect of Domestic or Small Works, the Adjudicator may determine any dispute in connection with or arising out of the Contract.

A copy of the appropriate form for applying for the selection/ appointment of an Adjudicator by The Institution of Civil Engineers may be obtained from:

The Dispute Administration Service, The Institution of Civil Engineers, One Great George Street, Westminster, LONDON SW1P 3AA

Telephone: +44 - (0)171 - 222 - 7722
Facsimile: +44 - (0)171 - 222 - 1403.

Adjudicator's agreement

THIS AGREEMENT is made on the .... day of .... 19..
between (the first Party):
of:

and (the second Party):
of:

and (where there is a third Party):
of:

(hereinafter called "the Parties") of the one part and:
of:

(hereinafter called "the Adjudicator") of the other part.

Disputes or differences may arise/have arisen* between the Parties under a
Contract dated .... and
known as:

and these disputes or differences shall be/have been* referred to adjudication in
accordance with The Institution of Civil Engineers' Adjudication Procedure (1997)
(hereinafter called "the Procedure") and the Adjudicator has been requested to
act.
* Delete as necessary
IT IS NOW AGREED as follows:
1. The rights and obligations of the Adjudicator and the Parties shall be as set
    out in the Procedure.
2. The Adjudicator hereby accepts the appointment and agrees to conduct the
    adjudication in accordance with the Procedure.
3. The Parties bind themselves jointly and severally to pay the Adjudicator's fees
    and expenses in accordance with the Procedure as set out in the attached
    Schedule.
4. The Parties and the Adjudicator shall at all times maintain the confidentiality
    of the adjudication and shall endeavour to ensure that anyone acting on their
    behalf or through them will do likewise, save with the consent of the other
    Parties which consent shall not be unreasonably refused.
5. The Adjudicator shall inform the Parties if he intends to destroy the
    documents which have been sent to him in relation to the adjudication and he
    shall retain documents for a further period at the request of either Party.

Signed on behalf of:

First Party:

Name:

Signature:

Date:

Second Party:

Name:

Signature:

Date:

Third Party (where there is a third Party)**:**

Name:

Signature:

Date:

Adjudicator:

Name:

Signature:

Date:

SCHEDULE to the ADJUDICATOR'S AGREEMENT

1. The Adjudicator shall be paid at the hourly rate of £   in respect of all time spent upon, or in connection with, the adjudication including time spent travelling.
2. The Adjudicator shall be reimbursed in respect of all disbursements properly made including, but not restricted to:
   (*a*) Printing, reproduction and purchase of documents, drawings, maps, records and photographs.
   (*b*) Telegrams, telex, faxes, and telephone calls.
   (*c*) Postage and similar delivery charges.
   (*d*) Travelling, hotel expenses and other similar disbursements.
   (*e*) Room charges.
   (*f*) Charges for legal or technical advice obtained in accordance with the Procedure.
3. The Adjudicator shall be paid an appointment fee of £   . This fee shall become payable in equal amounts by each Party within 14 days of the appointment of the Adjudicator. This fee will be deducted from the final statement of any sums which shall become payable under item 1 and/or item 2 of this Schedule. If the final statement is less than the appointment fee the balance shall be refunded to the Parties.
4. The Adjudicator is/is not* currently registered for VAT.
5. Where the Adjudicator is registered for VAT it shall be charged additionally in accordance with the rates current at the date of invoice.
6. All payments, other than the appointment fee (item 3) shall become due seven days after receipt of invoice, thereafter interest shall be payable at 5% per annum above the Bank of England base rate for every day the amount remains outstanding.

   * Delete as necessary

ICE
Dispute
Administration
Service

Application for the selection/appointment of an Adjudicator

Dispute Administration Service
The Institution of Civil Engineers
One Great George Street
Westminster
London SW1P 3AA   Date

The dispute and/or difference described in the attached Notice of Adjudication Reference _____
has arisen and since an Adjudicator has not been agreed between the Parties I/we hereby apply to
you to select/appoint an Adjudicator who has experience in:

     Civil Engineering   Building   Process Engineering *

I/we agree to meet all the reasonable costs incurred by the person selected/appointed by you if I/we
am/are not entitled to make this application in accordance with the agreement between the parties.

I/we enclose a cheque for £_____ + VAT in respect of the charge made by the Institution towards
the administrative cost in connection with this application.

Yours faithfully

For and behalf of:
....

Name:
....

Address:
....

....

                                       *Please delete whichever is not appropriate

Notes

    *1. The Institution will make a selection/appointment upon the application of any person using this form. The validity of the
       application will not be investigated.*

    *2. In making this application the Applicant undertakes to meet the reasonable charges of the person selected/appointed by the
       Institution pursuant to this application should the adjudication not proceed.*

    3. If the validity of the application is challenged then the person appointed and the parties involved must resolve the challenge.

Selection/appointment of an Adjudicator by the Institution of Civil Engineers

To (Name and Address of Applicant):

I hereby select/appoint:

of

Adjudicator for the dispute or difference described in the Notice of Adjudication attached to this application.

Dated:

On behalf of the Institution of Civil Engineers

Copies for information:
The Adjudicator
The Parties (other than the Applicant)

Notice of intention to refer a dispute to adjudication

To: *(Name of Responding Party)*
        (Address of Responding Party)

Date:

Dear Sir

**NOTICE OF ADJUDICATION
(Reference   )**

We consider that a dispute or difference has arisen between us under:

(a)   *(Contract Name:)*
        (Contract Date:)
        (Contract Location:)

(b)   Included as Appendix A are the issues which the Adjudicator is being asked to decide

(c)   Included as Appendix B are the details of the nature and extent of the redress sought

We now give notice that we require this dispute or difference to be referred to adjudication.

To act as Adjudicator the following person(s)

        has been named in the contract and has been sent a copy of this Notice [1]
        has/have agreed to act and is/are proposed for your consideration [2]

Name(s) of Adjudicator(s)
Address

Within 4 days of the date of this Notice

        the named Adjudicator has been requested to confirm he is able and willing to act[1]
        you are required to agree in writing to the appointment[2]

failing which within a further 3 days The Institution of Civil Engineers will be requested to select/appoint the Adjudicator.

Yours faithfully

For and on behalf of
(Referring Party)

1 and 2   Select either option 1 or option 2

Appendix 8

Amendments to 'Blue Form' of Subcontract 1991 (for use with the ICE 6th Edition)

Clause 1

Add new sub-clause 1(1)(h):

"insolvent" has the following meaning. A company becomes insolvent on the making of an administration order against it under Part II of the Insolvency Act 1986, on the appointment of an administrative receiver or a receiver or manager of its property under Chapter I of Part III of that Act, or the appointment of a receiver under Chapter II of that Part, on the passing of a resolution for voluntary winding up without a declaration of solvency under section 89 of that Act, or on the making of a winding-up order under Part IV or V of that Act. A partnership becomes insolvent on the making of a winding-up order against it under any provision of the Insolvency Act 1986 as applied by an order under section 420 of that Act, or when sequestration is awarded on the estate of the partnership under section 12 of the Bankruptcy (Scotland) Act 1895 or the partnership grants a trust deed for its creditors. An individual becomes insolvent on the making of a bankruptcy order against him under Part IX of the Insolvency Act 1986, or on the sequestration of his estate under the Bankruptcy (Scotland) Act 1895 or when he grants a trust deed for his creditors. A company, partnership or individual shall also be treated as insolvent on the occurrence of any event corresponding to those specified above under the law of Northern Ireland or of a country outside the United Kingdom.

Clause 10

Delete Sub-Clause 10(2) and insert the following:

10. (2) (*a*) Subject to the Subcontractor's complying with this sub-clause 10(2), the Contractor shall take all reasonable steps to secure from the Employer such contractual benefits, if any, as may be claimable in accordance with the Main Contract on account of any adverse physical conditions or artificial obstructions that may affect the execution of the Subcontract Works and the Subcontractor shall in sufficient time afford the Contractor all information and assistance that may be requisite to enable the Contractor to claim such benefits.

(*b*) Where the Contractor has claimed additional payment under the Main Contract on account of adverse physical conditions or artificial obstructions affecting the execution of the Subcontract Works and the Engineer has determined a sum due to the Contractor by reason of such conditions or obstructions, the Contractor shall within 28 days from such determination by the Engineer determine and notify in writing to the Subcontractor such proportion of any such sum which it is in all the circumstances fair and reasonable to pay to the Subcontractor. Provided that the Contractor shall have no liability to make any such payment to the Subcontractor to the extent that the Engineer has determined a sum due to the Contractor by reason of adverse physical conditions or artificial obstructions but the Employer is insolvent and has failed to make payment to the Contractor in respect of such determination.

(c) Where the Contractor has claimed an extension of time under the Main Contract on account of adverse physical conditions or artificial obstructions affecting the execution of the Subcontract Works and the Engineer has determined an extension of time to which the Contractor is entitled by reason of such conditions or obstructions, the Contractor shall determine such proportion of any such extension which it is in all the circumstances fair and reasonable to pass on to the Subcontractor.

(d) Save as aforesaid the Contractor shall have no liability to the Subcontractor in respect of any condition, obstruction or circumstance that may affect the execution of the Subcontract Works and the Subcontractor shall be deemed to have satisfied himself as to the correctness and sufficiency of the Price to cover the provision and doing by him of all things necessary for the performance of his obligations under the Subcontract. Provided always that nothing in this Clause shall prevent the Subcontractor claiming for delays in the execution of the Subcontract Works solely by the act or default of the Main Contractor on the ground only that the Main Contractor has no remedy against the Employer for such delay.

Clause 15

Delete existing clause and insert the following:

15. (1) (a) The Subcontractor shall not less than 7 days before the date specified in the First Schedule (the "Specified Date") or otherwise as agreed submit to the Contractor a written statement of the value of all work properly done under the Subcontract and of all materials delivered to the Site for incorporation in the Subcontract Works and if allowable under the Main Contract the value of off-site materials for incorporation in the Subcontract Works at the date of such statement. The statement shall be in such form and contain such details as the Contractor may reasonably require and the value of work done shall be calculated in accordance with the rates and prices, if any, specified in the Subcontract, or if there are no such rates and prices, then by reference to the Price.

(b) The statement submitted by the Subcontractor as provided in the preceding sub-clause shall constitute a "valid statement" for the purposes of this Clause but not otherwise.

(2) (a) The Contractor shall make applications for payment in accordance with the Main Contract and subject to the Subcontractor having submitted a valid statement shall include in such applications claims for the value of work and materials set out in such statement.

(b) In any proceedings instituted by the Contractor against the Employer to enforce payment of monies due under any certificate issued by the Engineer in accordance with the provisions of the Main Contract there shall be included all sums certified and unpaid in respect of the Subcontract Works.

(3) (a) Within 35 days of the Specified Date or otherwise as agreed but subject as hereinafter provided, there shall be due to the Subcontractor in respect of the value of the work and materials if included in a valid statement payment of a sum calculated and determined by the Contractor in accordance with the rates and prices specified in this Subcontract, or by reference to the Price, as the case may require, but subject to a deduction of previous payments

and of retention monies at the rate(s) specified in the Third Schedule hereto until such time as the limit of retention (if any) therein specified has been reached. The Contractor shall notify the Subcontractor in writing of the amount so calculated and determined within 35 days of the Specified Date. The final date for payment shall be 3 days later.

(b) Subject to Clauses 3(4), and 10(3) and 17(3) and as hereinafter provided and without prejudice to any rights which exist at Common Law the Contractor shall be entitled to withhold or defer payment of all or part of any sums otherwise due pursuant to the provisions hereof where:

(i) the amounts or quantities included in any valid statement together with any other sums to which the Subcontractor might otherwise be entitled do not exceed the minimum amount stated in the Third Schedule, or

(ii) the amounts or quantities included in any valid statement together with any sums which are the subject of an application by the Contractor in accordance with Clause 15(2) are insufficient to justify the issue of an interim certificate by the Engineer under the Main Contract, or

(iii) the amounts or quantities included in any valid statement are not certified in full by the Engineer, providing such failure to certify is not due to the act or default of the Contractor, or

(iv) the Contractor has included the amounts or quantities set out in the valid statement in his own statement in accordance with the Main Contract and the Engineer has certified but the Employer is insolvent and has failed to make payment in full to the Contractor in respect of such amounts or quantities, or

(v)   a dispute arises or has arisen between the Subcontractor and the Contractor and/or the Contractor and the Employer involving any question of measurement or quantities or any matter included in any such valid statement.

(c)   Any payment withheld under the provisions of sub-clauses (b) (iii), (iv) or (v) above shall be limited to the extent that the amounts in any valid statement are not certified, not paid by the Employer or are the subject of a dispute as the case may be.

(d)   The provisions of this Clause with regard to the time for payment shall not apply to the amounts or quantities in any valid statement by the Subcontractor which are included in the Contractor's statement of final account to the Employer under the provisions of the Main Contract. In respect of any such amounts or quantities the Contractor shall determine and notify in writing to the Subcontractor the amount due to the Subcontractor, within 28 days of the issue by the Engineer of a certificate stating the amount due to or from the Contractor pursuant to the Main Contract Conditions in respect of the Contractor's statement of final account. Payment of the amount determined by the Contractor shall be due to the Subcontractor upon such determination and notification. The final date for payment shall be 7 days later. Provided that the Contractor shall have no liability to make such payment of such amount to the extent that the Engineer has certified such amount or any part thereof pursuant to the provisions of the Main Contract, but the Employer is insolvent and has failed to make payment in full to the Contractor in respect of such certified amount.

(e) In the event of the Contractor failing to make payment of any sum properly due and payable to the Subcontractor, the Contractor shall pay to the Subcontractor interest on such overdue sum at the rate payable by the Employer to the Contractor under the provisions of the Main Contract. Provided that where the Contractor fails to make payment of any sum properly due and payable to the Subcontractor and where the Engineer has certified such amount or any part thereof pursuant to the provisions of the Main Contract, then to the extent that the Employer is insolvent and has failed to make payment to the Contractor in respect of such certified amount, the Contractor shall have no obligation to pay interest to the Subcontractor.

(f) Notwithstanding sub-clause (e) the Subcontractor shall be paid any interest actually received by the Contractor from the Employer which is attributable to monies due to the Subcontractor.

(4) The Contractor shall have power to omit from any determination of the value of work and materials included in a valid statement the value of any work done, goods or materials supplied or services rendered with which he may for the time being be dissatisfied and for that purpose or for any other reason which to him may seem proper may delete, correct or modify any sum previously determined by him as due for payment to the Subcontractor.

(5) (a) Within 35 days of the issue by the Engineer of a Certificate including an amount in respect of payment to the Contractor of the first half of the retention monies or where the Main Works are to be completed by sections for any section in which

the Subcontract Works are comprised there shall be due to the Subcontractor the first half of the retention monies under this Subcontract and the Contractor shall so notify the Subcontractor in writing. The final day for payment shall be 7 days later. Provided that the Contractor shall have no liability to make such payment if the Employer is insolvent and has failed to release the first half of the retention monies due under the Main Contract.

(b) Within 28 days of the date of issue of the Defects Correction Certificate under the Main Contract, there shall be due to the Subcontractor the second half of the retention monies under this Subcontract. The Contractor shall so notify the Subcontractor in writing within the same 28 day period. The final date for payment shall be 7 days later. Provided that the Contractor shall have no liability to make such payment if the Employer is insolvent and has failed to release the second half of the retention monies due under the Main Contract.

(6) Within three months after the Subcontractor has finally performed his obligations under Clause 13 (Outstanding Work and Defects), or within 14 days after the Contractor has recovered full payment under the Main Contract in respect of the Subcontract Works, whichever is the sooner and provided that one month has expired since the submission by the Subcontractor of his valid statement of final account to the Contractor, the Contractor shall determine the amount finally due under the Subcontract from the Contractor to the Subcontractor or from the Subcontractor to the Contractor as the case may be, after giving credit to the Subcontractor for the Price and/or any other sums that may have become due under the Subcontract and after giving credit to the Contractor for all amounts previously paid

by the Contractor and for all sums to which the Contractor is entitled under the Subcontract. The Contractor shall notify the Subcontractor in writing of the amount so determined within the same period. The final date for payment shall be 7 days later.

Provided always that if the Contractor shall have been required by the Main Contract to give to the Employer or to procure the Subcontractor to give to the Employer any undertaking as to the completion or maintenance of the Subcontract Works, the Subcontractor shall not be entitled to payment under this Subcontract until he has given a like undertaking to the Contractor or has given the required undertaking to the Employer, as the case may be.

(7)   The Contractor shall not be liable to the Subcontractor for any matter or thing arising out of or in connection with this Subcontract or the carrying out of the Subcontract Works unless the Subcontractor has made written claim in respect thereof to the Contractor before the Engineer issues the Defects Correction Certificate in respect of the Main Works, or, where under the Main Contract the Main Works are to be completed by sections, the Defects Correction Certificate in respect of the last of such sections in which the Subcontract Works are comprised.

(8)   Every written notification given by the Contractor to the Subcontractor of amounts of payments due to the Subcontractor under this Subcontract shall specify the amount (if any) of the payment made or proposed to be made and the basis on which that amount was calculated.

(9)   In the event of the Contractor withholding any payment after any final date for payment hereunder, he shall notify the Subcontractor of his reasons in writing not less than one day before the final date for payment specifying the

amount proposed to be withheld and the ground for withholding payment or if there is more than one ground each ground and the amount attributable to it.

Clause 17
At sub-clause 17(1), after "(1) If: ", add a new sub-clause:
> "(*a*) the Subcontractor is in breach of the Subcontract in suspending performance of his obligations under the Subcontract; or".

Renumber the existing sub-clauses (*a*) to (*e*) as (*b*) to (*f*).

Clause 18
Delete existing Clause and insert the following:

18. (1) If any dispute or difference shall arise between the Contractor and the Subcontractor in connection with or arising out of the Subcontract, or the carrying out of the Subcontract Works (excluding a dispute concerning VAT but including a dispute as to any act or omission of the Engineer) whether arising during the progress of the Subcontract Works or after their completion it shall be settled in accordance with the following provisions.

(2) (*a*) Where the Subcontractor seeks to make a submission that payment is due of any amount exceeding the amount determined by the Contractor as due to the Subcontractor, or that any act, decision, opinion, instruction or direction of the Contractor or any other matter arising under the Subcontract is unsatisfactory, the Subcontractor shall so notify the Contractor in writing, stating the grounds for such submission in sufficient detail for the Contractor to understand and consider the Subcontractor's submission.

(*b*) Where in the opinion of the Contractor such a submission gives rise to a matter of dissatisfaction under the Main Contract, the Contractor shall so notify the Subcontractor in writing as soon as possible. In that event, the Contractor shall pursue the matter of dissatisfaction under the Main Contract promptly and shall keep the Subcontractor fully informed in writing of progress. The Subcontractor shall promptly provide such information and attend such meetings in connection with the matter of dissatisfaction as the Contractor may request. The Contractor and the Subcontractor agree that no such submission shall constitute nor be said to give rise to a dispute under the Subcontract unless and until the Contractor has had the time and opportunity to refer the matter of dissatisfaction to the Engineer under the Main Contract and either the Engineer has given his decision or the time for the giving of a decision by the Engineer has expired.

(3) (*a*) The Contractor or the Subcontractor may at any time before service of a Notice to Refer to arbitration under sub-clause 18(7) by notice in writing seek the agreement of the other for the dispute to be considered under the Institution of Civil Engineers' Conciliation Procedure (1994) or any amendment or modification thereof being in force at the date of such notice.

(*b*) If the other party agrees to this procedure any recommendation of the conciliator shall be deemed to have been accepted as finally determining the dispute by agreement so that the matter is no longer in dispute unless a Notice of Adjudication under sub-clause 18(4) or a Notice to Refer to arbitration under sub-clause 18(7) is served within 28 days of receipt by the dissenting party of the conciliator's recommendation.

(4) (*a*) The Contractor and the Subcontractor each has the right to refer any dispute under the Subcontract for adjudication and either party may at any time give notice in writing (hereinafter called the Notice of Adjudication) to the other at any time of his intention to refer the dispute to adjudication. The Notice of Adjudication and the appointment of the adjudicator shall, save as provided under sub-clause 18(10)(b), be as provided at paragraphs 2 and 3 of the Institution of Civil Engineers' Adjudication Procedure (1997). Any dispute referred to adjudication shall be conducted in accordance with the Institution of Civil Engineers' Adjudication Procedure (1997) or any amendment or modification thereof being in force at the time of the appointment of the adjudicator.

(*b*) Unless the adjudicator has already been appointed he is to be appointed by a timetable with the object of securing his appointment and referral of the dispute to him within 7 days of such notice.

(*c*) The adjudicator shall reach a decision within 28 days of referral or such longer period as is agreed by the parties after the dispute has been referred.

(*d*) The adjudicator may extend the period of 28 days by up to 14 days with the consent of the party by whom the dispute was referred.

(*e*) The adjudicator shall act impartially.

(*f*) The adjudicator may take the initiative in ascertaining the facts and the law.

(5) The decision of the adjudicator shall be binding until the dispute is finally determined by legal proceedings or by arbitration (if the Subcontract provides for arbitration or the parties otherwise agree to arbitration).

(6) The adjudicator shall not be liable for anything done or omitted in the discharge or purported discharge of his

functions as adjudicator unless the act or omission is in bad faith and any employer or agent of the adjudicator shall similarly not be liable.

(7) (*a*) All disputes arising under or in connection with the Subcontract, other than failure to give effect to a decision of an adjudicator, shall be finally determined by reference to arbitration. The party seeking arbitration shall serve on the other party a notice in writing (called the Notice to Refer) to refer the dispute to arbitration.

(*b*) Where an adjudicator has given a decision under sub-clause 18(4) in respect of the particular dispute the Notice to Refer must be served within three months of the giving of the decision, otherwise it shall be final as well as binding.

(*c*) The date upon which the Notice to Refer is served shall be regarded as the date upon which the arbitral proceedings are commenced.

(8) (*a*) The arbitrator shall be a person appointed by agreement of the parties.

(*b*) If the parties fail to appoint an arbitrator within 28 days of either party serving on the other party a notice in writing (hereinafter called the Notice to Concur) to concur in the appointment of an arbitrator the dispute shall be referred to a person to be appointed on the application of either party by the President for the time being of the Institution of Civil Engineers.

(*c*) If an arbitrator declines the appointment or after appointment is removed by order of a competent court or is incapable of acting or dies and the parties do not within one month of the vacancy arising fill the vacancy then either party may apply to the President for the time being of the Institution of

Civil Engineers to appoint another arbitrator to fill the vacancy.

(d) In any case where the President for the time being of the Institution of Civil Engineers is not able to exercise the functions conferred on him by this clause the said functions shall be exercised on his behalf by a Vice-President for the time being of the said Institution.

(9) (a) Any reference to arbitration under this clause shall be deemed to be a submission to arbitration within the meaning of the Arbitration Act 1996 or any statutory re-enactment or amendment thereof for the time being in force. The reference shall be conducted in accordance with the procedure set out in the Second Schedule or any amendment or modification thereof being in force at the time of the appointment of the arbitrator. In the event of any inconsistency between the procedure set out in the Second Schedule and this Clause, this Clause shall prevail.

(b) Neither party shall be limited in the arbitration to evidence or argument put to any adjudicator pursuant to sub-clause 18(4).

(c) The award of the arbitrator shall be binding on the parties.

(d) Unless the parties otherwise agree in writing any reference to arbitration may proceed notwithstanding that the Subcontract Works are not then complete or alleged to be complete.

(e) The arbitrator shall have full power to open up, review and revise any decision, opinion, instruction, direction or valuation of the Contractor or an adjudicator.

(10) (a) If, when a dispute in connection with the Main Contract (hereinafter called a Main Contract

Dispute) is referred to a conciliator or an adjudicator under the Main Contract, and the Contractor is of the opinion that the Main Contract Dispute has any connection with the Subcontract Works then the Contractor may by notice in writing require that the Subcontractor shall as soon as is practicable provide such information and attend such meetings in connection with the Main Contract Dispute as the Contractor may request.

(b) If a Main Contract Dispute has been referred to conciliation or adjudication under the Main Contract and the Contractor is of the opinion that the Main Contract Dispute has any connection with a dispute which is to be (but has not yet been) referred for conciliation or adjudication under this Subcontract (hereinafter called a Connected Dispute), the Contractor may by notice in writing require that the Connected Dispute be referred to the conciliator or adjudicator to whom the Main Contract Dispute has been referred.

(c) If the Contractor is of the opinion that a Main Contract Dispute has any connection with a dispute in connection with the Subcontract (hereinafter called a Related Subcontract Dispute) and the Main Contract Dispute is referred to an arbitrator under the Main Contract, the Contractor may by notice in writing require that the Subcontractor provide such information and attend such meetings in connection with the Main Contract Dispute as the Contractor may request. The Contractor may also by notice in writing require that any Related Subcontract Dispute be dealt with jointly with the Main Contract Dispute and in like manner. In connection with any Related Subcontract Dispute the Subcontractor shall be bound in like manner as the Contractor by any award by an arbitrator in relation to the Main Contract Dispute.

(d) If a dispute arises under or in connection with the Subcontract (hereinafter called a Subcontract Dispute) and the Contractor is of the opinion that the Subcontract Dispute raises a matter or has any connection with a matter which the Contractor wishes to refer to arbitration under the Main Contract, the Contractor may by notice in writing require that the Subcontract Dispute be finally determined jointly with any arbitration to be commenced in accordance with the Main Contract. In connection with the Subcontract Dispute, the Subcontractor shall be bound in like manner as the Contractor by any award by an arbitrator concerning the matter referred to arbitration under the Main Contract.

(11) All matters and information placed before a conciliator pursuant to a reference under sub-clause 18(3) shall be deemed to be submitted to him without prejudice and the conciliator shall not be called as witness by the parties or anyone claiming through them in connection with any adjudication, arbitration or other legal proceedings arising out of or connected with any matter so referred to him.

Second Schedule

Add at end:

(D) Arbitration procedure:*

Add footnote to "Arbitration procedure": "*Insert Main Contract arbitration procedure or other as desired."

Third Schedule

Add after "The Price"[1] a footnote, to read: "[1] Where payment is to be made by reference to the Price, set out here stage payment dates or milestone events."

Add at end:

(D) Minimum payment amount.[2] Add a footnote to read "[2]See Clause 15(3)(b)(i)."

Appendix 9

The New Engineering Contract (NEC) Option Y(UK)2: The Housing Grants, Construction and Regeneration Act 1996 (Addendum)

Y2.1   In this Option

● the Act means The Housing Grants, Construction and Regeneration Act 1996 and

● periods of time stated in days are reckoned in accordance with Section 116 of the Act.

Y2.2   **Clause 51 is amended as follows:**

Clause 51.1   the first sentence is deleted and replaced with the following sentence:

'The *Project Manager* certifies a payment on or before the date on which a payment becomes due.'

Clause 51.2   the first sentence is deleted and replaced with the following sentence:

'Each certified payment is made on or before the final date for payment.'

Y2.3   **The following clauses are added**

Dates for Payment 56

56.1   For the purpose of Sections 109 and 110 of the Act,

- the *Project Manager's* certificate is the notice of payment from the *Employer* to the *Contractor* specifying the amount (if any) of the payment made or proposed to be made, and the basis on which that amount was calculated,
- the date on which a payment becomes due is seven. days after the assessment date and
- the final date for payment is
  - ○ twenty one days or
  - ○ if a different period for payment is stated in the Contract Data, the period stated

  after the date on which the payment becomes due.

56.2 If the *Employer* intends to withhold payment after the final date for payment of a sum due under this contract, he notifies the *Contractor* not later than seven days (the prescribed period) before the final date for payment by specifying

- the amount proposed to be withheld and the ground for withholding payment or
- if there is more than one ground, each ground and the amount attributable to it.

Y2.4   **The following is added to clause 60**

60.7 Suspension of performance is a compensation event if the *Contractor* exercises his right to suspend performance under the Act.

Y2.5   **Clause 90 is deleted and replaced by the following:**

Avoidance and settlement of disputes

90.1 The Parties and the *Project Manager* follow this procedure for the avoidance and settlement of disputes.

90.2 If the *Contractor* is dissatisfied with an action or a failure to take action by the *Project Manager*, he notifies his dissatisfaction to the *Project Manager* no later than

- four weeks after he became aware of the action or
- four weeks after he became aware that the action had not been taken.

Within two weeks of such notification of dissatisfaction, the *Contractor* and the *Project Manager* attend a meeting to discuss and seek to resolve the matter.

90.3 If either Party is dissatisfied with any other matter, he notifies his dissatisfaction to the *Project Manager* and to the other Party no later than four weeks after he became aware of the matter. Within two weeks of such notification of dissatisfaction, the Parties and the *Project Manager* attend a meeting to discuss and seek to resolve the matter.

90.4 The Parties agree that no matter shall be a dispute unless a notice of dissatisfaction has been given and the matter has not been resolved within four weeks. The word dispute (which includes a difference) has that meaning.

90.5 Either Party may give notice to the other Party at any time of his intention to refer a dispute to adjudication. The notifying Party refers the dispute to the *Adjudicator* within seven days of the notice.

90.6 The Party referring the dispute to the *Adjudicator* includes with his submission information to be considered by the *Adjudicator*. Any further information from a Party to be considered by the *Adjudicator* is provided within fourteen days of referral.

90.7 Unless and until the *Adjudicator* has given his decision on the dispute, the Parties and the *Project Manager* proceed as if the action, failure to take action or other matters were not disputed.

90.8 The *Adjudicator* acts impartially. The *Adjudicator* may take the initiative in ascertaining the facts and the law.

90.9   The *Adjudicator* reaches a decision within twenty eight days of referral or such longer period as is agreed by the Parties after the dispute has been referred. The *Adjudicator* may extend the period of twenty eight days by up to fourteen days with the consent of the notifying Party.

90.10   The *Adjudicator* provides his reasons to the Parties and to the *Project Manager* with his decision.

90.11   The decision of the *Adjudicator* is binding until the dispute is finally determined by the *tribunal* or by agreement.

90.12   The *Adjudicator* is not liable for anything done or omitted in the discharge or purported discharge of his functions as adjudicator unless the act or omission is in bad faith and any employee or agent of the *Adjudicator* is similarly protected from liability.

Y2.6   **Clause 91 is amended as follows:**

Side heading: 'The adjudication' is replaced with **'Combining procedures'**

Clause 91.1 is deleted and replaced by the following:

91.1   If a matter causing dissatisfaction under or in connection with a subcontract is also a matter causing dissatisfaction under or in connection with this contract, the subcontractor may attend the meeting between the Parties and the *Project Manager* to discuss and seek to resolve the matter.

Clause 91.2 line 4 'settles' is replaced with 'gives his decision on'

Y2.7   **Clause 92 is amended as follows:**

Clause 92.1 line 1 'settles' is replaced with 'gives his decision on'
Clause 92.2 line 6 'settle' is replaced with 'decide on'
Clause 92.2 line 7 'had not been settled' is replaced with 'a decision had not been given'

Y2.8   **Contract Data Part 1 – Optional statements**

The fifth optional statement is deleted and replaced by the following:

'If the period for payment is not twenty one days

The period within which payments are made is . . . days'

Appendix 10

The Joint Contracts Tribunal (JCT) Adjudication Scheme

Standard Form of Building Contract 1980 Edition
With and Without Quantities versions
(Incorporating Amendments 1 to 13 and 15 and
including Amendments 14, 16 and 17)

Amendment 18
and Guidance Notes

Issued April 1998

Amendments arising out of proposals in
'Constructing the Team'
by Sir Michael Latham (the 'Latham Report') issued July
1994

Amendments to comply with the provisions of the
**Housing Grants, Construction and Regeneration Act
1996: Part II Construction Contracts**

Amendments arising from 1996 Act are marked ●

Contents

Amendment 18 consists of 22 items making the amendments referred to below:

Item Clause etc.

1 **Articles** Addition to Second recital: priced **Activity Schedule.**

Additional recital (Sixth: Fifth in XQ): provision to Contractor of an **Information Release Schedule.**

Additional recital (Seventh: Sixth in XQ): bond terms.

New Article 5: **reference to adjudicator.**

Revised Article 5 re-numbered as Article 7A: disputes or difference – arbitration – 'JCT 1988 edition of the Construction Industry Model Arbitration Rules (CIMAR)' – and as Article 7B – legal proceedings.

2 **1.3** Additional definitions.

3 – New clause 1.5:
Giving or service of notices or other documents.
New clause 1.6:
Reckoning periods of days.
New clause 1.7:
Employer's Representative.
New clause 1.8:
Applicable law.

4 **5.4** Drawings or details:
revised clause – **Information Release Schedule.**

20 **41** New clause 41A: **'Adjudication'**; revised clause 41, re-numbered as clause 41B 'Arbitration', **new clause 41C, 'Legal Proceedings'.**

21 **Appendix** Additional entries pursuant to items 1, 12, 13, 14 and 20.

22 **VAT Agreement** Consequential amendments.

Guidance Notes

followed by:

Example of priced Activity Schedule (see item 13)

Text of JCT Adjudication Agreement

Advice on the choice between arbitration and litigation (see item 20)

Amendments to clause 41A where the parties wish to name an Adjudicator in the Contract (see item 20)

Text of JCT Adjudication Agreement (Named)

1:	Articles of Agreement

At the end of the Second recital **insert:**

[b.2] and has provided the Employer with a priced Activity Schedule;

Insert additional recitals (Fifth and Sixth in XQ):

[b.2] Sixth	the Employer has provided the Contractor with a schedule ('Information Release Schedule') which states what information the Architect will release and the time of that release;
Seventh	if the Employer requires any bond to be on terms other than those agreed between the Joint Contracts Tribunal and the British Bankers' Association the Contractor has been given copies of these terms;

Insert footnote **[b.2]**;

[b.2] Delete if not provided.

● **Insert** as Article 5:

● **Article 5**

Dispute or difference – Adjudication	If any dispute or difference arises under this Contract, either Party may refer it to adjudication in accordance with clause 41A.

Delete the existing Article 5 and **insert** additional Articles 7A and 7B:

Article 7A

Dispute or
difference –
arbitration

Where the entry in the Appendix stating that 'clause 41B applies' has not been deleted then, subject to Article 5, if any dispute or difference as to any matter or thing of whatsoever nature arising under this Contract or in connection therewith, except in connection with the enforcement of any decision of an Adjudicator appointed to determine a dispute or difference arising thereunder, shall arise between the Parties either during the progress or after the completion or abandonment of the Works or after the determination of the employment of the Contractor except under clause 31 (*statutory tax deduction scheme*) to the extent provided in clause 31.9, or under clause 3 of the VAT Agreement, it shall be referred to arbitration in accordance with clause 41B and the JCT 1998 edition of the Construction Industry Model Arbitration Rules (CIMAR). **[g.3]**

Article 7B

Dispute or
difference –
legal
proceedings

Where the entry in the Appendix stating that 'clause 41B applies' has been deleted, then, subject to Article 5, if any dispute or difference as to any matter or thing of whatsoever nature arising under this Contract or in connection therewith shall arise between the Parties either during the progress or after the completion or abandonment of the Works or

after the determination of the employment of the Contractor it shall be
determined by legal proceedings and
clause 41C shall apply to such proceedings.

Use of Amendment 18

Either   amend the Form of Contract in accordance with
Amendment 18 and exe-
cute the Contract as so
amended. Each amend-
ment should be initialled
by or on behalf of the
parties.

or   cut out the following
pages 5 to 31 and attach
to the Form of Contract;
and insert in the Articles
an additional article
which states:

*Article. . .
'Amendment 18 – The conditions shall
incorporation   have effect as
modified by the
amendments in
Amendment 18
attached hereto.'
*Allocate the next
available article
number

If users only wish to incorporate the
amendments which arise from the

Housing Grants, Construction and Regeneration Act 1996: Part II Construction Contracts they should:

Either   amend the Form of Contract in accordance with
Amendment 18 marked
● and execute the Con-
tract as so amended. Each
amendment should be
initialled by or on behalf
of the parties.

or   cut out the following
pages 5 to 31, delete all
amendments not marked
● and insert in the Arti-
cles an additional article
which states:

*Article. . .

'Amendment 18 – The Conditions shall
incorporation   have effect as
modified by the
amendments in
Amendment 18
attached hereto.'
*Allocate the next
available article
number

Insert footnote [g.3]:

[g.3] The JCT 1998 edition of the
Construction industry Model Arbitration Rules (CIMAR) contain procedures
for beginning an arbitration and the

appointment of an arbitrator, the con-
solidation or joinder of disputes including related disputes between different
parties engaged under different contracts
on the same project, and for the conduct
of arbitral proceedings. The objective of
CIMAR is the fair, impartial, speedy,
cost effective and binding resolution of
construction disputes. The JCT 1998
edition of the Construction Industry
Model Arbitration Rules (CIMAR)
includes additional rules concerning
the calling of preliminary meetings and
supplemental and advisory procedures
which may, with the agreement of the
parties, be used with Rules 7 (short
hearing), 8 (documents only) or 9 (full
procedure).

Local Authorities versions only:

in footnote **[c]** **delete** 'Architects
Registration Acts 1931 to 1969' and
insert 'Architects' Act 1997'.

2:	Clause 1.3 **Definitions**

Insert in alphabetical order the following
definitions:

Activity Schedule:	the schedule of activities as attached to the Appendix with each activity priced and with the sum of those prices being the Contract

Sum excluding provisional sums, prime cost sums and any Contractor's profit thereon [and the value of work for which Approximation Quantities are included in the Contract Bills]: **see clause 30.2.1.**

Words in [square brackets] = With Quantities only

● Adjudication see **clause 41A.2.1.**
Agreement:

● Adjudicator: any individual appointed pursuant to **clause 41A** as the Adjudicator.

Information the schedule referred to
Release in the **Sixth recital** or as
Schedule: varied pursuant to **clause 5.4.1.**

● Party: The Employer or the Contractor named as the Employer or the Contractor in the Articles of Agreement.

● Parties: The Employer and the Contractor named as the Employer and the Contractor in the Articles of Agreement.

	Price Statement:	see **clause 13.4.1.2 Alternative A.**
●	Public Holiday:	Christmas Day, Good Friday or a day which under the Banking and Financial Dealings Act 1971 is a bank holiday. **[g.4]**
	Valuation:	A valuation by the Quantity Surveyor pursuant to **clause 13.4.1.2 Alternative B** or the amount of any Price Statement or any part thereof accepted pursuant to **clause 13.4.1.2 paragraph A2** or amended Price Statement or any part thereof accepted pursuant to **clause 13.4.1.2 paragraph A4.2.**

Insert footnote **[g.4]**

● **[g.4]** Amend as necessary if different Public Holidays are applicable.

19: **Clause 38** **Fluctuations: Contribution, levy and tax fluctuations: Landfill tax**

After clause 38.2.2 **insert**:

Landfill tax 38.2 .3. 1 The prices contained in the Contract Bills are [XQ: The Contract

Sum is] based upon the incidence and rate of landfill tax (as referred to in the Finance Act 1996) on waste deposited on a licensed landfill site and for which at the Base Date the landfill site operator is accountable to HM Customs and Excise.

.3. 2 If in respect of waste arising out of the carrying out and completion of the Works which the Contractor after the Base Date deposits on a licensed landfill site the price charged by the operator of that site to the Contractor for such deposit is increased or decreased by reason only of a change in the incidence or rate of landfill tax effective after the Base Date from what would have been charged before that effective date the net amount of that increase or decrease shall, as the case may be, be paid to or allowed by the Contractor.

.3. 3 No payment pursuant to clause 38.2.3.2 shall be made if the Contractor could reasonably be expected to have disposed of the waste other than to a licensed landfill site.

Consequential amendment

38.4.1

After clause 38.4.1.3 **insert**:
'.1 .4 clause 38.2.3'

and **re-number** clause 38.4.1.4 as
38.4.1.5.

| 20: | **Clause 41** | **Settlement of disputes – Arbitration** |

Re-draft the heading:

**'Part 4: Settlement of disputes –
Adjudication – Arbitration – Legal
Proceedings'**

Insert new clause 41A:

● 41A   **Adjudication**

Application
of clause 41A

41A.1   Clause 41A applies where, pursuant to
Article 5, either Party refers any dispute
or difference arising under this Contract
to adjudication.

Identity of
Adjudicator

41A.2   The Adjudicator to decide the dispute or
difference shall be either an individual
agreed by the Parties or, on the application of either Party, an individual to be
nominated as the Adjudicator by the
person named in the Appendix ('the
nominator'). Provided that **[y.1]**

41A.2 .1   no Adjudicator shall be agreed or
nominated under clause 41A.2.2 or
clause 41A.3 who will not execute
the Standard Agreement for the
appointment of an Adjudicator
issued by the Joint Contracts
Tribunal (the 'JCT Adjudication
Agreement') with the Parties, **[y.1]**
and

41A.2   .2   where either Party has given notice of his intention to refer a dispute to adjudication then

—   any agreement by the Parties on the appointment of an Adjudicator must be reached with the object of securing the appointment of, and the referral of the dispute or difference to, the Adjudicator within 7 days of the date of the notice of intention to refer (*see clause 41A.4.1*);

—   any application to the nominator must be made with the object of securing the appointment of, and the referral of the dispute or difference to, the Adjudicator within 7 days of the date of the notice of intention to refer;

41A.2   .3   upon agreement by the Parties on the appointment of the Adjudicator or upon receipt by the Parties from the nominator of the name of the nominated Adjudicator the Parties shall thereupon execute with the Adjudicator the JCT Adjudication Agreement.

Insert new footnotes:

[y.1]: The nominators named in the Appendix have agreed with the Joint Contracts Tribunal that they will comply with the requirements of clause 41A on the nomination of an adjudicator including the requirement in clause 41A.2.2 for the nomination to be made with the object of securing the appointment of, and the referral of the dispute or difference to, the Adjudicator within 7 days of the date of the notice of intention to refer; and will only nominate adjudicators who will enter into the 'JCT Adjudication Agreement'.

† The JCT Adjudication Agreement, whose text is set out in the Guidance Notes to this Amendment, is available from the retailers of JCT Forms.

Death of Adjudicator – inability to adjudicate

41A.3 If the Adjudicator dies or becomes ill or is unavailable for some other cause and is thus unable to adjudicate on a dispute or difference referred to him, the Parties may either agree upon an individual to replace the Adjudicator or either party may apply to the nominator for the nomination of an adjudicator to adjudicate that dispute or difference; and the Parties shall execute the JCT Adjudication Agreement with the agreed or nominated Adjudicator.

Dispute or difference – notice of intention to refer to Adjudication – referral

41A.4 .1 When pursuant to Article 5 a Party requires a dispute or difference to be referred to adjudication then that Party shall give notice to the other Party of his intention to refer the dispute or difference, briefly identified in the notice, to adjudication. Within 7 days from the date of such notice or the execution of the JCT Adjudication Agreement by the Adjudicator if later, the Party giving the notice of intention shall refer the dispute or difference to the Adjudicator for his decision ('the referral'); and shall include with that referral particulars of the dispute or difference together with a summary of the contentions on which he relies, a statement of the relief or remedy which is sought and any material he wishes the Adjudicator to consider. The referral and its accompanying documentation shall be copied simultaneously to the other Party.

41A.4 .2 The referral by a Party with its accompanying documentation to the Adjudicator and the copies thereof to be provided to the other Party shall be given by actual delivery or by FAX or by registered post or recorded delivery. If given by FAX then, for record purposes, the referral and its accompanying documentation must forthwith be sent by first class post or given by actual delivery. If sent by registered post or recorded delivery the referral and its accompanying documentation shall, subject to proof to the contrary, be deemed to have been received 48 hours after the date of posting subject to the exclusion of Sundays and any Public Holiday.

Conduct of the Adjudication

41A.5 .1 The Adjudicator shall immediately upon receipt of the referral and its accompanying documentation confirm the date of that receipt to the Parties.

41A.5 .2 The Party not making the referral may, by the same means stated in clause 41A.4.2, send to the Adjudicator within 7 days of the date of the referral with a copy to the other Party, a written statement of the contentions on which he relies and any material he wishes the Adjudicator to consider.

41A.5 .3 The Adjudicator shall within 28 days of his receipt of the referral and its accompanying documentation under clause 41A.4.1 and acting as an Adjudicator for the purposes of S.108 of the Housing Grants, Construction and Regeneration Act 1996 and not as an expert or an arbitrator reach his decision and forthwith send that decision in writing to the Parties. Provided that the Party who has made the referral may consent to allowing the Adjudicator to extend the period of 28 days by up to 14 days; and that by agreement between the Parties after the referral has been made a longer period than

28 days may be notified jointly by the Parties to the Adjudicator within which to reach his decision.

41A.5 .4 The Adjudicator shall not be obliged to give reasons for his decision.

41A.5 .5 In reaching his decision the Adjudicator shall act impartially, set his own procedure and at his absolute discretion may take the initiative in ascertaining the facts and the law as he considers necessary in respect of the referral which may include the following:

.5 .1 using his own knowledge and/or experience;

.5 .2 opening up, reviewing and revising any certificate, opinion, decision, requirement or notice issued given or made under the Contract as if no such certificate, opinion, decision, requirement or notice had been issued given or made;

.5 .3 requiring from the Parties further information than that contained in the notice of referral and its accompanying documentation or in any written statement provided by the Parties including the results of any tests that have been made or of any opening up;

.5 .4 requiring the Parties to carry out tests or additional tests or to open up work or further open up work;

.5 .5 visiting the site of the Works or any workshop where work is being or has been prepared for the Contract;

.5 .6 obtaining such information as he considers necessary from any employee or representative of the Parties provided that before obtaining information from an employee of a Party he has given prior notice to that Party;

.5 .7 obtaining from others such information and advice as he considers necessary on technical and on legal matters subject to giving prior notice to the Parties together with a statement or estimate of the cost involved;

.5 .8 having regard to any term of the contract relating to the payment of interest, deciding the circumstances in which or the period for which a simple rate of interest shall be paid.

41A.5 .6 Any failure by either Party to enter into the JCT Adjudication Agreement or to comply with any requirement of the Adjudicator under clause 41A.5.5 or with any provision in or requirement under clause 41A shall not invalidate the decision of the Adjudicator.

	41A.5 .7	The Parties shall meet their own costs of the Adjudication except that the Adjudicator may direct as to who should pay the cost of any test or opening up if required pursuant to clause 41A.5.5.4.
Adjudicator's fee and reasonable expenses – payment	41A.6 .1	The Adjudicator in his decision shall state how payment of his fee and reasonable expenses is to be apportioned as between the Parties. In default of such statement the Parties shall bear the cost of the Adjudicator's fee and reasonable expenses in equal proportions.
	41A.6 .2	The Parties shall be jointly and severally liable to the Adjudicator for his fee and for all expenses reasonably incurred by the Adjudicator pursuant to the Adjudication.
Effect of Adjudicator's decision	41A.7 .1	The decision of the Adjudicator shall be binding on the Parties until the dispute or difference is finally determined by arbitration or by legal proceedings or by an agreement in writing between the Parties made after the decision of the Adjudicator has been given. [y.2]
	41A.7 .2	The Parties shall, without prejudice to their other rights under the Contract, comply with the decisions of the Adjudicator; and the Employer and the Contractor shall

ensure that the decisions of the Adjudicator are given effect.

41A.7 .3   If either Party does not comply with the decision of the Adjudicator, the other Party shall be entitled to take legal proceedings to secure such compliance pending any final determination of the referred dispute or difference pursuant to clause 41A.7.1.

Insert new footnote:

[y.2] The arbitration or legal proceedings are not an appeal against the decision of the Adjudicator but are a consideration of the dispute or difference as if no decision had been made by an Adjudicator.

Immunity   41A.8 The Adjudicator shall not be liable for anything done or omitted in the discharge or purported discharge of his functions as Adjudicator unless the act or omission is in bad faith and this protection from liability shall similarly extend to any employee or agent of the Adjudicator.

Delete clause 41 and **insert** clause 41B:

41B   **Arbitration**

A reference in clause 41B to a Rule or Rules is a reference to the JCT 1998 edition of the Construction Industry Model Arbitration Rules (CIMAR) current at the Base Date.

41B.1 .1 Where pursuant to Article 7A either Party requires a dispute or difference to be referred to arbitration then that Party shall serve on the other Party a notice of arbitration to such effect in accordance with Rule 2.1 which states:

'Arbitral proceedings are begun in respect of a dispute when one party serves on the other a written notice of arbitration identifying the dispute and requiring him to agree to the appointment of an arbitrator;'

and an arbitrator shall be an individual agreed by the parties or appointed by the person named in the Appendix in accordance with Rule 2.3 which states:

'If the parties fail to agree on the name of an arbitrator within 14 days (or any agreed extension) after:

(*i*) the notice of arbitration is served, or

(*ii*) a previously appointed arbitrator ceases to hold office for any reason, either party may apply for the appointment of an arbitrator to the person so empowered.'

By Rule 2.5:

'the arbitrator's appointment takes effect upon his agreement to act or his appointment under Rule 2.3, whether or not his terms have been accepted.'

41B.1 .2 Where two or more related arbitral proceedings in respect of the Works fall under separate arbitration agreements Rules 2.6, 2.7 and 2.8 shall apply thereto.

41B.1 .3 After an arbitrator has been appointed either Party may give a further notice of arbitration to the other Party and to the Arbitrator referring any other dispute which falls under Article 7A to be decided in the arbitral proceedings and Rule 3.3 shall apply thereto.

41B.2 Subject to the provisions of Article 7A and clause 30.9 the Arbitrator shall, without prejudice to the generality of his powers, have power to rectify this Contract so that it accurately reflects the true agreement made by the Parties, to direct such measurements and/or valuations as may in his opinion be desirable in order to determine the rights of the Parties and to ascertain and award any sum which ought to have been the subject of or included in any certificate and to open up, review and revise any certificate, opinion, decision, requirement or notice and to determine all matters in dispute which shall be submitted to him in the same manner as if no such certificate, opinion, decision, requirement or notice had been given.

41B.3 Subject to clause 41B.4 the award of such Arbitrator shall be final and binding on the Parties.

41B.4 The Parties hereby agree pursuant to Section 45(2)(a) and Section 69(2)(a) of the Arbitration Act, 1996, that either Party may (upon notice to the other Party and to the Arbitrator):

41B.4 .1 apply to the courts to determine any question of law arising in the course of the reference; and

41B.4 .2 appeal to the courts on any question of law arising out of an award made in an arbitration under this Arbitration Agreement.

41B.5 The provisions of the Arbitration Act 1996 or any amendment thereof shall apply to any arbitration under this Contract wherever the same, or any part of it, shall be conducted. **[y.3]**

41B.6 The arbitration shall be conducted in accordance with the JCT 1998 edition of the Construction Industry Model Arbitration Rules (CIMAR) current at the Base Date. Provided that if any amendments to the Rules so current have been issued by the Joint Contracts Tribunal after the Base Date the Parties may, by a joint notice in writing to the Arbitrator, state that they wish the arbitration to be conducted in accordance with the Rules as so amended.

Insert revised footnote:

[y.3] It should be noted that the provisions of the Arbitration Act 1996 do not extend to Scotland. Where the site of the Works is situated in Scotland then the forms issued by the Scottish Building Contract Committee which contain Scots proper law, adjudication and arbitration provisions are the appropriate documents. The SBCC issues guidance in this respect.

Consequential amendments

1.3

In the definition of Arbitrator **delete** 'clause 41' and **insert** 'clause 41B'

4.2

Lines 5 to 7 **delete** the words in brackets and **insert** between the brackets:

'neither party before such compliance having invoked the relevant procedures under the Contract to the resolution of disputes or differences in order that it may be decided whether the provision specified by the Architect empowers the issue of the said instructions'

8.4.1

Delete the existing text and **insert**:

'notwithstanding the power of the Architect under clause 8.4.2 issue instructions in regard to the removal from the site of all or any of such work, materials or goods; and/or'

31.9 Line 1 **delete** 'The provisions of article 5' and **insert** 'The relevant procedures applicable under the Contract to the resolution of disputes or differences'

Delete existing side heading and **insert**:

Application of dispute procedures

After clause 41B **insert**:

41C Legal Proceedings

41C.1 When any dispute or difference is to be determined by legal proceedings, then insofar as the Conditions provide for the issue of a certificate, or the expression of an opinion or the giving of a decision, requirement or notice such provision shall not prevent the Court, in determining the rights and liabilities of the Parties hereto, from making any finding necessary to establish whether such certificate was correctly issued or opinion correctly expressed or decision, requirement or notice correctly given on the facts found by the Court; nor shall such provision prevent the Court establishing what certificate ought to have been issued or what other opinion should have been expressed or what other decision, requirement or notice should have been given as if no certificate, opinion, decision, requirement or notice had been issued, expressed or given.

● Adjudication – nominator of Adjudicator (if no nominator is selected the nominator shall be the President or a Vice-President of the Royal Institute of British Architects)

41A.2   President or a Vice-President or Chairman or a Vice-Chairman:
* Royal Institute of British Architects
* Royal Institution of Chartered Surveyors
* Construction Confederation
* National Specialist Contractors' Council

Settlement of disputes – Arbitration – appointor (if no appointor is selected the appointor shall be the President or a Vice-President of the Royal Institute of British Architects)

41B.1   President or a Vice-President:
* Royal Institute of British Architects
* Royal Institution of Chartered Surveyors
* Chartered Institute of Arbitrators

* Delete all but one

22:   **Consequential amendments: Supplemental Provisions (the VAT Agreement)**

Clause 5   **Delete** side heading and **insert** 'Awards in dispute procedures'

Line 1 **delete** 'under article 5' and **insert** 'pursuant to article 7A'

Line 1 **delete** 'a court' and **insert** 'legal proceedings'

Line 2 **delete** 'court proceedings' and **insert** 'legal proceedings'

Clause 6   Line 1 **delete** 'article 5' and **insert** 'article 7A'

Local Authorities versions only

In this Amendment 18 the term 'the Architect' wherever appearing is deemed to have been deleted and the term 'the Architect/the Contract Administrator' is deemed to have been substituted.

Guidance Notes

on items 1 to 22 in Amendment 18 to the Standard Form of Building Contract 1980 Edition With and Without Quantities versions

Note: Unless otherwise stated a reference to 'the Act' in these Notes is to the Housing Grants, Construction and Regeneration Act 1996, Part II Construction Contracts.

Item No.

1:   **Articles of Agreement**

For comment on the addition to the Second recital **see the Guidance Note on item 13;** on the new Sixth recital **see** the **Guidance Note on item 4**; on the new Seventh recital see items 12 and 14; and on the new text for Article 5 and the additional Articles 7A and 7B, **see the Guidance Notes on item 20.**

2: Clause 1.3 Definitions

The items in the Amendment to which these additional definitions relate are:

Activity Schedule:	item 13
Adjudication Agreement and Adjudicator:	item 20
Information Release Schedule:	item 4
Party and Parties:	item 20
Price Statement:	item 5 – re-drafted clause 13.4.1
Public Holiday:	item 3 – new clause 1.6

Any necessary comment on these definitions is included in the guidance on the item to which the definitions relate.

3:      Clause 1   **Interpretation, definitions etc.: new
                   clauses
                   1.5 Service of notices or other
                        documents
                   1.6 Reckoning period of days
                   1.7 Employers' Representative
                   1.8 Applicable law**

Clause 1.5 is included to give effect to S.115 of the Act which provides:

Service of   115. (1) The parties are
notices, etc.   free to agree on the man-
                 ner of service of any notice
                 or other document re-
                 quired or authorised to be
                 served in pursuance of the
                 construction contract or
                 for any of the purposes of
                 this Part.
                 (2) If or to the extent that
                 there is no such agreement
                 the following provisions
                 apply.
                 (3) A notice or other
                 document may be served
                 on a person by any effec-
                 tive means.
                 (4) If a notice or other
                 document is addressed,
                 pre-paid and delivered by
                 post –
                 (*a*) to the addressee's last
                 known principal residence

or, if he is or has been carrying on a trade, profession or business, his last known principal business address, or

(b) where the addressee is a body corporate, to the body's registered or principal office,

it shall be treated as effectively served.

(5) This section does not apply to the service of documents for the purposes of legal proceedings, for which provision is made by rules of court.

(6) References in this Part to a notice or other document include any form of communication in writing and references to service shall be construed accordingly.

The Conditions in certain clauses e.g., in clause 27.1 and in clause 41A.4.2 (see item 18) prescribe the manner of service of the documents referred to; and this is permitted by S.115(1). Clause 1.5 only therefore applies where no manner of service is prescribed in the Conditions, e.g., the issue of the Architect's instruction under clause 4.1.1, the provision of the Contractor's Statement under clause 42.4. In these circumstances service has to be by 'any effective means'; and if served as described in clause 1.5 then that is an 'effective means' though any other means that are effective are equally valid.

Clause 1.6 is included to give partial but extended effect in the Conditions to S.116 of the Act; it is 'partial' in that it applies only to periods of days and 'extended' in that it applies to matters outside the scope of Part II of the Act. S.116 provides:

Reckoning periods of time	116. (1) For the purposes of this Part periods of time shall be reckoned as follows:
	(2) Where an act is required to be done within a specified period after or from a specified date, the period begins immediately after that date.
	(3) Where the period would include Christmas Day, Good Friday or a day which under the Banking and Financial Dealings Act 1971 is a bank holiday in England and Wales or, as the case may be, in Scotland, that day shall be excluded.

The clause only applies to 'periods of days' e.g., clause 28.2.3 (period of continuance of a specified default or specified suspension event), clause 30.1.1.1 in item 11 (calculation of the final date for payment of an Interim Certificate). Where periods are expressed in periods other than days, e.g., the length of the Defects Liability Period under clause 17.2 and the relevant Appendix entry, the period under clause 30.6.1.1 for the Contractor to provide all documents necessary for the adjustment of the Contract Sum, then, in the event of any dispute over the matter, to the extent that the dispute relates to matters within Part II of the Act S.116 will apply in reckoning the commencement and expiry of the period.

20:   **Clause 41 Settlement of disputes – Arbitration**

Part 4 has been extensively amended as a result of:

(*a*) the statutory right given by S.108(1) of the Act to a party to a construction contract to refer a dispute or difference arising under the contract for adjudication; see also Article 5;

(*b*) a decision of the Tribunal's constituent bodies to give a choice to the parties of omitting the agreement to take disputes to arbitration so that disputes would be the subject of legal proceedings; see Article 7B;

(c) the provisions of the Arbitration Act 1996 and the decision to replace the current JCT Arbitration Rules by the 'JCT 1998 edition of the Construction Industry Model Arbitration Rules (CIMAR)'.

Adjudication

Ss.108(1) to (5) of the Act provide:

Right to refer disputes to adjudication

108. (1) A party to a construction contract has the right to refer a dispute arising under the contract for adjudication under a procedure complying with this section.
For this purpose 'dispute' includes any difference.
(2) The contract shall –
(*a*) enable a party to give notice at any time of his intention to refer a dispute to adjudication;
(*b*) provide a timetable with the object of securing the appointment of the adjudicator and referral of the dispute to him within 7 days of such notice;

(c) require the adjudicator to reach a decision within 28 days of referral or such longer period as is agreed by the parties after the dispute has been referred;

(d) allow the adjudicator to extend the period of 28 days by up to 14 days, with the consent of the party by whom the dispute was referred;

(e) impose a duty on the adjudicator to act impartially; and

(f) enable the adjudicator to take the initiative in ascertaining the facts and the law.

(3) The contract shall provide that the decision of the adjudicator is binding until the dispute is finally determined by legal proceedings, by arbitration (if the contract provides for arbitration or the parties otherwise agree to arbitration), or by agreement.

The parties may agree to accept the decision of the adjudicator as finally determining the dispute.

(4) The contract shall also provide that the adjudicator is not liable for anything done or omitted in the discharge or purported discharge of his functions as adjudicator unless the act or omission is in bad faith, and that any employee or agent of the adjudicator is similarly protected from liability.

(5) If the contract does not comply with the requirements of subsections (1) to (4), the adjudication provisions of the Scheme for Construction Contracts apply.

As the new Article 5 and clause '41A Adjudication' comply with Ss. 108(1) to (4), S.108(5) will not therefore be applicable to the Standard Form 1980 Edition.

The following points should be noted:

(*a*) By Article 5 either Party (a new defined term in item 2 of Amendment 18) by notice to the other Party may refer a dispute or difference to Adjudication; such reference does not require an agreement between the Parties. The Adjudication is then carried out under the terms of clause 41A.

Article 5 follows S.108(1) in giving a right to refer to adjudication a dispute arising 'under' the Contract. Leading Counsel referred to the use of the term 'under' in the Section and contrasted that with the phrase used in Article 7A (and in the pre-Amendment 18 Article 5) – Arbitration – any dispute . . . arising under this Contract or in connection therewith'. He advised that disputes as to, for example, the existence of a contract or the right to sue for misrepresentation would be outside the jurisdiction of an Adjudicator pursuant to S.108(1) and to Article 5 as not arising 'under' the Contract.

(b) The appointment of the Adjudicator is **either** by agreement between the Parties **or** by either party applying to the nominating body named in the Appendix (see item 21) to nominate an Adjudicator: **clause 41A.2**.
The nominating bodies have each agreed to nominate in accordance with the time table for appointment in clause 41A which reflects the time table in S.108; and only to nominate persons who will enter into the JCT Standard Agreement for the appointment of an Adjudicator (the 'Adjudication Agreement'). A copy of this Agreement

is **reproduced on pages 49–52 of these Notes**. An Adjudicator agreed by the Parties must also have agreed to enter into the Adjudication Agreement.
If the Parties wish to name an Adjudicator in the Contract then amendments to clause 41A are required as set out on pages 55–56 of this Note. A version of the Adjudication Agreement for use with a named Adjudicator is set out on pages 57–60 of this Note.

(c) The Adjudication Agreements state the fee of the Adjudicator which is either a lump sum or an hourly rate.

(d) The next step after a Party has given notice of his intention to refer a dispute to adjudication is for that Party to refer the dispute or difference to the Adjudicator. The details in **clause 41A.4** of this referral must be followed as they are in compliance with the requirements of S.108(2).

(e) The conduct of the Adjudication including the time for the Adjudicator to give his decision is set out in **clause 41A.5** which complies with S.108. The Tribunal has provided in clause 41A.5.3 that the 28 day period for the Adjudicator to reach his decision is to run from the date of receipt by the Adjudicator of the referral notice which the Adjudicator under clause 41A.5.2 has to confirm to the Parties. This appeared to the Tribunal to be a realistic and practicable method of dealing with any problems of delay outside the control of the Parties (e.g. postal strikes) while not conflicting with S.108(2) of the Act. Particular attention is called to **clause 41A.5.3** which states that the Adjudicator, in carrying out the Adjudication and giving his decision, is 'acting as an Adjudicator for the purposes of S.108 of 'the Housing Grants, Construction and Regeneration Act 1996' and not as an expert or an arbitrator'; and to **clauses 41A.5.5.1 to .8**.

(*f*) The Adjudicator is entitled to his fee and to 'reasonable expenses'; and the liability of the Parties for payment of the Adjudicator is stated in **clause 41A.6**. The Parties may submit sealed letters to the Adjudicator, to be opened after he has reached his decision, if they wish him to consider particular matters before reaching his decision on apportionment of his fee and reasonable expenses under clause 41A.6.1 and under clause

41A.5.7 on payment of the cost of any test or opening up.

(g) **Clause 41A.7** Effect of Adjudicator's decision – follows the provisions of S.108(3). The important footnote **[y.2]** stresses that any arbitration or legal proceedings finally to settle the dispute or difference are **not** an appeal from the Adjudicator's decision; they will be a **new** hearing of the dispute or difference.

(h) **Clause 41A.7.3** specifically provides that if a Party does not comply with an Adjudicator's decision the other Party can take legal proceedings. Article 7A, the arbitration agreement of the Parties, specifically excepts from the right to refer any dispute or difference to arbitration a dispute or difference 'in connection with the enforcement of any decision of an Adjudicator'. Thus even if the Parties have retained arbitration for the determination of disputes, the inclusion of this exception has removed from the arbitration agreement the enforcement of Adjudicator's decisions and the arbitration agreement could not be used to stay legal proceedings in the courts for such enforcement.

(i) **Clause 41A.8** complies with S.108(4) of the Act.

Text of JCT Adjudication Agreement

JCT Adjudication Agreement

This Agreement

is made on the _____ day of _____ 19___

BETWEEN ('the Contracting Parties')

Insert names and
addresses of the
Contracting Parties

(1) _____

_____

_____

_____

(2)

_____

_____

_____

_____

and ('the Adjudicator')

Insert name and
address of
Adjudicator

_____

_____

_____

_____

Whereas

the Contracting Parties have entered into a
*Contract/Sub-Contract/Agreement (the 'contract') for

Brief description of the
works/the sub-contract
works

_____

_____

_____

_____

_____

on the terms of

Insert the title of the JCT
Contract/Sub-Contract/
Agreement and any
amendments thereto
incorporated therein

_____

_____

_____

_____

in which the provisions on adjudication ('the Adjudication
Provisions') are set out in clause _____

And Whereas
a dispute or difference has arisen under the contract which the
Contracting Parties wish to be referred to adjudication in
accordance with the said Adjudication Provisions.

*Delete as appropriate.

Now it is agreed that

Appointment and acceptance

1. The Contracting Parties hereby appoint the Adjudicator and the Adjudicator hereby accepts such appointment in respect of the dispute briefly identified in the attached notice.

Adjudication Provisions

2. The Adjudicator shall observe the Adjudication Provisions as if they were set out in full in this Agreement.

Adjudicator's fee and reasonable expenses

3. The Contracting Parties will be jointly and severally liable to the Adjudicator for his fee as stated in the Schedule hereto for conducting the adjudication and for all expenses reasonably incurred by the Adjudicator as referred to in the Adjudication Provisions.

Unavailability of Adjudicator to act on the referral

4. If the Adjudicator becomes ill or becomes unavailable for some other cause and is thus unable to complete the adjudication, he shall immediately give notice to the Contracting Parties to such effect.

Termination

5. .1 The Contracting Parties jointly may terminate the Adjudication Agreement at any time on written notice to the Adjudicator. Following such termination the Contracting Parties shall, subject to clause 5.2, pay the Adjudicator his fee

or any balance thereof and his expenses reasonably incurred prior to the termination.

.2 Where the decision of the Contracting Parties to terminate the Adjudication Agreement under clause 5.1 is because of a failure by the Adjudicator to give his decision on the dispute or difference within the time-scales in the Adjudication Provisions or at all, the Adjudicator shall not be entitled to recover from the Contracting Parties his fee and expenses.

As Witness
the hands of the Contracting Parties and the Adjudicator

Signed by or on behalf of:

the Contracting Parties
(1) _____

in the presence of _____

(2) _____

in the presence of _____

Signed by:

the Adjudicator

_____

in the presence of _____

Schedule

Fee   The lump sum fee is £_____
            or
            The hourly rate is £_____

Appendix
Delete the entry with reference to clause 41A.2.

Insert an additional entry:
Adjudication   41A.2   Name and address of Adjudicator

_____

_____

_____

_____

Fee of Adjudicator
*Lump sum £_____
or

*Hourly rate £_____

*Complete as applicable

Text of JCT Adjudication Agreement

JCT Adjudication Agreement
for an ADJUDICATOR NAMED in a Contract/Sub-Contract/
Agreement

This Agreement

is made on the _____day of _____ 19___

BETWEEN ('the Contracting Parties')

Insert names and
addresses of the
Contracting Parties

(1)_____

_____

_____

(2)_____

_____

_____

_____

and ('the Adjudicator')

Insert name and
address of
Adjudicator

_____

_____

_____

Whereas

the Contracting Parties have named the Adjudicator in the said
contract.

Brief description of
the works/the sub-
contract works

_____

_____

_____

_____

on the terms of

Insert the title of the
JCT Contract/Sub-
Contract/Agreement
and any amendments
thereto incorporated
therein

_____

_____

_____

in which the provisions on adjudication ('the Adjudication
Provisions') are set out in clause _____

And Whereas

a dispute or difference has arisen under the contract which the Contracting Parties wish to be referred to adjudication in accordance with the said Adjudication Provisions.

*Delete as appropriate.

Now it is agreed that

Appointment and acceptance

1. The Contracting Parties hereby appoint the Adjudicator and the Adjudicator hereby accepts such appointment in respect of any dispute that may arise on the said contract and the Adjudicator will use his best endeavours to be available to consider any referral to him by either party to the contract.† If a dispute or difference arises under a nominated or named sub-contract entered into pursuant to the aforementioned contract which the parties to such sub-contract require to be referred to adjudication, the Adjudicator will, if so required, execute an agreement in similar terms to this Agreement to act as Adjudicator thereon.

Adjudication Provisions

2. The Adjudicator shall observe the Adjudication Provisions as if they were set out in full in this Agreement.

Adjudicator's fee and reasonable expenses

3. The Contracting Parties will be jointly and severally liable to the Adjudicator for his fee as stated in the Schedule hereto for

---

† Delete if the contract is in respect of a sub-contract.

conducting the adjudication and for all expenses reasonably incurred by the Adjudicator as referred to in the Adjudication Provisions.

Unavailability of Adjudicator to act on the referral

4. If the Adjudicator becomes ill or becomes unavailable for some other cause and is thus unable to complete the adjudication he shall immediately give notice to the Contracting Parties to such effect.

Termination

5. .1 The Contracting Parties jointly may

.1 terminate the Adjudication Agreement at any time on written notice to the Adjudicator;

.2 terminate an adjudication at any time and immediately give written notice to the Adjudicator thereof.

Following such termination the Contracting Parties shall, subject to clause 5.2, pay the Adjudicator his fee or any balance thereof and his expenses reasonably incurred prior to the termination.

.2 Where the decision of the Contracting Parties to terminate the Adjudication Agreement under clause 5.1 is because of a failure by the Adjudicator to give his decision on the dispute or difference within the time-scales in the Adjudication Provisions or at all, the Adjudicator shall not be entitled to recover from the Contracting Parties his fee and expenses.

As Witness
the hands of the Contracting Parties and the Adjudicator

Signed by or on behalf of:

the Contracting Parties
(1) _____

in the presence of _____

(2) _____

in the presence of _____

Signed by:

the Adjudicator

_____

in the presence of _____

Schedule

Fee   The lump sum fee is £_____
or
The hourly rate is £_____

Appendix 11

The Construction Industry Council (CIC) Model Adjudication Procedure: First Edition

General principles
Object
1. The object of adjudication is to reach a fair, rapid and inexpensive decision upon a dispute arising under the Contract and this procedure shall be interpreted accordingly.

Impartiality
2. The Adjudicator shall act impartially.

The Adjudicator's role
3. The Adjudicator may take the initiative in ascertaining the facts and the law. He may use his own knowledge and experience. The adjudication shall be neither an arbitration nor an expert determination.

Decision binding in interim
4. The Adjudicator's decision shall be binding until the dispute is finally determined by legal proceedings, by arbitration (if the contract provides for arbitration or the parties otherwise agree to arbitration), or by agreement.

Implementation of the decision

5. The Parties shall implement the Adjudicator's decision without delay whether or not the dispute is to be referred to legal proceedings or arbitration.

Application

Application

6. If this procedure is incorporated into the Contract by reference, the reference shall be deemed to be to the edition current at the date of the Notice.

Conflict

7. If a conflict arises between this procedure and the Contract, unless the Contract provides otherwise, this procedure shall prevail.

Appointment of the Adjudicator

Notice of adjudication

8. Either Party may give notice at any time of its intention to refer a dispute arising under the Contract to adjudication by giving a written Notice to the other Party. The Notice shall include a brief statement of the issue or issues which it is desired to refer and the redress sought. The referring Party shall send a copy of the Notice to any adjudicator named in the Contract.

Time for appointment and referral

9. The object of the procedure in paragraphs 10–14 is to secure the appointment of the adjudicator and referral of the dispute to him within 7 days of the Notice.

Appointment

10. If an adjudicator is named in the Contract, he shall within 2 days of receiving the Notice confirm his availability to act. If no

adjudicator is named, or if the named adjudicator does not so confirm, the referring Party shall request the body stated in the Contract, if any, or if none, the Construction Industry Council, to nominate an Adjudicator within 5 days of receipt of the request. The request shall be in writing, accompanied by a copy of the Notice and the appropriate fee. Alternatively the Parties may, within 2 days of the Notice, appoint the Adjudicator by agreement.

Adjudicator unable to act

11. If, for any reason, the Adjudicator is unable to act, or fails to reach his decision within the time required by this procedure, either Party may request the body stated in the Contract, if any, or if none, the Construction Industry Council, to nominate a replacement adjudicator.

Adjudicator's terms and conditions

12. Unless the Contract provides otherwise, the Adjudicator shall be appointed on the terms and conditions set out in the attached Agreement and shall be entitled to a reasonable fee and expenses.

Objection to appointment

13. If a Party objects to the appointment of a particular person as adjudicator, that objection shall not invalidate the Adjudicator's appointment or any decision he may reach.

Conduct of the Adjudication

Statement of case

14. The referring Party shall send to the Adjudicator within 7 days of the Notice (or as soon thereafter as the Adjudicator is appointed) and copy to the other Party, a statement of its case including a copy of the Notice, the Contract, details of the circumstances giving rise to the dispute, the reasons why it is

entitled to the redress sought, and the evidence upon which it relies.

Date of referral

15. The date of referral shall be the date on which the Adjudicator receives this statement of case.

Period for decision

16. The Adjudicator shall reach his decision within 28 days of the date of referral, or such longer period as is agreed by the Parties after the dispute has been referred. The Adjudicator may extend the period of 28 days by up to 14 days with the consent of the referring Party.

Procedure

17. The Adjudicator shall have complete discretion as to how to conduct the adjudication, and shall establish the procedure and timetable, subject to any limitation there may be in the Contract or the Act. He shall not be required to observe any rule of evidence, procedure or otherwise, of any court or tribunal. Without prejudice to the generality of these powers, he may:

   (*i*)   request a written defence, further argument or counter argument

   (*ii*) request the production of documents or the attendance of people whom he considers could assist

   (*iii*) visit the site

   (*iv*) meet and question the Parties and their representatives

   (*v*)   meet the Parties separately

   (*vi*) limit the length or time for submission of any statement, defence or argument

   (*vii*) proceed with the adjudication and reach a decision even if a Party fails to comply with a request or direction of the Adjudicator (*viii*) issue such further directions as he considers to be appropriate.

Parties to comply

18. The Parties shall comply with any request or direction of the Adjudicator in relation to the adjudication.

Obtaining advice

19. The Adjudicator may obtain legal or technical advice, provided that he has notified the Parties of his intention first. He shall provide the Parties with copies of any written advice received.

Matters to be determined

20. The Adjudicator shall decide the matters set out in the Notice, together with any other matters which the Parties and the Adjudicator agree shall be within the scope of the adjudication.

Adjudicator to apply the law

21. The Adjudicator shall determine the rights and obligations of the Parties in accordance with the law of the Contract.

Joining third parties

22. Any Party may at any time ask that additional parties shall be joined in the adjudication. Joining of additional parties shall be subject to the agreement of the Adjudicator and the existing and additional parties. An additional party shall have the same rights and obligations as the other Parties, unless otherwise agreed by the Adjudicator and the Parties.

Resignation

23. The Adjudicator may resign at any time on giving notice in writing to the Parties.

The Decision

Reasons

24. The Adjudicator shall reach his decision within the time limits in paragraph 16. The Adjudicator may withhold delivery of his decision until his fees and expenses have been paid. He shall not be required to give reasons.

Late decisions

25. If the Adjudicator fails to reach his decision within the time permitted by this procedure, his decision shall nonetheless be effective if reached before the referral of the dispute to any replacement adjudicator under paragraph 11 but not otherwise. If he fails to reach such an effective decision, he shall not be entitled to any fees or expenses (save for the cost of any legal or technical advice subject to the Parties having received such advice).

Power to open up certificates

26. The Adjudicator may open up, review and revise any certificate, decision, direction, instruction, notice, opinion requirement or valuation made in relation to the Contract.

Interest

27. The Adjudicator may in any decision direct the payment of such simple or compound interest from such dates, at such rates and with such rests, as he considers appropriate.

Costs

28. The Parties shall bear their own costs and expenses incurred in the adjudication.

Adjudicator's fees and expenses

29. The Parties shall be jointly and severally liable for the Adjudicator's fees and expenses, including those of any legal or technical adviser appointed under paragraph 19, but the Adjudicator may direct a Party to pay all or part of the fees and expenses. If he makes no such direction, the Parties shall pay them in equal shares. The Party requesting the adjudication shall be liable for the Adjudicator's fees and expenses if the adjudication does not proceed.

Enforcement

30. The Parties shall be entitled to the redress set out in the decision and to seek summary enforcement, whether or not the dispute is to be finally determined by legal proceedings or arbitration. No issue decided by the Adjudicator may subsequently be referred for decision by another adjudicator unless so agreed by the Parties.

Subsequent decision by arbitration or court

31. In the event that the dispute is referred to legal proceedings or arbitration, the Adjudicator's decision shall not inhibit the right of the court or arbitrator to determine the Parties' rights or obligations as if no adjudication had taken place.

Miscellaneous provisions

Adjudicator not to be appointed arbitrator

32. Unless the Parties agree, the Adjudicator shall not be appointed arbitrator in any subsequent arbitration between the Parties under the Contract. No Party may call the Adjudicator as a witness in any legal proceedings or arbitration concerning the subject matter of the adjudication.

Immunity of the Adjudicator

33. The Adjudicator is not liable for anything done or omitted in the discharge or purported discharge of his functions as Adjudicator (whether in negligence or otherwise) unless the act or omission is in bad faith, and any employee or agent of the Adjudicator is similarly protected from liability.

Reliance

34. The Adjudicator is appointed to determine the dispute or disputes between the Parties and his decision may not be relied upon by third parties, to whom he shall owe no duty of care.

Proper law

35. This procedure shall be interpreted in accordance with the law of England and Wales.

Definitions

'Act' means the Housing Grants, Construction and Regeneration Act 1996.

'Adjudicator' means the person named as such in the Contract or appointed in accordance with this Procedure.

'Contract' means the contract between the Parties which contains the provision for adjudication.

'Notice' means the notice given under paragraph 8.

'Party' means a party to the Contract, and any additional parties joined under paragraph 22. 'Referring Party' means the Party who gives notice under paragraph 8.

AGREEMENT

THIS AGREEMENT is made on the ....day of.................................19............

Between

1.   ....

      of ....

      .... (the referring Party)

2.   ....

      of ....

      .... (the other Party)

(together called the Parties)

3.   ....

      of ....

      .... (the Adjudicator)

A dispute has arisen between the Parties under a Contract between them dated ....
in connection with ....

This dispute has been referred to adjudication in accordance with the CIC Model Adjudication Procedure (the Procedure) and the Adjudicator has been requested to act.

IT IS AGREED that

1.   The rights and obligations of the Adjudicator and the Parties shall be as set out in this Agreement.

2.   The Adjudicator agrees to adjudicate the dispute in accordance with the Procedure.

3.   The Parties agree jointly and severally to pay the Adjudicator's fees and expenses as set out in the attached schedule and in accordance with the Procedure.

4.   The Adjudicator and the Parties shall keep the adjudication confidential, except so far as is necessary to enable a Party to implement or enforce the Adjudicator's decision.

5. The Parties acknowledge that the Adjudicator shall not be liable for anything done or omitted in the discharge or purported discharge of his functions as Adjudicator (whether in negligence or otherwise) unless the act or omission is in bad faith, and any employee or agent of the Adjudicator shall be similarly protected from liability.

Signed on behalf of the referring Party

....

Signed on behalf of the other Party

....

Signed on behalf of the Adjudicator

....

6. This Agreement shall be interpreted in accordance with the law of England and Wales.

Schedule

1. The Adjudicator shall be paid £........... per hour in respect of all time spent on the adjudication, including travelling time with a maximum of £............. per day.

2. The Adjudicator shall be reimbursed his reasonable expenses and disbursements, in respect of travelling, hotel and similar expenses, room charges, the cost of legal or technical advice obtained in accordance with the Procedure and other extraordinary expenses necessarily incurred.

3. The Adjudicator is/is not * currently registered for VAT. Where the Adjudicator is registered for VAT, it shall be charged additionally in accordance with the rates current at the date of the work done.

* delete as applicable.

Index